An Element of Trust

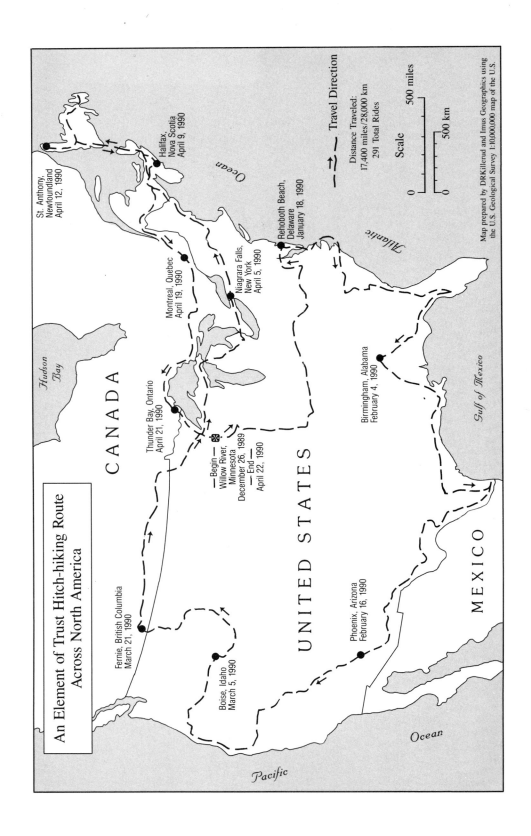

An Element of Trust Hitch-hiking Route
Across North America

St. Anthony,
Newfoundland
April 12, 1990

Halifax,
Nova Scotia
April 9, 1990

Hudson
Bay

CANADA

Ocean

Montreal, Quebec
April 19, 1990

Thunder Bay, Ontario
April 21, 1990

Niagrara Falls,
New York
April 5, 1990

Rehoboth Beach,
Delaware
January 18, 1990

—Begin—
Willow River,
Minnesota
December 26, 1989
—End—
April 22, 1990

Atlantic

Birmingham, Alabama
February 4, 1990

UNITED STATES

Gulf of Mexico

Fernie, British Columbia
March 21, 1990

Boise, Idaho
March 5, 1990

Phoenix, Arizona
February 16, 1990

MEXICO

Pacific

Ocean

Travel Direction

Distance Traveled:
17,400 miles/28,000 km
291 Total Rides

Scale

0   500 miles

0   500 km

Map prepared by DR Killerud and Imus Geographics using
the U.S. Geological Survey 1:10,000,000 map of the U.S.

An Element
of
Trust

Douglas R Killerud

Douglas R Killerud (signature)

To Linda Whang,
May your life's journey lead you to peace.
Enjoy the ride! Doug K
Lake McDonald MT
6/25/97

FROZEN REEF
BOOKS
West Glacier, Montana

All of the events described in this book actually took place. Entirely at the author's discretion, for reasons of privacy, the indentities of certain characters have been altered.

Shelter From the Storm, by Bob Dylan,
Copyright © <u>1974, 1975 by Ram's Horn Music.</u>
All rights reserved. International copyright secured. Reprinted by permission.

Cover designed by Daniel J. Smith, EARTHTALK Communication Studios.
Author photograph by Barbara Killerud.
Front cover photograph by Scott Killerud.

Published in 1994 by
Frozen Reef Books
P.O. Box 31
West Glacier, MT 59936-0031

In association with EARTHTALK Communication Studios, Bozeman, Montana.

Library of Congress Catalog Card Number 94-70050
International Standard Book Number 0-9640872-0-0

Printed in the United States of America
10 9 8 7 6 5 4 3 2 1

To order additional copies of *An Element of Trust* and for information
on other Frozen Reef Books titles please write to:
Frozen Reef Books
P.O. Box 31
West Glacier, MT 59936-0031

Contents

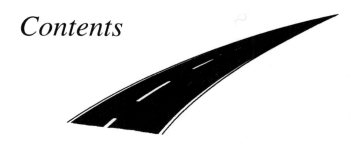

List of Maps

This book is dedicated to those drivers
who cared to look beyond their fear.

In a world of steel-eyed death
And men who are fighting to be warm
"Come in," she said, "I'll give you
Shelter from the Storm."
                    - Bob Dylan

Chapter One

220 Minnesota Miles:
A Full Day's Work

The temperature along the windswept highway had warmed up to minus 10°F. The surrounding forest of white pine, tamarack, and the skeletal remains of deciduous oak, maple, and aspen were covered with a fresh layer of snow. During the previous night, these otherwise silent sentinels shattered the quiet with crackling and popping as the freezing water within the living tree expanded beyond the flexibility of the wood fibers. Even at daylight, with the sun attempting to warm their outsides, they strained to maintain their internal integrity as the encroaching ice attempted to rend their core. The stark blackness of temporarily dormant oak limbs against the brilliant whiteness of the snow was a grim reminder of the power of winter. As I looked back down the roadway toward the occasional approaching car, I began to ponder the absurdity of standing at the base of this freeway entrance ramp, challenging winter.

Snow covered everything except portions of pavement where the highway snowplows and sand trucks were able to meet their own challenges. Temperatures had been so cold of late that the salt/sand mixture used on the road surface to promote melting did little to break the grip of well established ice. I stood facing north with one foot on the paved shoulder and the other on the frozen brown grass exposed by a plow's blade. Hemmed in by a snow berm to the left, there was only a six foot margin of safety between me and fast moving freeway traffic. Oncoming cars passed by with the loud crunch of ice chunks exploding under their tires and fine snow crystals billowing up in the slipstream behind them. Carried on an icy wind generated by mysterious arctic forces, and pulled even faster by gusts from each passing vehicle, these crystals would strike my face. I was tempted to turn away from the onslaught, but had to keep my attention directed toward the traffic if I ever hoped to get out of there.

My hitchhiking technique that morning included the use of a small, hand-held sign. Poorly designed on a square piece of brown cardboard, it nonetheless carried the day's destination emblazoned across it in black felt tip pen. With all of its crazy vowels, Winona was impossible to abbreviate so I had written it in hyphenated form. Perhaps the people who drove by thought I was some kind of high school sports booster, out on the freeway exhorting a team, from the previously unknown village of Ona, to win!

The freeway shoulder I straddled was on Interstate 35 in the east-central Minnesota town of Willow River. Fifty miles to the north was the western tip of Lake Superior, the city of Duluth, and the northerly terminus of I-35. Just east of Willow River was the location of my parents' and brother's farm. It was there I went for the Thanksgiving and Christmas holidays after quitting my job in Salem, Oregon. Having worked in an office tethered to a drafting table for the past two years, I felt a desperate need for an escape to wider spaces. I had no further employment respon-sibilities, nor social obligations following the holiday season, and found myself free to seek the wide open spaces I desired. The first order of busi-ness was to get away from the cold. The freezing temperatures had actu-ally strengthened my resolve to begin travelling. The day after Christmas I was on the road, determined to head south.

My method of travel, though common for the 1960s, was unusual for the 1990s, and generally frowned upon by responsible people and law enforcement personnel. I almost had a chance to find out how serious the law was about prohibiting pedestrians from using the freeway right-of-way. Just moments before I had illegally entered the freeway as a pedestrian, my parents and I observed a maroon and white Minnesota Highway Patrol car turn onto the entrance ramp heading south. If my folks had dropped me off a few minutes earlier I would have undoubtedly received a stern lecture at the very least, and a jail term at the very most, for standing around ducking ice shards. In a punishment even worse than the monetary loss involved in paying a fine, I would have been evicted from my spot and forced to stand at the top of the entrance ramp to wait for a ride. In a hopelessly tiny town like Willow River there would have been only a car or two entering the freeway in the time it would have taken me to freeze to death, or die of boredom! As long as that State Trooper was safely ahead of me I walked onto the right-of-way, and having done this very thing many times before, continued my life of crime.

Dropping me off at a convenient hitchhiking location was nothing new for my parents. Not having the kind of money it took to jet me around Europe while I attended college, but understanding my wanderlust, they were subjected to numerous departures, similar to this one, as I spent my summers exploring North America. They didn't exactly encourage hitchhiking trips, but felt it would have been unfair to forbid me the travel opportunities available in my young adulthood. After dropping me off they would patiently wait until my first ride came along. We'd wave our final goodbyes, then I'd disappear down the road in the company of a stranger.

Now, on the day after Christmas, fifteen years after they had begun dropping me off on corners and waving goodbye, my parents sat in their comfortably heated car on the overpass, and waited. They were, no doubt, worried about how I would fare on this particular adventure. It was one thing to set their son on the road for a few weeks in the summer splendor of June, quite another to drop him off in the depths of winter and not expect to see him again for four months. They must have surely felt that their thirty-three year-old son would have been much better off tethered to a cluttered desk, laboring under the white freeze of fluorescent light tubes in a large, warm office building, than freezing his feet along the roadside. No matter what they felt at the time, after a fifteen minute wait, they watched their son escape.

A small station wagon slowed and gingerly drifted onto the slippery shoulder. The driver of my first ride had averted the disaster of spinning out and landing in the ditch. I felt confident it would be a safe ride on dangerous roads. I hoisted fifty pounds of gear off the road and walked up to the passenger door. When I opened it I was bombarded by music. The driver, Alan, was listening to the so-called supergroup, The Travelling Wilburys, so-called because the personnel consisted of the likes of Bob Dylan, Tom Petty and George Harrison. The tunes were coincidentally appropriate and I was sure I'd enjoy Alan's company. Through the haze of cold car exhaust and my own condensed breath, I jammed my gear into the back seat, waved a last goodbye to my folks, and climbed in.

Alan's car was full of skis and other cold weather stuff. On his way back home to Minneapolis, he was disappointed about having spent his little Christmas holiday up north with a bunch of people he wasn't very fond of. He didn't say how he had gotten tangled up in that situation, only that he was happy to be headed home.

As we drove toward the Twin Cities of Minneapolis and St. Paul, a small white kitten suddenly appeared on the back of my seat. I was startled by this surprise visitor. Sharing a ride with a driver's dog wasn't unusual, but I hadn't encountered many people who would take their pet cats with them on weekend trips. This little one travelled well and prowled around all the exciting stuff in back. Normally, cat hair would give me a fitful allergic reaction, but the kitten stayed out of my face so I remained dry eyed.

I was thrilled to be on my way. Poor Alan was subjected to a flurry of conversation that was primarily adrenaline induced. When I told him of my relief at no longer living in a medium sized city like Salem, he mentioned his concerns about the social problems facing a large city like Minneapolis. Most importantly for him and his family was the apparent failure of the public education system to provide an environment conducive to learning and personal growth. As the schools presently exist, the environment is one of fear, intimidation, stress, and cultural and intellectual deficiencies. He wasn't willing to let his kids be guinea pigs in hit and miss experiments by school systems, while administrators determined the best way to educate students. He had pulled his kids out of the public schools and enrolled them in a private school, under the assumption that it was capable of providing the optimum learning atmosphere. The results of his own experimentation wouldn't be available for at least ten years.

Our conversation ended seventy-five miles later. We split up where I-35 became I-35W to Minneapolis and I-35E to St. Paul. After Alan dropped me off on the shoulder I hustled across two lanes of traffic to reach the I-35E spur. Respect for the dangerously cold weather led me to consider my options at that point. Willow River had been no worry because of an interchange gas station, and, of course, my parents idling away in their car. Alan was suddenly gone and I was on my own. Although

I stood at a major junction, there were no gas stations or houses this far out of town to provide emergency shelter. It was up to me and my WINONA sign to coax a driver to stop. If it couldn't be done in a reasonable amount of time I would have to start walking to avoid the deadly effects of hypothermia. This threat added an interesting dimension to my reliance upon the goodwill of others. It was not a threat to be taken lightly.

There was no test of my cold weather endurance--that time. Chester Lehman stopped shortly after Alan left me. Even though I had used my sign to attract drivers, Chester said he stopped without noticing what it said. The effectiveness of even an ideally constructed sign is often doubtful. Still, sometimes the shabbiest sign imaginable can work miracles in getting the ride you want.

CHESTER LEHMAN
St. Paul, Minnesota

Chester was approximately thirty years old with short brown hair, wire-rimmed glasses, and an intense, introspective manner. I wasn't at all surprised to learn that he possessed an undergraduate degree in philosophy. He fit neatly into my stereotypical image. His employment as a carpenter, however, was unanticipated. When asked about the incongruity of his field of study with his profession, he disagreed, arguing that the two went hand in hand. His interest in carpentry and architecture stemmed from a desire to build "socially conscious housing." What he perceived as a social and cultural injustice, the lack of simple, decent shelter for low- and no-income Americans, led him to concentrate his efforts on solving the problem. It was an admirable physical response to an internal, philosophical call to action.

I-35E was incomplete through downtown St. Paul. Chester was able to navigate a messy little urban detour to return us to a brand new section of highway. By the time we had reached the southern suburb of Eagan, I needed to get out of his car to make another road connection. The highway I wanted crossed over I-35E, but there was no interchange. Chester pulled onto the shoulder at the overpass. I grabbed my gear, thanked him, and slogged up the steep, snow covered embankment to trade one highway right of way for another.

It was mid-morning and the weather was warming up. Being 100 miles south of my starting point made a big difference in temperature, too. These were positive contributions to my attitude as I faced the slight complication of route finding.

Making a couple of turns, or even backtracking to get from one highway to another, is a relatively simple procedure for someone in control of an automobile. A hitchhiker has a far more difficult time making those types of connections. Communicating his needs to passing motorists is usually limited to the abbreviated name of a town on a beat-up cardboard sign. Listing the most convenient route is rarely an option for the hitchhiker.

I fully expected to walk the three miles to U.S. Highway 52 through a mixed rural/suburban landscape. Hitchhiking in suburbia is something to be avoided if at all possible. Mothers hauling kids in station wagons are unlikely to pick up people who could possibly do them harm. It was already too late for me to avoid the inconvenient location so I simply began walking in the direction of my new route.

While walking along I would frequently check behind me for approaching vehicles. When any vehicle would come to within a hundred yards of my position, I would turn to flash them my sign and a smile. If they didn't stop, I turned again and continued walking until the next vehicle approached.

Scott McKnite made my life easy that morning by stopping after I'd strolled a mere half-mile. This guy was all smiles and questions. As for most people, picking up hitchhikers was an uncommon business for Scott. He was curious about what I was doing out and about in such cold weather. He also expressed genuine concern for my personal safety. The possibility of my being robbed, injured, or even killed, was worrisome to him. From his unselfish perspective he had forgotten that those same things could have happened to him under different circumstances.

Different circumstances could have been any of a million scenarios in which our safety was at stake. Those scenarios nearly always included irresponsible, unscrupulous people with little respect for life, taking what they could get away with. If those people did get away with some infraction that caused harm to someone else, they would be pleased that they didn't get caught and would be willing to do it again. Of course, the results would be at the expense of someone else. On the other hand, if caught, they would be quick to place blame on others, or a cultural situation which ultimately led them to wrongdoing. Our population has become so inundated with these whiny little people that we, as a society, have fallen into a quagmire of blame. It is acceptable, even fashionable, to place blame on the next guy for our own errors. Nobody, it seems, is capable of making and then taking responsibility for their own decisions. It is the sort of cultural environment in which lawyers get rich.

Whom are we supposed to trust in a population that feels no responsibilities and has twisted priorities? Where can we turn when our institutions are failing us, and around every corner is another shyster waiting to take us for all we're worth? In a world of senseless lawsuits and random violence we can no longer trust our neighbors, business associates, religious leaders, perhaps even our parents and spouses. This shabbiness of our combined cultural moral character is affecting progressively younger generations, thereby turning children into criminals. I wouldn't go so far as claiming the world was better off at any other time in human history, it's just that we are supposed to be advancing toward a more civilized society. It seems as though our achievement of that noble goal is long past due.

Constant exposure to this darker side of human nature by our media institutions leaves little time in our lives for hope. Engorged with the force-fed brutality of life that makes sensational news copy, I had nearly lost faith in life, liberty, and the pursuit of happiness. Those inspirational words were beginning to sound like nothing more than a storybook fantasy rather than the guidelines of democratic rights!

I just had to believe, despite the unending barrage of lousy news, that not everyone was locked into bewildering lives of hate, fear, and dishonesty. There must have been people out there who were peaceful, cooperative, and willing to rise above the fears perpetuated by our cultural mistrust. Turning to the road, as pilgrims had for centuries before, I found myself seeking a better way. I sought the trust residing in those people who would take a chance on sharing a few moments of their lives with a stranger and receive no tangible reward for such an effort. As they opened their car doors the drivers opened a small portion of their lives to me. With my reciprocity, through each ride experience, we would heal a bit of the large wound that was bleeding our national conscience to death.

Scott made the correct turn on U.S. 52 and I rode with him south to Cannon Falls. Assuring him that my vast hitchhiking experience had prepared me well for a safe continental excursion, Scott was amenable to letting me out to continue.

Things were looking good. I hadn't had to do any serious walking, the weather was turning fine, the rides had been pleasant and of reasonable distances, and after only a few minutes in Cannon Falls I had a ride to Rochester, home of the world renowned Mayo Clinic.

Gordon Pratt was returning home from the Twin Cities after visiting his kids and grandkids for the holidays. He had spent forty of his previous years working for IBM in Rochester. Now, basking in a well earned retirement, he spends his summers motorcycle touring.

Winona was now off to the east. Gordon brought me to the east edge of town, on U.S. 14, thereby saving me a potentially long walk.

By then the sky had turned gray. Already spoiled by short waits, after a mere one hour wait in Rochester my mood matched the sky. Without the sun to warm my face the cold started creeping in. Jim Pyfferoen was the driver who took me in and warmed me up. A friendly postal employee, he was heading home after working the 3:00 am to 11:30 am shift. When he dropped me off at a remote intersection it felt as though there would be another long wait ahead of me. It must have just been my nerves. Those solitary spots made me impatient, especially since there was more snow here than 170 miles north, in Willow River.

Despite the light traffic, one of the first few cars to approach came to a stop. There was no shoulder on this narrow highway but Bill Sholes squeezed as far to the right as possible. With so few cars passing by there wasn't much danger of a collision.

My sign may have read Winona but I was actually going to a friend's house in a rural area just north of the city. Bill volunteered to take me to a pay phone that was very close to my ultimate destination. He was from the area and knew all of the backroads. I sat there in the passenger seat watching unfamiliar scenery along unfamiliar roads until we pulled up to the pay phone in Minnesota City.

Having made prior arrangements to spend the night with friends, I called them up. This was my warm-up day on the road and I wanted it to finish in comfort. Unsure of the weather, I didn't want to take a chance on spending the night out-of-doors in below zero temperatures.

On my first nationwide hitchhiking trip, back in 1975, the outcome of day one wasn't nearly as pleasant. It had been a marginal day at best, barely making over 100 miles. I found myself surrounded by the Minnesota northwoods as the sun went down. It was a cool spring evening and bloodthirsty mosquitoes were out hunting for their next victim. I must have been the only living flesh around because it seemed as though every insect in the forest was doing a kamikaze dive into my face. That harassment was bad enough but even worse was the endless, annoying whine as they hovered around my ears.

My gear back in those days was basic, including a canvas boyscout-issue backpack, a light nylon sleeping bag, and a $24.95 JC Penney pup tent. Woe and misery to the poor neophyte! A few hours after I had escaped the demented insects by retiring into my tent, the weather began to rage. A cold hard rain and its attendant wind pummelled my camp.

The tent site was located on soft, boggy soil to protect my precious back, sort of a Princess and the Pea syndrome. The rain came down and filled up the surrounding peat moss like a massive sponge. The trees provided little protection from the wind. It seemed to follow the same path as the rain and came blasting straight down out of the sky.

By 3:00 am I was trying to sleep in a small, cold, nylon lake. The tent that was once a miniature, movable structure, was no longer standing. It had been reduced to so much wet material flopping around in the wind and mud. Sleep was impossible. Too cold and stunned to do anything else, I gathered the gritty, wet nylon together, jammed everything into the slimy canvas pack, and started walking down the highway. It was daybreak before somebody stopped to haul my weary bones to the next town.

This day, in contrast, had been outstanding. I wasn't sure if I wound up sleeping in a warm bed because of my excellent preparation, roadside savvy, thousands of miles of experience, or just dumb luck. Not wanting to look a gift horse in the mouth, I just hoped that whatever it was would keep on coming!

Chapter Two

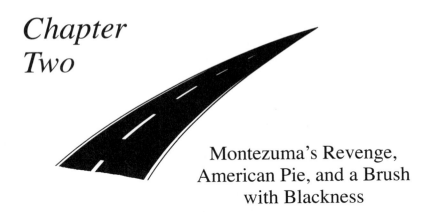

Montezuma's Revenge, American Pie, and a Brush with Blackness

In my search for an element of trust, the trip I had planned would take me to over half of the forty-eight continental United States and nine of the twelve Canadian provinces and territories. The route was fashioned on the basis of three factors: the weather, the location of acquaintances who were willing to harbor me for a day or two, and a geographic interest in certain areas I had never before travelled.

My departure date being in the middle of winter forced me to go south immediately. I had already taken enough chances with Old Man Winter by leaving northern Minnesota on the day after Christmas. Having no desire to face any more of his abuse I would remain in the southern half of the United States for the next two months. When signs of spring began to appear, the plan was to move north, along with the migrating birds.

The location of acquaintances across the country was also an important factor. On a trip of 17,000 miles that would take as long as four months to complete, I knew fatigue would take its toll on body and soul. My minuscule budget of $500 would not allow the extravagance of cushy nights in motels. I was depending on friends to lift my sagging spirit, share in my tales of good fortune and excitement, and provide shower and shelter. I intended to make good use of their hospitality.

It wasn't anything to bank on but I expected to spend an occasional night at a driver's home, too. Having experienced this type of generosity on previous trips I hoped it would happen often during this one.

Between those rest stops I was prepared to sleep wherever I landed. This time, equipped with a decent tent and warm sleeping bag, I could deal with nearly any sort of inclement weather. It was absolutely necessary to carry this type of gear because there was no way of predicting where the last ride of the day would end. Many times it would be in a very remote area. Whether it was in the Manitoba northwoods, on the high Texas desert plain, along the Pacific coast, or mired in deep snow on a mountain pass, good equipment and thorough preparation was the key to a safe, comfortable night's rest.

The remaining influence upon route design was my interest in geography. As a youngster, maps and globes held a particular fascination for me. There was no question that the strange names attached to cities, rivers, mountain ranges, lakes, canyons, and innumerable other geographic features, existed on something more tangible than a two-dimensional map. I knew they were actually out there. The map brought them to me in abstract form and provided me with the information it took to locate the features of interest in the real world. It was up to me to propel myself through space to fill in the abstraction. Only by feeling the heat, smelling the air, hearing the birds sing or the factories roar, and seeing, with the precious gift of my own two eyes, could I complete the mental map I carried with me at all times.

Having very little money but a burning desire to fill in the vast gaps of my geographic knowledge, I began hitchhiking. Now, many years after my first hitchhiked ride, in addition to passing through familiar western states, I intended to cover thousands of miles in the eastern half of the United States and Canada. Knowledge of that huge area had escaped me because during earlier years of travel I concentrated on seeing the plains and mountains of the western half. I was just as excited about seeing new highways as I was about re-travelling highways I regarded as old friends.

The most important part of all those route considerations was trust. Travelling to the corners, and across broad stretches of North America, I placed a complete reliance upon the good nature and trust within people at every stop of the way. I could have walked the route and seen all the same things and visited all my friends along the way, but that wasn't the point. I chose hitchhiking as my method of travel to force people to make a decision and give them an opportunity to express their kindness by offering me a ride.

Rational observation and logical decision making eludes many bright people when faced with picking up a hitchhiker. I'm reminded of an incident in Glacier National Park, Montana, where a small airplane had crashed in a snowstorm on a high mountain pass. A surviving woman eventually struggled her way through snow across unfamiliar terrain to reach the highway that traversed the park. She approached a passenger car that was parked on one of the many turnouts along that high elevation, scenic road. The occupants looked at her through their closed windows. They listened to her plead for help for a few seconds before taking off, leaving her standing in the snow.

The mind struggles to understand the driver's reaction. If the circumstances were altered ever so slightly, in terms of place and personalities, we might well find ourselves in the driver's seat, ignoring the same cries for help.

If we don't look into a hitchhiker's eyes it is easy to convince ourselves that they just don't exist. Like walking down a crowded sidewalk, with our eyes focused on infinity, we are unaware of the individual components of the humanity surrounding us. As we drive by we avoid the hitchhiker's eyes so if, perchance, they reflect trustworthiness, we simply won't be tempted to actually make a decision to stop. No recognition, no problem, no decision. We remain safe and sound. Any potential threat to our personal safety is retreating at 65 miles-per-hour. The rear-view mirror reflects a humanoid form that apparently had no face.

Of course, there are a million good reasons to drive by hitchhikers. I must have heard them all and have even used some of them as excuses myself. Most are legitimate, proper, and intelligent reasons which would make it irresponsible for me to encourage everyone to pick up people at every opportunity. That stack of reasons not to pick someone up is also why a successful hitchhike is such a remarkable event. I feel qualified to make that claim because of the surprise and relief that never fails to strike my emotions with every single ride encountered.

I would never imply that the people who passed me by were unkind. What can be said with complete confidence, regarding anyone driving a vehicle, is that picking up a hitchhiker requires a giant leap of faith. Believe it or not that leap of faith is the smaller of two hurdles. A larger wall to be scaled is the actual performance of hitting the brakes and pulling over. Decision without action is meaningless. If the driver makes the decision to stop and takes the steps to halt the vehicle, they suddenly find themselves waiting for a stranger to enter their vehicle. That is the moment when the fear and second guessing sets in.

The accompanying emotional rush from the fear and second guessing of your decision is powerful. To pick up a hitchhiker is to break taboo. Societal convention has certainly discouraged, and in some places even banned ride-sharing between strangers. It is only natural that when overcoming years of instinctual and learned fears our emotional reaction would be memorable.

I was standing on I-90 west of Winona, heading west, when Ralph pulled his rig over. Despite the preceding argument, when Ralph Young picked me up I was sure his emotional reaction was something less than memorable. The poor guy was nearly asleep! Even so, he must have been somewhat relieved at the prospect of breaking the monotony of his drive with a little company.

Pulling his rig over to the shoulder looked like no easy task. The rig Ralph piloted consisted of the unusual conglomeration of a small truck hauling a long trailer. That trailer in turn had smaller trailers stacked upon it a couple high. While he strained the brakes to maneuver it all over to the highway side, I rejoiced at getting the first ride of day two.

Starting that outfit up again from a dead stop taxed the worn out engine to the limit. Poor old Ford! I held my breath hoping my stuff and I wouldn't be the straw that broke the camel's back. It was a good thing we weren't on an uphill stretch or both Ralph and I would have been out hitch-hiking.

Ralph was also taxed to the limit. Driving all night on his 500 mile route from Elkhart, Indiana, he had run into bad weather and terrible road conditions. He was heading to St. Paul to deliver the trailers. He hadn't had any sleep since leaving and was bored and very tired. Nearly everyone knows of the stress involved with driving in bad weather. Ralph had the added stress of pulling a trailer assembly that was too much for a little truck and an illegal seven feet over length. He was avoiding truck weigh stations because he couldn't afford a fine. Once he'd been slapped with a $700 fine. He could deal with none of that now. He just wanted to deliver his load and relax. Needless to say, it wasn't an easy day for him; one of many he had faced as a truck driver.

Like most truckers, he was constantly on the road. That meant missing holidays with his family and friends. He was glad for the company, even for a mere half hour. I didn't envy his job.

Where Ralph turned north toward the Twin Cities I was still eight miles away from U.S. 63. It was a bad, in-between, spot. I waited for over two hours in 20°F temperatures and gusty winds. I was so chilled I had to begin walking toward the next exit which also happened to be the junction with U.S. 63.

After a mile long walk Greg Harlos stopped. This guy was too much! Greg possessed an indomitable spirit. He lived back in Winona, and travelled all over the United States installing and repairing stained glass windows. He was on his way to Mason City, Iowa, for a church job. South on 63 wasn't the most direct route for him, but he was willing to take a slight detour on my behalf. Once, Greg had gone 300 miles out of his way for the benefit of a hitchhiker. After hearing that story, it didn't seem like such a big deal for him to take me 20 miles out of his way this time. He enjoyed picking people up and rarely passed them by.

GREG HARLOS
New Hampton, Iowa

Greg was an extremely friendly and generous man with an interesting vocation. He had been working with stained glass since he was 17 years old and was supremely confident in his craftsmanship and abilities. He was glad to be on this job alone. He didn't have the energy to deal with a crew that morning. At 26 years of age, he supervised a crew of drunks and wanted to get rid of the whole bunch of them. He had plans to buy his own shop in Kentucky, as soon as possible. That was one sure way to dump his crew.

In the autumn of 1989 he had worked in Charleston, South Carolina, in the aftermath of hurricane Hugo. Needless to say, Hugo raised unholy hell with the stained glass windows in town. Charleston could have used about twenty guys just like him. While there, Greg was in his glory doing what he knew best.

Greg left me in New Hampton, Iowa after making the southern cut on 63. There weren't any route complications between where I stood and St. Louis. It was the next scheduled site of rest and relaxation.

In New Hampton, Ben Beckman almost passed me by, assuming I wouldn't be interested in a relatively short, six mile ride. He stopped to check nonetheless. Many people will pass by because they don't think they're going far enough to satisfy me. Often a short ride will provide much needed momentum. In Ben's case he was taking me to a safe, well travelled intersection.

Bedecked in khaki camouflage from head to toe, Ben was on his way to do some bow hunting for deer. He served in the army with an airborne unit stationed in Waterloo, Iowa. He was so extroverted and loquacious, I would have sworn he was a recruiter! He probably could have talked me into joining. Nah, maybe not.

Ben had taken a little hitchhiking trip around northeastern Iowa with some buddies back when he was in high school. They'd had a great time and those happy memories stuck with him. I was glad to have been the catalyst in his recall. One of the first things people mention to me, on or off the road, are their own hitchhiking experiences. Memories are often sparked by a stranger interested in hearing about long buried adventures.

While waiting just south of New Hampton I nearly scared my next ride away. The driver approached slowly and gave me a very close look. Perturbed by his apparent scowl and condescending stare, I scowled back and shrugged my shoulders to ask the universal question, "Why not?"

He had not been frightened away and I got the answers to my questions when he stopped. Mike Miller and his dog Quincy were not being critical with their looks as I had originally assumed, but calculating. He had been busy comparing the small amount of space he had left in his car with the amount of gear I was carrying. Success! He figured I'd fit, so stopped to squeeze me in. Much to the dismay of the big black lab, Quincy, I swiped his front row seat. I doubted he'd ever forgive me.

Both Mike and I seemed to have lived nearly parallel lives up until the month prior to our meeting. We were in our early thirties, raised in the midwest, attended college in the western United States to study engineering and science, possessed masters degrees, and found ourselves returning to our adolescent homes. It was there our paths suddenly diverged. Mike was continuing on a career track by working at an engineering firm. I, on the other hand, had derailed my career a month earlier by quitting my job as a cartographer with the state of Oregon. With so much in common up to that point our conversation was fast and furious.

The holidays must have put Mike in a generous state of mind. While visiting family over the past few days he had obtained quite a stash of Christmas goodies. Twisting my arm until I could stand it no longer, I accepted the almonds and homemade toffee he offered. Both items were excellent travelling food: durable, light and sweet. The toffee didn't last 24 hours but I was able to ration the almonds for a week.

Mike took exception to the pathetic little atlas I used as a map. He pulled out an excellent, glove-compartment-sized road atlas and insisted I take it. It proved to be an invaluable navigation and planning aid throughout the entire trip. I still have it, though much worse for wear.

Our pleasant visit ended a few miles south of Waterloo, Iowa, in the small town of Hudson. Quincy reclaimed the front seat and I was back on the road.

The temperature was a balmy 35°F. The shoulder consisted of slush covered dirt. On my left was a filling station. As I stood there looking around, getting a feel for my new spot, I noticed a fuel customer glancing my way. It is only natural for people to look at anomalies so I never think too much about people staring at me. If I was anything, I was definitely a curiosity for most folks.

A couple of minutes later a big, old Cadillac Coupe deVille slowly approached. As it passed by I noticed it was driven by the kid at the gas station who had looked me over from there. We made eye contact briefly and I waved. He returned the wave but kept on driving. A few minutes following our momentary communication of mutual friendliness he pulled up and offered a ride.

There didn't seem to be that many drivers in fancy cars willing to give people rides. Because it didn't happen all that often, climbing into nice cars always made me nervous. The feeling was similar to entering a house decorated in a museum motif. You couldn't touch anything for fear of breaking, smudging, or creasing any artifacts or furniture.

The driver of the Cadillac, Eric Schumacher, ignored my request to put my stuff in the trunk and said it would be fine in the back seat. He was the boss. Fortunately, my big backpack was still relatively free of road grime.

Eric was the first of a disappointingly few young people who picked me up. I don't think he had ever picked anybody up before. Perhaps there was the occasional ride to other kids around his hometown, but never some unknown guy out along the highway. Hence the caution exhibited by driving past to get a closer look at me and see if I displayed a bad attitude. Scowling drunks, panhandlers, people with chips on their shoulders and a generally unfriendly disposition are easy to spot with a single pass. He was, after all, driving his parents' car. He had to exhibit some measure of responsibility! I was fortunate he stopped. Not because of the ride itself, but for the opportunity to meet Eric.

ERIC SCHUMACHER
Toledo, Iowa

Only a junior in high school, Eric was the youngest driver to ever pick me up. We must have looked like quite a team cruising in the old Caddy. He sported the usual trappings of a high schooler: baseball cap, a black tee shirt decorated with the horrifying faces of a rock group, and a green army surplus jacket. His hair was of a conservative length and he wore large, dark rimmed glasses which gave him the appearance of a budding intellectual. He was of medium height and slight of build.

Over twice his age, I wasn't a pretty sight adorning the highway shoulder. At 6'3", 180 pounds, with my long hair in a ponytail and prematurely graying dark beard, I cut a rather intimidating figure. With my three to four layers of warm clothing I probably appeared to weigh closer to 250 pounds. Most people frankly admit they would never even consider picking me up. Can't say I blame them.

Both Eric and I were explorers. I had set my fears aside to place myself at the mercy of the population. It was the only way to seek the knowledge I needed. Eric also set his fears aside for the purpose of discovery. By picking me up he expected to get a taste of a lifestyle previously foreign to him. He drilled me with unending questions about the structure and details of my life. Not anything really personal, just chronological.

Of particular interest was the transition between high school and college. He was formulating his future plans and wanted to hear of my experience. Trying not to sound too negative I told him my undergraduate university experience was a terrible, but necessary one. My alma mater, the University of Minnesota, was an overwhelmingly large student factory. I was the type of student who had to study constantly to squeeze out a C average. As the quarters went by my enthusiasm waned. My graduation seemed to have set a pattern for life. Finishing a particular job, or course of study, I couldn't get away from it fast enough. It was on to the next thing. No real plan, just on to the next thing.

Eric loved high school and was a good student. What made me encourage him to attend college was the necessity of good communication skills in today's information society. I assured Eric that his high school background would serve him well in college. Colleges were made for enquiring kids like Eric.

The daylight hours were short this close to the winter solstice and it was dark when we arrived at a department store parking lot in Toledo, Iowa. As Eric drove away I hoped that the rest of his generation was as bright and thoughtful. Eric reminded me that they have to put up with a lot of criticism. They face a continuous barrage of reports on poor standardized test scores, geographic ignorance, and the three R's being ignored by school systems and students alike. It's such a shame to resign them to failure, by our own failures as a society. Not all of our youth are drug addled, violence prone, troublemakers. They are simply a reflection of their environment.

So, there I was, standing in a discount department store parking lot in an unfamiliar town, in the dark. Fortunately, small towns in Iowa weren't very threatening. I wasn't going to be hitchhiking anywhere else that night so started looking for a place to spend the night. I walked about 200 yards south and came across a huge high school athletic playing field complex. Perfect. I set up my tent in a remote corner to avoid being bothered, or bothering anyone. Trees surrounded my site and a slight rise interfered with the view from the houses along the road. There isn't a more secure feeling than being invisible, and on that winter's night, I was.

Even though I was very tired, it took hours to fall asleep. After all, it was my first night out in the wilds of middle America, and I felt like a live wire!

A hitchhiking trip makes the location of your next bed a real mystery. You awaken each morning with the hope of arriving at a particular goal. In my case I would usually leave a place with my next friend's house in mind. Sometimes I would make it there while other times I would still be hundreds of miles away at day's end. All you can do is go until you stop. You are completely out of control of forward motion. What you can control is when to quit for the day. Darkness and fatigue would usually force me to begin looking for a discreet tent site.

In finding a good camp site the thing to look for is cover. Trees, bushes, field crops, hills, and sometimes buildings can protect you from detection. Undeniably, the best cover is darkness. Darkness enables you to move about, finding quiet little places in the blackest of shadows. It sounds kind of slinky and sleazy, and I suppose it is, reflecting sort of an underworld existence. The whole purpose of the exercise is legitimate enough: to obtain the privacy and quiet required for a very tired person to get plenty of rest.

Arising at dawn to be on the road as soon as feasible keeps you out of trouble just in case you had been sleeping on private property. After spending a few nights on the road much of this information would be self-evident. I actually looked forward to the daily challenge of finding a place to put my simple, but adequate bed. It broke the monotony of going from car to car, constantly moving.

On the fourth morning of the trip, I awoke in Toledo to a world devoid of sound. I poked my nose out of the tent into a gray, wet, blanket of fog. I neglected to mention above what good cover fog makes. Good cover, but bad housekeeping. The dampness made everything cold and clammy. I had erected my tent on snow so both the rain fly and tent floor were soaked. There wasn't even the slightest breeze that morning to help dry the nylon. I had no choice but to pack everything up wet. I was not looking forward to pulling all of that stuff out later in the day and trying to set it up. The small town of Warrenton, Missouri, was the location of my next planned stop. Just west of St. Louis, Warrenton was a little more than 300 miles away. It would take a long day and the best of luck to hip-hop through the small towns of Iowa and northern Missouri to make it. The possibility of sleeping in a dry bed that night seemed hopelessly remote at that damp and dreary moment.

Arriving at the road dressed in full rain gear, I lamented leaving my warm, cozy sleeping bag. The fog gave what little I could see of Toledo a look of desolation. It could have easily been mistaken for the radioactive remnant of the long anticipated nuclear holocaust. Its drippy gray fingers clung onto every visible thing and created a haunted, eerie atmosphere. With everything so quiet and little sign of life along main street, I would have rather ignored the world with my head under the covers.

Of the people who were out, nobody seemed to be going south. I walked a mile across the remainder of Toledo, then another half mile into Tama before a man pulled over, driving an old, beat up Plymouth Colt. It too looked like a remnant of a bomb blast. The driver of that pitiful heap of rust was turning off at the edge of town, but could drop me off at a good junction. He said he was surprised to see me out on the road, claiming that nobody around there ever picked up hitchhikers. Despite his skepticism, I tried to remain hopeful. There was no other choice.

Justifying my hope, a driver hit the brakes of his five ton truck as he topped the hill where I stood waiting. The cab was so tall, I couldn't even see who was driving. As I teetered beneath the unwieldy bulk of my 50 pound pack, trying to push it up into the cab, I saw this enormous hand reach out to grab it and haul it effortlessly upward. I followed it up. When I climbed into the narrow passenger seat, I was met by a huge, hairy (grizzly bear comes to mind) man behind the wheel. His name was Jack Eckstein.

Jack was in his late thirties. He had long black hair and a long, curly black beard. Massive, he nearly filled his half of the cab. It was impossible to tell if he was smiling through his beard. His dark eyes gave no hint as to his demeanor. I did not want this man angry at me! He wouldn't have looked out of place decked out in greasy black leather, riding a chopped, customized '65 Harley, with a motorcycle mamma glued to his back.

His temperament didn't match his rough-hewn appearance. It's funny how guys who look so intimidating can turn out to be so soft-spoken. The old maxim about reading books by their covers continues to be good advice.

Jack was only going about 20 miles, to the intersection of U.S. 63 and I-80, near Malcom. It felt great to be out of the cold drizzle, for a little while anyway.

Malcom, Iowa, seemed like the perfect hitchhiking spot. There was traffic coming off the interstate, and there were also a couple of busy truck stops at the intersection. I promptly positioned myself in the optimum location to catch a lift. There was plenty of room to pull over, traffic was just beginning to accelerate to speed, and there were no visual obstructions so approaching drivers had plenty of time to view me and decide. Unfortunately, despite the seemingly perfect location, things were deteriorating rapidly.

The weather had quickly turned colder, windier, and wetter. It was an ugly combination. To make matters worse, whenever the rare southbound vehicle did pass by, I would get a little shower of road grime. It would mist up off of the tires, get caught in the strong head wind, and come straight for me. I was wearing a teal colored parka that was slowly turning brown. My glasses soon looked like an automobile windshield that needed a good squeegee cleaning. I was getting hungry, too. I needed some fuel to fend off the cold, but conditions were bad enough that I didn't feel like opening up my pack. I snacked on the almonds thoughtfully provided by Mike Miller, the day before.

After enduring two full hours of that misery, I was relieved when a couple of guys stopped to take me away. Their car was so full of stuff, it took a while to make space. I folded myself in, enjoyed the warmth, and considered myself lucky. It turned out that they were only going to the next town, about eight miles away. Oh well, it could have been only three!

They left me in the middle of Montezuma, Iowa. It appeared to be a nice enough, little, working class town. I stood there for yet another two hours, under the same lousy conditions, before deciding I'd better take a break. I felt like an icicle that had been dropped into dirt.

I walked across the street to a convenience store/gas station and bought a cup of hot chocolate. I was so cold I could barely speak. I did manage to ask the cashier if he minded if I drank the stuff inside the store, giving me a couple of minutes to warm up. He said no, I couldn't. Well, I was shocked! Some sweet little geek in some sweet little mid-western town didn't have the civility to let me enjoy their product under their roof. I didn't think my request was at all extravagant or intrusive. It wasn't as though I had just purchased a magnum of muscatel and planned on getting drunk and passing out in a corner of the store.

My guess was that his friends could come in and hang out as long as they wanted. They probably talked about important stuff like cheerleaders and fast cars. I was infuriated and dejected. Was this the kinder and gentler America our politicians wanted us to become? Long waits for rides and no friendly faces to be experienced, right here in Heartland, USA. It was probably a blessing in disguise that my lips were frozen. Imagine the trouble I might have gotten into if I'd been able to give him a piece of my mind!

Fuming with anger, I went back to my spot on the corner, drank the hot chocolate, walked back to the store, threw the paper cup into a trash can, came back to my pack, picked it up and started walking south. I had seen about all I could stand of Montezuma, Iowa.

When I move and think so deliberately, I realize how mad I can get. Unfortunately, a hitchhiker must constantly keep emotions under control. You're so visible. Everything you do, including the slightest display of negative emotions could affect a driver's decision to stop. You must remain cool. Each approaching vehicle must be met with a smile upon your face. The only thing that matters is the next ride. A ticket to the fast car out of town can't be obtained with a glower.

After nearly five hours of standing in a freezing drizzle, I figured it was time for some better luck. It came, in less than a half mile of walking, in the form of Henry Schaper. He was driving a huge diesel pick-up truck christened "THUMPER." He lived in Eddyville, which gave me about 45 minutes to warm up and chill out.

Henry was a power house construction contractor. Business was booming and he resented the errand that was bringing him home. A former employee was suing him for some alleged injury that had occurred on the job. He took it in stride though; he'd counter-sue the bastard! He was confident of his legal position and thought the whole thing a lot of foolishness. Here was a man getting sued by a former employee, who didn't hesitate at stopping for a stranger who could possibly cause him even more trouble. Henry must have had a deep faith in the good nature of people despite his disaffected worker.

Henry was a man who liked to work and worked hard to support his family of nine kids. I can't even imagine being married, and this guy's got nine kids! How could anyone like to work that hard?

I hadn't even set my pack down at the corner in Eddyville when Larry T. Williams stopped. He was from Bussey, Iowa, and worked for Pella Windows. He'd spent 19 years at the same plant and figured he helped produce the finest windows in the world. He was a real talker and I noticed a slight southern drawl. I wondered how he had retained it after being in the midwest for so many years.

He seemed to be a real do-gooder. He told me of the many people he had helped out when they were faced with financial hardship. He clearly didn't squander any of his money on himself. He was a middle-aged bachelor, wore second hand store clothes and drove an old, rusted out Pontiac Grand Prix. He made sure I had plenty of food and water before he set me on the road again. I admired him because his heart was so huge. Larry took me to a great spot to catch a lift, on the southern edge of Ottumwa. Things were definitely looking up! There was even a little break in the drizzle that seemed to be waiting at every intersection I landed on.

Another Larry stopped almost immediately. Larry Marshall was the epitome of the midwestern man. He owned and operated a farm that primarily raised shorthorn cattle. In addition to ranching, he labored at a meat packing plant. He was a union man, proud of his work and responsibilities. His family lived in Bloomfield, and he was headed home from his day's work in the city.

Larry was a pleasant, happy, and handsome man in his mid-forties. He cut quite a profile with his baseball cap, clean cut face and easy smile. He looked sharper after working all day at a packing plant than I would have looked at a wedding. It was nice to experience this slice of apple pie. Larry was what I had expected to find earlier that day, in Montezuma. It was worth the wait. The wholesome spirit of America's heartland, as expressed through Larry Marshall's kindness, didn't let me down.

Larry's ride brought me to a good intersection, south of Bloomfield. Seasonally short daylight hours, with five of them totally wasted on long waits that morning, left little time before dark. The overcast sky sped the night even closer. A solitary Pizza Hut was the only sign of life. The weather was getting bad again, so I donned my rain pants once more and prepared for the worst. Some guy in a decrepit, green Dodge Dart was out driving around trying to charge up his battery. He took me a few miles to another good intersection. As he dropped me off the clouds could no longer contain their burden. I got hammered by a torrential downpour.

I was already soaked when two guys in a little pick-up truck and canopy let me ride in back. Perfect. I could stretch out and relax under the sealed canopy. I needed the break. I kicked back and listened to the water swoosh around the vehicle as big, fat raindrops drummed on the canopy roof.

They turned off the highway to stop at a farm house where they bought some eggs. It didn't matter to me. I was in no hurry. There was no sense trying to race the darkness that had already fallen. They were only going 16 miles down U.S. 63 and left me on the edge of nowhere.

Gary Robinson watched me get dropped off and I flagged him down. There was no light at that intersection and I have no doubt that if he hadn't noticed me and stopped I would have spent the night at that spot. I would have set my wet tent up on a frozen farm field covered with pools of rain water. Ever since my ride with Henry Schaper out of Montezuma, my momentum had been carrying me along. The good fortune continued.

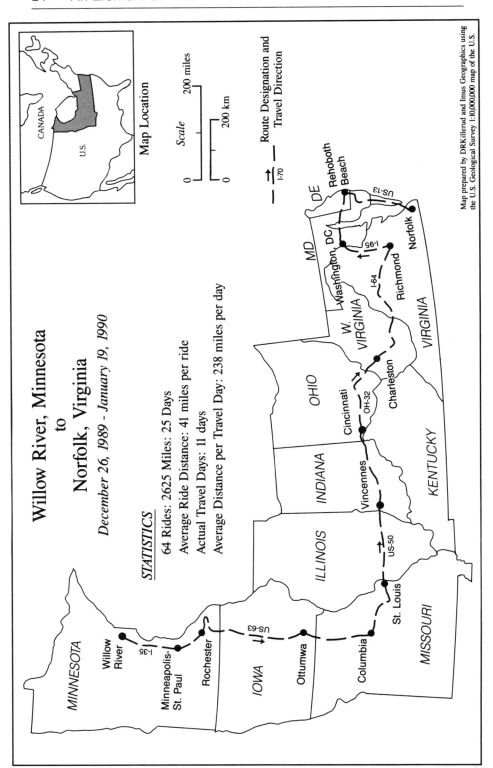

Willow River, Minnesota
to
Norfolk, Virginia

December 26, 1989 - January 19, 1990

STATISTICS

64 Rides: 2625 Miles: 25 Days
Average Ride Distance: 41 miles per ride
Actual Travel Days: 11 days
Average Distance per Travel Day: 238 miles per day

Map Location

Scale

0   200 miles

0   200 km

I-70

Route Designation and
Travel Direction

Map prepared by DRKillerud and Imus Geographics using
the U.S. Geological Survey 1:10,000,000 map of the U.S.

Kirksville is home to North East Missouri State College. Although Gary wasn't a student there at the moment, he was heading there to tend to some school business. Unemployed at the time, he could no longer attend school due to a lack of funds.

Gary had an untapped adventurous streak inside of him. He loved trains and had romantic visions of travelling the countryside by hopping freights. He spoke endlessly and affectionately of his knowledge of trains. He told me about technical things like lighting, speed, company origins of various rail lines, grades, and the latest information on the demise of certain routes. Where I would always have a Rand McNally road atlas at my fingertips, Gary would have a Rand McNally Railroad Atlas at his. He showed me the copy he carried in his car. I hadn't even realized that they published such a thing.

He dropped me at a perfect spot in Kirksville. There was a stop light to slow traffic down, a wide shoulder, a bright street light, and best of all, it was at the southern edge of town. A lot of cars drove past me, despite my great location. It was still raining steadily and I began to think about spending the night there. Across the road was a huge cemetery with a solitary light illuminating a structure. I started walking that way, to check it out. I was hoping for an overhanging roof or some sort of drive-through port, where I could stay reasonably dry.

I had never slept in a cemetery before. The weather provided a perfect backdrop for my vivid imagination. As I contemplated walking across the street, my mind began to replay scenes from old horror movies involving graveyards. Mummys, grave robbers, vampires, the living dead, and other evil creatures chased all reason out of me. Even though I was tired and my body ached for some relief, I decided I wasn't quite capable of steeling myself for a long, dismal night chasing ghouls. Returning to the security of the street lamp, clinging onto my little spot, I wished someone would notice me.

It was a wise and fortunate move. A young man named Ross stopped soon thereafter. He was going the entire 95 miles into Columbia, Missouri. I had escaped sleeping with the dead, so far.

Ross had had his first hitchhiking experience just a couple of days earlier. He had driven his car a few miles outside of town when the alternator quit. He tried hitching back to town but wound up walking the whole way. He just couldn't understand why nobody stopped; a common complaint among hitchhikers! Now that he had wheels again, he wasn't about to leave the next guy standing along the road.

Ross was a business student at North East Missouri State. He also played third string on their football team, which wasn't always a rewarding vocation. The coach would call his number to play when the team was either winning by a safe margin, or getting crushed. If it was a close game he got to watch without getting beat up. I don't think Ross lay awake all night worrying about his, and the team's, football performance. He was cool about it.

He was on the road that nasty night, with his new, $100 alternator humming along, to visit one of his best friends. This friend had grown up with Ross in Lake Ozark, Missouri, a little town southwest of Jefferson City. His friend was black but had a white wife. Ross, a caucasian, claimed there was a lot of racial prejudice in central Missouri. Landlords would turn the couple away, as they looked for apartments, because they were racially mixed. Growing up with close, racially diverse friends, Ross never really saw color and was saddened at the underlying bigotry existing around him. Many of us feel that same sadness, no matter what color we are.

Columbia, Missouri, was still 66 miles from Warrenton, where my friends lived. So close, yet so far, as I was reaching the limits of my endurance. My momentum had been so good I had to try pressing onward. Relying on adrenaline, I waited in a lousy place. It was getting late, pitch-dark, no street lamp on this entrance ramp to I-70, and no place to camp immediately visible amongst the suburban sprawl. I was tired, and it was still raining! I definitely did not want to set up my tent that night. I was thinking of making a deal with the devil as I stuck out my thumb. I hoped someone would see me through their wipers and stop before I would give in to any such arrangement!

After a half hour of feeling invisible, the driver (speak of the devil!) of The Black Death Monte Carlo angled over. Angled over meaning he left most of the vehicle in the roadway. This was especially dangerous because the vehicle was completely black with no visible tail-lights or rear reflectors. When it had come to a complete stop, the passenger door flew open. I stood there in the cold rain, exhausted, looking at this battered black beast rumbling only ten paces away, trying to decide whether to walk up and step into the belly of the beast or turn and run. The entire situation was like a scene right out of a slice and dice horror flick. The only difference was that I was playing the lead role!

In the movies the characters are so stupid. They always start down the hallway, open a cobwebbed, rusty hinged door to enter the cellar and continue down squeaky, rotten stairs. With plenty of opportunities to go back and have a piece of pie and coffee in town, they continue, driven by the hand of a twisted screenwriter to a harrowing demise. All the while the movie goers are telling the person next to them that nobody, but nobody, is stupid enough to go through that many hoops to their potential doom!

Despite being warned by a hundred movies of what not to do in these real life situations, I sucked up a deep breath and approached the door. The trust I was seeking, across the country, had to begin with me.

I was only seeing shadows, but was able to distinguish two human forms in the front seat and piles of debris in the back. There was no dome light. Before I stuck my head in I noticed a couple of cars swerve at the last second to avoid the nearly invisible Black Death. In the momentary passing of traffic their headlights illuminated the backs of the occupants heads but not their faces. I may as well have been blindfolded.

Monte Carlos have only two doors. The passenger didn't want to get out into the rain, so leaned forward and pulled the seat-back with him. This allowed me to get my pack into the back seat but not me. The driver and I had to shove all the stuff in the back seat aside so I could climb in. I sat holding my pack on my lap for the entire ride. I shuffled my feet around to find a comfortable position to carry the weight of the backpack. The floor was piled high with pop and beer cans. That made for even less leg room than a Monte Carlo normally provides. Hey, I didn't even care. It was warm and dry in there and they were headed all the way into St. Louis. Their next stop was Warrenton, to drop me off.

The wild man behind the wheel (I never did catch either of their names) liked to drive fast. I thought it a proper strategy since the car had no tail lights. Being so completely cloaked, we didn't want anybody approaching us from the rear. That way there was no chance of getting the Black Death's trunk slammed, creating a screaming inferno of twisted metal. Not to mention the human toll of such an event.

No automobile of the Black Death genre would be complete without a sound system capable of very high volume and very low fidelity. Add this feature to the noise emanating straight from the manifold into a non-existent exhaust system, and there isn't much opportunity for an intellectual discussion of world events. This barrage of industrial strength decibels made sign language the only reasonable method of communication, except it was dark and I wasn't fluent. Communication on my part was reduced to yelling things like, "Oh, yeah," "For sure," "I know what you mean," and "Right on, man," in response to unheard questions or comments. I simply figured I'd better agree with them.

The Black Death had some handling idiosyncracies I found interesting. At speeds above 75 mph the front end developed mysterious shakes and rattles. It also had the obnoxious habit of transmission slippage for no apparent reason; accompanied by the uncontrolled revving that occurs when the load is removed from an engine at a high rpm. The driver would be trying to pass some 70 mph tortoise with the throttle mashed to the floor and the darn tranny would slip. We'd coast for a few seconds with the engine howling in protest, before the transmission would grab hold again. I never really got used to it. My heart would jump into my throat each time it happened. The cold sweats didn't come and go, they just stayed.

Hurtling through the thick fog at 80 mph reminded me of an earlier trip, across Nebraska. I was riding in a rust-consumed Pontiac Safari station wagon with a driver who never spoke. It was only Nebraska, so I didn't care that I never saw it. In fact, I couldn't even tell you where I got picked up or dropped off on that ride. The Twilight Zone never ran such eerie episodes! In this particular installment, heading for St. Louis, I was simply interested in surviving the next forty minutes.

It was clear to me that we needed to go 80 mph because most of the other traffic was going 75. There was simply no way this guy was going to let any of these "Show Me" staters beat him to ol' St. Louiee. It was interesting to note that these guys were from Marshalltown, Iowa, home of our young pal, Eric Schumacher.

I was able to decipher the driver's mission. He was registering for truck drivers school (God save us all!!), and his friend was just along for the ride. I couldn't believe his friend didn't have anything better to do than risk life and limb on this joy ride in a rainstorm. (I couldn't believe I didn't have anything better to do!) Once he had checked in, they were returning home immediately. I never did quite comprehend the whole sequence of events required for this school registration. In fact I didn't understand much of anything at that point, nor did I care!

Warrenton was fast approaching in this suicidal race and we were in the outside lane. Along with its many other deficiencies, I had no reason to believe this car had any brakes. I simply slouched down in the back seat, behind my pack, and closed my eyes. When I opened them again, we were parked under the glimmering lights of a convenience store. I cracked a smile and breathed a sigh of relief.

As I unloaded my gear, one of Missouri's finest came walking up to us with a look of consternation on his face. I quickly scanned the area for flashing lights and a S.W.A.T. team commander preparing a shoot to kill order. The officer had noticed the missing tail lights as we entered the parking lot and politely advised the driver to repair the problem before proceeding any farther down the road.

THAT'S IT?! My brain screamed at me! You mean you're not going to haul us all into some roach infested Missouri jail and beat us about the head and shoulders with hickory truncheons for violating, if not the letter, at least the spirit of all traffic laws? Hell, just being near that car could be considered gross negligence. God only knows what other violations were being perpetrated; perhaps transportation of controlled substances, no insurance, registration, or license, in addition to the obvious open container and vehicle safety laws.

As it was on that particular Friday night, the driver kindly thanked the officer for bringing the light problem to his attention and set about fixing it. I thanked them for the ride, found the nearest phone and was quickly whisked away by friends, to a quiet place with a dry bed, and a glass of warm milk.

The smile I had barely cracked in the back of the Monte Carlo had finally turned into a big, stupid grin.

Chapter Three

The Corn Belt to the D.C. Beltway

I went to a party on the night of December 31st, to usher in the New Year. After being introduced around I commenced talking to a few party-goers about the hitchhiking tour I was in the midst of. A guy named Avery got all hot and defensive about the fact that he never picks up hitchhikers anymore. Avery was determined, in a really convoluted way, to make me defend his position on the matter. Well, at one point in my life I did consider going to law school. Perhaps that was enough to qualify me to take his case. A further boost to my resume was the fact that I understood nearly every aspect and idiosyncracy regarding driver conduct. Perhaps I could speak objectively enough to convince him that he was correct in passing right by hitchhikers. Of course, by making an excellent case, I was running the risk that he'd probably drive right by me some day!

The argument I used was one of peer identity. When he was younger, poorer, and without the responsibility of a family , he was free to be a ramblin' sort of guy. Back then, young ramblin' sorts were easy to recognize. They had long, greasy hair, wore sandals, colorful tie-dyed clothes, beads, and carried a pocketful of pot. If you happened to be driving along in your flower-power Volkswagen bus and saw someone along the road who looked a lot like you, you figured they were safe because you recognized a compatriot. You pulled over, gave them a lift, shared a joint and bitched about Nixon and the war. It was cool, man. No Problem.

On the other hand, if the hitchhiker you were approaching had a butch haircut and "square clothes" you would drive by laughing and questioning the propriety of letting Nazis roam freely in a democracy. Even then you discriminated on the basis of a stranger's appearance. You didn't recognize the attitude or style, so that hitchhiker was a threat. There was nothing to immediately grasp and understand about that person, so you drove by. It was easy to drive by then and even easier now!

I have found that even the tiniest link of recognition can establish a relationship worthy of an element of trust. An attractively drawn destination sign, the pleasant color of my teal parka, plain glasses that make me look intellectual or less threatening, the orderliness of my gear, awful weather, or any of a thousand possible variables that might strike a chord of recognition with a driver.

Most people are trying just as hard to find a reason to pick you up as they are to leave you standing. Many people confess that it breaks their hearts to drive past someone. The internal struggle that these people experience affects the hitchhiker's emotions as well. The fleeting seconds of eye contact that exist with the approach of a vehicle is very revealing. I witness that turmoil on the faces of sensitive drivers at nearly every corner. The hitchhiker needs to help make each driver's decision as easy as possible.

Avery, selling out to the establishment, was now a Volvo-driving yuppie with a wife and kids. A lot of the questionable characters along the roadside were clearly not his recognizable peers. Unless he came upon a disabled Mercedes with husband, wife, and kids with their thumbs out (wearing designer emblems on nearly every article of clothing), offering a lift was just not in the cards. Which is just fine. A true hitchhiker understands this sort of psychology and spends little, or no time contemplating tortures for drivers who pass you by; except, of course, for entertainment purposes during those few long waits. We never expect anyone to actually stop, we're just fortunate and pleasantly surprised when they do.

Our discussion convinced Avery he needn't fret any longer. There was no sense losing sleep after passing by a hitchhiker. The hitchhiker is plenty used to watching traffic go by. We toasted the New Year with hopes of a successful trip, for my sake and that of our society.

A couple of days later, the tenth day out of Willow River, I found myself on a corner in O'Fallon, Illinois, watching traffic go by. I had deemed St. Louis far enough south for now. In O'Fallon, just east of East St. Louis, I hooked up with U.S. 50. I planned to take highway 50, east across Illinois and Indiana.

It was an hour wait at a grimy intersection before Dave Shake took me a short distance into Trenton, Illinois. As a member of the armed forces, he was stationed on Shemya Island, Alaska. Shemya is a 2 1/2 by 4 1/2 mile rock at the far western end of the Aleutian Islands. The sole purpose of the 600 men and women there was to watch out for the Russians. Dave was stationed there on a one year assignment. Originally from southern Illinois, he was back visiting his family on a one week leave. He escaped out of the Anchorage airport only moments before Mt. Redoubt, in the Aleutian mountain range, erupted for the second time in as many weeks. Had his plane been grounded, perhaps he would have been forced to hitchhike the Alaska Highway. Nah. That's probably a little too far to go on a week's leave. If he had tried to do it the attempt would certainly have given him a different perspective on an element of trust!

Insurance salesman Mark Schuette short-hopped me to Aviston, Illinois. With a chilly wind, slate gray skies, light traffic and long waits, Illinois wasn't exactly treating me like a king.

The monotony snapped when a Lincoln Mark V stopped. Seventy-six-year-old Bud Welker treated me to the first and only Lincoln ride I'd ever had. I rode with him to Salem, Illinois. He was the kind of man who had been in control positions most of his life. He possessed the confidence of an oil company executive. He looked the part of the sophisticate in his pin striped suit and full pate of wavy, white hair.

In his youth, Bud slaved in the northern Michigan oil fields for next to nothing. He climbed his way up the industrial ladder until he owned his own oil company. He ran afoul of the federal government when he failed to register a particular real estate transaction. This was enough of a transgression to land him in jail for three years. While it wasn't exactly hard labor and even though the facility resembled a college dorm, he was not a free man. He was attempting to sue his former lawyers for malpractice and was furious because the court kept postponing his trial dates. The court's most recent postponement was for ten months. He assumed the court was putting it off long enough for him to die of old age. Out of sight, out of mind. It was no joke. This silver lion still had his claws and was going to live to be 100-years-old, just to spite the lawyers, judges and insurance executives who had been thorns in his paw over the past thirty years.

After spending so much time maneuvering through our judicial system, he was frustrated by its apparent lack of justice. He felt that lawyers, judges, and money were the main deterrents to justice. I concurred claiming there seemed to be no room for truth in the crowded courtrooms in this country. "Do you promise to tell the truth, the whole truth and nothing but the truth, so help you God?" Fat chance. The truth was nothing but a hinderance to a judicial bargain.

Bud anticipates a revolution in the United States. Not a revolt against economics or government, nor on racial or religious grounds, but against an obsolete, ineffective, corrupt and otherwise worthless justice system. I, too, welcomed the thought of rebellion. I only hoped it would take place before Bud turned 100.

I was surprised when he declined to have his picture taken. He practically blushed. I bet that didn't happen too often. He volunteered his car and I photographed my one and only Lincoln. Cadillac drivers, unlike their Lincoln driving counterparts, give rides fairly frequently. Leave it to Bud to break the mold. He was the sort of man who could always make an exception to pointless rules. He didn't live by the book.

A couple of short rides from Bob Helm and Dale Jones brought me into Flora, Illinois. It was already dark when Dale dropped me off. I was wasted after a long day with little progress. It was one of my lowest mileage days. It had taken eight hours to travel a paltry seventy-four miles. Less than ten miles an hour is about as bad as it can get!

The temperature was dropping as I snooped around for a place to camp. North of the highway were some cultivated fields that had not yet been swallowed up by residential expansion. Along the far edge was a strip of trees that could provide the cover I desired. Aided by the ethereal light of a Pizza Hut sign, I set up camp, and slept like a baby.

The morning of January 5th was frost laden after temperatures had dipped into the low 20s overnight. Trees, cars, the highway, and my tent were all concealed under a heavy white rime.

Preston Parrish, a full gospel, non-denominational, charismatic Christian, brought me the 20 miles to Olney, Illinois. He spent much of his time travelling around preaching. He was very honest and caring and promised to say a prayer, or two, for me. I thanked him assuming I needed all the help I could get!

Before I became too cold in Olney, Brad Cummins stopped to take me a few more miles to tiny Sumner.

My ride from Sumner into Vincennes, Indiana, was with James and Lanna Kay Norton. They were accompanied by another hitchhiker, Bob Chapdeaux, of Minneapolis. Bob hitched to Louisville, Kentucky twice a year to receive free cancer treatment. It had taken him a week to get to central Illinois from Minneapolis. He wasn't even making 100 miles a day. Very poor luck. Surprising, considering how handsome and well dressed this old timer was. In his narrow black tie, worsted wool overcoat, and strawberry blond hair slicked back with Brylcream, he cut a dapper figure on the roadway. He wouldn't have posed a threat to a fly. It should have taken him less than four days to reach Louisville. One can never tell; the road isn't always generous.

James and Lanna Kay were quite a couple. There was no hesitation abut picking me up. There was no decision to be made. It had already been made years earlier. They had room and were going my direction, so, of course, they stopped. It was just like the days of yore. I appreciated their considerate attitude.

LANNA KAY AND JAMES NORTON AND
BOB CHAPDEAUX
Vincennes, Indiana

James wasn't at all concerned about dropping me off on a narrow cloverleaf exit ramp and taking the time to snap a photo. They were all completely relaxed while I frantically hauled out my gear, fearing a rear-end collision and flaming death. I wonder if they knew something I didn't. Not a vehicle went by.

The weather was exceptionally warm and sunny, but both rides and miles were harder to come by. After three more rides from Jim Upton, Greg and Sharon Smock, and Earl Crowder, the 40 miles to Shoals, Indiana were finally under my belt. Shoals was a real drag. There was a lot of traffic going by but no one was interested in me. After two hours of dump trucks blasting by at three to five minute intervals, I couldn't take another second of standing there and started walking.

I had walked only a half mile when a man named Tim stopped. Tim was really nice but endangered everyone by not pulling completely off the highway. My heart pumped hard as I ran up to where he waited. I kept looking over my shoulder, expecting some rig to come bearing down on us. Luck was with us that time. There were none of the notorious dump trucks screaming around that last blind curve, during the 45 seconds it took me to load up.

Being under that kind of fateful pressure was tremendously unpleasant. I hated that feeling of dread. It cropped up far too many times. I continually felt the urge to found a defensive driving school! It would have been a noble role, warning motorists about all of the mistakes some drivers inadvertently make that could be fatal. From my white line perspective I must have seen every unsafe maneuver imaginable. Travelling tens of thousands of miles while hitchhiking I never really feared for my life due to some sort of murderous personality. What put a real fear into me was the poor driving performance of so many drivers. It's no wonder traffic fatalities are such a major contributor to the death rates of Americans.

Tim got us safely to the near edge of Bedford, Indiana, where two guys in a ratty, old pick-up truck took me across town. They wanted to get me to the eastern city limits, to keep the cops from hassling me. Apparently they'd had some experience in dealing with them.

Derek Wray got me a few more miles, to the turn off to his farm. It was a very lonely intersection. While crossing Bedford in the ratty truck, I

DEREK WRAY
Bedford, Indiana

had noticed a structure that had been demolished by fire. Coincidentally, it was Derek's mother's house, but the situation hadn't dampened his smile at all. She was now living with him at his farm. It was just a house the family had lost, not their mother. The house was replaceable. His mother wasn't.

What is it about Monte Carlos? They seem to be out to get me. This next ride made the trip with Black Death Monte Carlo seem tame. I went from Derek's boyish smile and brand new truck to this sleazy, black $50 piece of scrap on fraying steel belts: the Car from Hell. That old dreadful feeling was back to haunt me!

I was standing on a downhill section of a rural two-lane highway at the junction of Derek's driveway. The Monte Carlo driver blew by me at what I estimated to be about 80 mph. I couldn't really be sure of the speed. Without a muffler, maybe it just sounded fast. You could have guessed it had only fragments of an exhaust system remaining. I shouldn't complain too much about noisy cars because I ride in a lot of them. Some, like this one, are nearly intolerable.

The driver's brain must have been reacting slowly that day. He was still mashing the accelerator to the floor as he passed me. When it clicked that I was hitchhiking he was already a hundred yards past me. Those electrical impulses that are processed by the brain and sent to the appropriate muscle group took another 50 yards to respond. By the time the vehicle actually stopped, it was about 200 yards down the road from where I stood.

As I was hurrying toward the car, he was backing up, more or less. I grit my teeth and slowed down my pace as I watched. The shoulder was about six feet wide and he only swerved out into the driving lane a couple of times. You try backing up at 25 mph, or so, drunk. I'll bet you couldn't keep it between the lines either.

Of course, I didn't realize he was drunk until after getting in. Getting in was a classic comedy scene.

I stuck my head in the passenger window and saw little room in the back seat for my pack. I asked if I could put it in the trunk. He turned off the car (blessed silence!) and gave me the keys, insisting I not wreck some shirt he had back there. I, of course, couldn't open the trunk. There's always a trick to it on cars like that. Its always something more than simply sticking in the key and turning the lock. I had to go back and ask him what the trick was. He grudgingly said he'd give me a hand. Great, I thought. We'd be cruising down the road at 80 in less than a minute.

It wasn't going to be as simple as you'd expect. The driver's side door was non-functioning. He struggled out from behind the steering wheel, crawled over the transmission console into the passenger seat and finally out the passenger door. He knew the trick to the trunk and sure enough, there lay the prized shirt. It was just a shirt! It was special because it was probably his last clean article of clothing and he would be wearing it at his new girlfriend's house. I was sure she'd be impressed.

Well, now that my pack was trapped in the trunk, there was no turning back. I watched him negotiate the passenger seat/transmission console obstacle course again. My heart sank as I guessed he had no more than twice the legal limit of alcohol in his blood stream. Add those numbers to recent divorce, boredom, and a generally confused state of mind and I found that this guy should have been institutionalized instead of mobilized!

I was practically paralyzed with anxiety. My seat didn't even have an operable seat belt! Perhaps I'd finally find out what it felt like to have ones rib cage crushed against a dashboard.

All went fine for a while. I hoped the carbon monoxide, which was flooding the passenger compartment from an engine exhaust leak, wouldn't do too much brain damage over the next thirty miles. That was the least of my worries. Losing a few brain cells was far preferable to massive head trauma.

The stereo system consisted of a portable cassette player which balanced precariously on the back seat. He could reach it between the front bucket seats. There were tapes laying all over the place and he was searching for one in particular. In his left hand he held a cocktail in a large plastic tumbler. His right hand was occupied with tasks such as holding and lighting cigarettes, doing the tape search and operating the cassette deck in the back seat. All the while he told me depressing stories of divorce, unemployment, and being evicted from his apartment. Under those challenging conditions, to have even kept his vehicle on pavement, much less between the lines, was a testimony to driving skills that were quite remarkable.

We had to slow down as we approached a slow moving truck, hauling roof trusses. The load was laying down, instead of on end. It was so wide it was missing highway signs by mere inches. I was sure that the driver of the Car from Hell wouldn't try passing. There was a lot of traffic in the other lane. It was the one time in my life I was hoping for very heavy traffic, making it impossible for the driver to pass. Unfortunately, he kept drifting across the center line trying to see around the load. This went on for about three miles. He wanted to go!

He finally saw his break and hit the gas. As we pulled into the oncoming lane it didn't look like that much of a break to me, but the old Monte Carlo showed its teeth. With the pedal to the floor, the 350 four-barrel blasted off and left the wide load in a cloud of blue/black smoke. A bit of the alcoholic swill that occupied the trough of the transmission console sloshed out onto the floor. The plastic tumbler he was sipping from also wound up spilled across the dashboard and into my lap. Apparently, I was destined to relive Hunter S. Thompson's original savage journey, described in his book *Fear and Loathing in Las Vegas.*

THE CAR FROM HELL
Near Seymour, Indiana

Although we were safely past the truck my driver felt we needed to make up for lost time. He ran at a steady 70 mph for a while. During that time, he began running optical experiments. He would close his left eye and try focusing with his right eye. It didn't work. He tried the other eye with similar results. After blinking numerous times with both eyes once again and still not focusing on anything other than a splitting headache he concluded the experiments a failure. As we drifted toward a long line of oncoming traffic he seemed to realize he couldn't drive any longer. It was a rather astute observation on his part. I thought the drunker you got, the nearer to invincible you became.

He inquired about my willingness to pilot the Car from Hell into Seymour, Indiana. I felt like telling him that he was doing a fine job of driving and ask him to join Tim, and others, in teaching a course at Doug's Defensive Driving School. Instead, I said that if he was feeling a tad sleepy, I'd be happy to take over the wheel on his behalf.

I climbed out. He climbed out. I performed the ungainly maneuver of dragging my 6'3" frame across the transmission console. The hard part was getting my legs under the steering wheel. The seat adjustment was broken so I had to slouch to keep my head from banging the headliner. I looked back out the passenger door to check on the ex-driver's progress. I slipped lower and lower in my seat, trying to make myself very small while he relieved himself alongside the car. This he did without the benefit of a tree, or even a fire hydrant!

Thank God I was in control of this big black weapon. All I could think about was how I was probably saving many drivers lives by sitting behind the wheel. There was a trick to getting it into gear and he had to use both hands from the passenger seat to do it. All I can say is that nobody died as a result of this ride.

In Seymour, I wanted to put as much distance as possible between that last ride and me, and I didn't care how. I started walking as soon as my pack burdened my back and my feet hit the ground. Sweet earth! Sweet cloudy sky and chilly wind! I had not a care in the world. I was alive!

It was rush hour and the only through street in Seymour was U.S. 50. Glorious rush hour! (The euphoria of my continued existence was still with me!) It seemed as though anybody who owned a car was in it, and on this street. They were lined up bumper to bumper the length of their city. As I walked along, moving faster than some of the traffic was, I got to feeling pretty smug. I would occasionally turn around to stick out my thumb. I assumed that if I did get a ride it would probably take longer to get out of town than if I kept on walking!

A couple of guys waiting at a stop light made positive eye contact and waved me up to their pick-up truck. Just as they did, the light changed. Traffic around them began to move. Not wanting to face any nasty looks or honking horns for slowing up traffic even more than its present snail's pace, I didn't have time to do anything gracefully. Running up to the truck I took a flying leap into the truck bed. The weight of my pack, still on my back, helped to pull me over the fender. I wound up on my back with arms and legs flailing in the air. While struggling to detach my hip belt and chest strap so I could sit upright, I felt much like the proverbial turtle on its back.

As all of this comedy was taking place, the woman in the car behind us looked on, aghast. I'm sure she assumed I was one of those madman hitchhikers who just jumped into any passing car he could catch. Who said Seymour, Indiana, wasn't an exciting place?

Tom Law and his son Clint were the occupants of the truck I had just leaped into. The next chance they had to stop they told me to come into the truck cab with them. They said they were on their way to watch a big basketball game in North Vernon. Actually, any basketball game in town would have been billed as The Big Game. Winter on the cornfields doesn't provide many recreational opportunities for Hoosiers. The pursuit of high school basketball in Indiana is serious business and considered akin to religion. Basketball is as much a part of Indiana's cultural fabric as hockey is to Minnesota and surfing is to California. People there lived for it. It was still an hour before game time and a huge traffic jam at the entrance of the high school parking lot was already firmly established.

Clint had just returned from National Guard training and Tom was a diesel mechanic. The day before, while at work, Tom had slipped a disc in his back. Stiff with pain, it was a real effort for him to turn his head and shoulders to look at me as we conversed. The last thing he should have been doing was sitting on a hard bleacher for two-and-a-half hours surrounded by exuberant fans. I was getting a crash course on Indiana priorities!

Neither Tom nor Clint had ever picked up a hitchhiker before and over a burger and fries I told them some stories. I always felt that "Virgin" drivers required a little extra attention to assure that they came away from the experience with a positive attitude. It was the best time to be a goodwill ambassador.

Darkness had set in by the time we finally reached North Vernon. It was too early to go to bed, however. Not really expecting to get a ride after dark I half-heartedly looked around for a place to camp while walking along with my thumb out. Despite the darkness, Ernie Kurtz pulled his eighteen-wheeler onto the shoulder and welcomed me aboard. It's always a pleasant surprise when a trucker pulls over. It doesn't happen nearly as often as most people would think.

Ernie was from Richmond, Indiana, and hauled plastic pellets out of a chemical plant in Cincinnati. He had driven all over the United States and Canada, and could remember practically every little town that he'd ever passed through. His geographic knowledge seemed bottomless. I'd been to a fair number of places myself, and every time I mentioned a town, he claimed to have been there only the week before, even remembering how many tons of pellets he'd hauled to some local manufacturing plant.

Ernie didn't need to drive a truck for a living. He did it because he loved it. After spending twenty-seven years in the Navy, he and a partner

ERNIE KURTZ
Addyston, Ohio

bought this semi-tractor. Ernie did all of the driving while his partner maintained a financial interest. The road was his place in the sun. Actually, any place Ernie went was sunny. In his early fifties, he was recently married and travelled through life with a tremendously positive attitude. He was full of curiosity and spoke with authority on a wide range of topics. You couldn't be around him without feeling refreshed. What a miserable place the world would be without people like him.

Addyston, Ohio, just west of Cincinnati, was home for me that night. Ernie was dropping off his trailer there and then heading north while I would continue east.

In Addyston I experienced my first large, industrial, chemical manufacturing plant. The Monsanto factory was massive and surreal in the surrounding darkness. Across the highway from the plant, houses were perched on the hills above the Ohio River. Somehow the residents slept amid the constant roar of the manufacturing process. Clouds of effluvium rose from the endless maze of tubing, valves, smoke stacks, pipes, and vehicles that existed beyond the high barbed-wire and chain link fence. It was all illuminated by flood lights and tall, slender towers with flames flickering at the summits, burning off remnant gases. Night came and went in Addyston every day, but it never got dark.

To find my bed for the night I climbed up into the wooded hills. The vegetation was so thick and the hills were so steep it was difficult to find an open, level spot. When I finally did it was 10:30 pm. That was late for me! I treated myself to a little snack and crashed out.

The next morning was Saturday and bus rides were cheap. When Ernie dropped me off last night, he pointed out the city bus stop. For a mere thirty-five cents I got to ride across Cincinnati. It was the sort of bargain that made trans-urban travel pleasant for a frugal hitchhiker. As the bus was nearly empty the driver was happy to act as a tour guide while the easy miles rolled past.

When I rode by Pete Rose Boulevard, I couldn't help wincing at the sudden ache in my heart. After a long, record setting career in professional baseball Rose was banned from the sport because of gambling allegations. Anyone who loves baseball and respected Rose's playing ability had to hurt, contemplating his professional demise. Hopefully Cincinnati will retain the street name as a reminder of the human fallibility of an immortal athlete.

When I stepped off the bus at its terminus I still wasn't free of the city. I had to walk a mile along a limited access highway and then through a suburban commercial district. Tom Cors wasn't sure what to make of this anomaly, walking down the suburban sidewalk. He was dying to talk to me because he had some road plans of his own. He was a student at Davidson College, near Charlotte, North Carolina. His plan was to study classical Greek and Roman in Europe, the following year. When he got there he wanted to hitchhike around as much of Europe as he could.

Tom got me a couple of miles farther, to Milford, Ohio.

At this point I was essentially lost in the tangle of roads surrounding Cincinnati. I was venturing into the blank spaces of my geographic knowledge of North America. When Wally Jones and his son Zachary stopped, that's exactly what I admitted.

I was forced to make another admission when Wally asked if I'd had breakfast or lunch that morning. Answering in the negative, he immediately invited me to lunch at his house. Wally bragged about his barbecued pork chops and wanted to prove how good they were. It would have been foolish to turn down such an offer so we wound our way down a series of roads to his house.

His wife, Brenda, was a great sport and welcomed this surprise visitor into her home. She was busily organizing her household after the hectic Christmas and New Year's holidays. Chaos reigned in their household with three kids, a dog and a cat. Smiles were on everyone's faces that warm Saturday afternoon.

Wally was a big, round man who could have easily stood in for Santa Claus. His jolly, generous disposition, thick blond beard and glasses, made him a dead ringer! His kindness and generosity was not limited to disoriented strangers along the road. Employed by the local school system he worked with learning disabled students, teaching special education.

This pleasant, young family opened up their refrigerator to offer me a huge repast. My plate was piled high with numerous helpings of his famous barbecued pork chops, au gratin potatoes, and applesauce raisin cake for dessert. When I finally said, "No more!" with enough conviction to be believable, Wally stopped filling my plate. He then set about filling a brown paper sack with goodies. He wasn't going to let me go without packing a little something for later that day.

My time with the Jones family was a refreshing reminder of how, given a chance, people step out of the ugliness of fear and into a realm of trust and cooperation. It made all the brutal news reports of the past seem like some sort of a joke.

Before leaving the house Wally helped me with a little route planning. We piled back into the car and to get me going in the right direction he took me to Williamsburg, setting me east on Ohio 32.

Joe Muthler, in a pick-up truck that was so high even I had trouble getting into it, took me about twenty miles east of Williamsburg. Despite his dislike of big cities, he had moved to Cincinnati from Philadelphia, six months ago. He was a bulldozer operator at a marina project. A workaholic by choice, he sometimes worked 80 hour weeks. The money was good but he confessed to spending it faster than he earned it.

There wasn't any real town where Joe had dropped me off and traffic was light. Even though I'd spent most of the day goofing off I wasn't at all concerned about making miles. I was enjoying the warm sun on my face when Jack, Tony, and Dorothy Hunt eased their car over to give me a lift. They were driving a big, old Oldsmobile. It was a typical old sled, with the tail nearly dragging along the ground. The suspension was shot to hell from hauling its own massive bulk around for twenty-five years. The driver, Dorothy, was a gray haired matron. The two men, in their late 20s, were her sons.

Jack had a couple of interesting tattoos. Emblazoned across the knuckles of one hand was the word LOVE. The other proclaimed HATE. I didn't bother asking about them. Normally, I try to avoid philosophical discussions on the larger questions of love and hate, with people in leather jackets wearing tattoos. I know that makes me sound just a little narrow-minded, but I figured there was no sense in stretching my luck!

Following a long, fast, smooth ride, the Hunts left me at an excellent spot near Jackson, on U.S. 35, which went straight into Charleston, West Virginia. A brief ride with Ed White quickly brought me to Rio Grande, Ohio.

I rode a short distance with Terry McClellan into Rodney, Ohio. Slender, with dark curly hair, goatee beard, black leather jacket and base-ball cap, he appeared to be in his late 30s. He was a very quiet man. He must have been a logger or mill worker because his clothes were full of dirt and sawdust. He was going home after his day's labor. We drove along with the radio tuned into a high-powered, Bible thumper station. I didn't get any other sense of a deeper spirituality during our short time together which increased my curiosity about this man.

The one thing that impressed me the most about my ride with Terry was the sense of fatigue I felt emanating from across the car. It was like an aura of complete weariness. I was unable to discern if the fatigue was due to physical, or mental stresses. I was disappointed the ride was so short. I nearly asked if he would be willing to let me stay at his place that night. I wanted to find out more about him. He had been kind enough to give me a lift and I decided it was best not to intrude any further. Regrettably, without giving him the chance to answer for himself, our paths diverged just north of Gallipolis, Ohio.

Terry dropped me off at a little truck stop and assured me it was a good spot. He was correct. Almost immediately a huge semi-truck, with three guys already in it, squeezed onto the highway shoulder. It was one of those household mover vans. They were heading for Roanoake, Virginia, having unloaded their freight earlier that day.

To break up the boredom of the long drive, the two guys in the sleeper unit had a mini-television and were trying to tune in a football game. I gathered that my old home team, the Minnesota Vikings, were getting waxed by the San Francisco 49ers. That was nothing new.

The drive was very intense. The narrow two lane highway followed the twisting course of the Kanawha River. It was extremely dark, the traffic was heavy, and these guys were in a big hurry to get home. Normally one feels pretty safe and secure in a big semi rig. In this case I was concerned for our safety, as well as that of the ant-like automobiles surrounding us.

My goal was a small town near Oak Hill, West Virginia. Lisa, a friend of a friend, lived there. I had no instructions on how to find her. All

I had was a work phone number but she was never in the office. I was determined to look her up because I wanted to spend some time in the mountains of West Virginia. I'd never seen those green, rolling hills before and wasn't about to let this opportunity slip through my fingers just because I didn't know where Lisa lived. When I actually did find her I was worried that it was going to be an etiquette disaster by showing up unannounced.

Not knowing exactly where to go I made a mistake by asking the semi driver to drop me off at one exit past where I actually should have been. From the Beckley interchange I tried a few different phone calls in an unsuccessful attempt to contact her. I suddenly found myself nervous. I wasn't confident and in control of things. This was one of the few situations where I felt afraid. There was nothing rational about my fear. I was just being a baby. I had become disoriented travelling in the darkness as we wound our way along the deep river valleys of West Virginia. If you ever want to be in an extremely dark place, go to rural West Virginia on an overcast winter night. Anything outside the perimeter of a man made light source was invisible. It was like a wall. Intriguing, but frightening at the same time.

Standing in Beckley, I knew I needed to be closer to the town of Oak Hill. On a fringe of light at the entrance ramp I quickly made a sign that said so. The first car to approach on that dark night, stopped. I was so thrilled I leaped for joy!

Jim Elmore was returning home to Oak Hill from working in Beckley. He had worked at a department store for the last fourteen years. As a way to escape that drudgery, he was studying to become a minister. He was nearly finished with his studies and looked forward to his new, spiritually oriented career.

Jim had been in a serious automobile accident recently. Although he looked fine to me, he claimed to have had several operations to repair his injured face. His final plastic surgery was coming up. Following his accident, the people Jim didn't trust any more were those already in cars. He felt that they were the dangerous ones; not someone standing alongside the road. That made me feel great!

I explained my predicament of trying to find my friend. He brought me to her work location, which was the one solid piece of information I had acquired. I set up camp on the lawn of the New River Gorge Visitor Center and slept until someone showed up the next morning. They were able to contact Lisa and she welcomed me into her home. Voila! I looked back and wondered why I had been so nervous earlier.

I spent the next three nights in Lisa's tiny, two level house. She lived far back in the hills. When it snowed all the following day, I wondered how she would make it home from work. The snow was nice and wet, perfect for snowballs and slick roads. When she finally did come home, she was greeted by a snowman. After reading next to a warm fire and walking around on backroads, I didn't have anything better to do, so building a snowman was as good an occupation as any.

Even though we had both worked for a couple of seasons in north-western Montana's Glacier National Park, we had never met. She had done seasonal work on a trail maintenance crew. It was the kind of work that required a tremendous amount of endurance. While she was digging steep trails out of ten feet of snow on a 7000' mountain pass, I was sitting in an office entering data for a computerized Geographic Information System. I love the outdoors but never coveted a trail dog's job. They woke up to the toughest environmental conditions imaginable, worked long and hard, returned to camp for some sleep, then got up and did it all again. This went on for ten days in a row before walking as many as 20 miles out of the backcountry to enjoy a few days off.

Lisa's hospitality was outstanding despite my ambush. She helped me prepare for a couple of cities that were coming up. She contacted some people in Richmond, Virginia, and Washington, D.C., who were willing to put me up for a couple of nights. That was just what this midwestern pup needed to feel comfortable venturing into some very unfamiliar territory. I had been on the road for two weeks when I left West Virginia for Richmond.

When Lisa dropped me off on her way to work, it was before dawn and snowing. I was on U.S. 60, southeast of U.S. 19. I'm still not exactly sure where I had been over the past couple of days. The geographic disori-entation from that previous dark night in Beckley remained. The darkness and snow I faced on the road that morning as I left the state was no help.

I stood at the lowest point, on the inside of a curve. Cars came down a hill toward me, then up a hill after passing me. I was blocked from their view by a steep, rocky slope until they were very close. If they failed to recognize me as a hitchhiker in a matter of a few seconds it would have been very difficult for them to stop and come back to get me.

A couple of cars went by before I caught someone's eye. The driver stopped up the road a bit, then backed down to get me. Saying my good-byes to the falling snow, I threw my pack in the back of the little red pick-up truck and opened the passenger door. I was pleasantly surprised to meet a young woman named Angelia "Angel" Tincher. I was surprised by two things. First, she had stopped despite the many factors working against hitchhikers that morning. It was early, cold, dark, snowy, and a very incon-venient place to stop. The second surprising aspect of the ride was that she was female! That was a nice change. I knew it would eventually happen, but Angel held the somewhat dubious distinction of being the first woman, alone in a vehicle, to offer me a ride. On that narrow mountain road, in wintry conditions, she welcomed me into her comfortable vehicle.

Angel was on her way to Rainelle, West Virginia where she worked as the music director and morning announcer at a local radio station. When I chided her for picking up strange men, she retorted that I didn't appear to be too strange. Besides, she had a reputation to maintain. Her friends and family claimed that she'd never met a stranger.

From the mid 1970s to the mid 1980s I had hitchhiked many thou-sands of miles in the U.S. and Canada. My luck seemed pretty good in years past, but I reasoned it was due to living in another era, the openness of the olden days. As time progressed it seemed as though our society was closing the door on intimacy. A complete fear of intimacy in the 1990s would surely slam the door on hitchhiking. A successful hitchhike is an intimate event. There you sit, two strangers suddenly thrust together, essentially inches apart. There is no reference here to physical intimacy. The intimacy implied is through communication. You can sit next to a stranger at a bar, baseball game, or even church, and not say a word to that person. An elevator ride with one other person comes close to intimacy except that, even then, no one is really compelled to communicate. In a car, however, both parties have asked to be with the other. You have an interest in satisfying your curiosity of one another through communica-tion, learning, and the intimacy of sharing. The cultural doors that were thought to be closing on intimacy are blown off their hinges with every ride. It is very satisfying for hitchhikers and their drivers to experience that reverse in a societal trend.

For women, in addition to the fear of a possible physical threat from the hitchhiker, opening up communication channels to a stranger would make the challenge of picking them up doubly difficult.

Angelia was unafraid. She was happy for the company and the opportunity to help me out. Even with the responsibility of raising her 13 month old child she was willing to take a chance on picking me up. There was no doubting her good faith in people. It was obvious to me that Angelia had an immense capacity for trust and would probably maintain her reputation of never having met a stranger.

I don't think the citizens of Rainelle saw too many hitchhikers. On that soggy morning, as I waited along the road in front of the bank, I got some pretty strange looks. Tolby Lowe gave me a look and saw exactly what he wanted: company. He hit the brakes. I rejoiced!

Not only did he want the intimacy of conversation with a stranger, he craved it. Tolby lived in the tree covered mountains, alone. Only thirty-nine, his three children were already grown up and on their own. He said he had married too young and the unhappy result was a divorce and a measure of loneliness.

Never having completed high school, Tolby has been a laborer all his life. For seven years he harvested timber from the thickly wooded ridges of Appalachia. There had been so much timber hauled out of this area that Rainelle, at one time, boasted the world's largest lumber mill. Not surprisingly, the town also claimed to have the largest church in the world built with chestnut wood.

Coal is also a natural resource that has played an important role in the West Virginia economy. Tolby has worked for coal companies over the years, but only in an above ground capacity. Even though the money is considerably better as an underground miner he affirmed his resolve to never work in a subterranean environment. The reason became clear when he mentioned his father was killed while setting timber in an underground mine. He figured peace of mind couldn't be bought by a couple of bucks per hour more in wages.

For a man who had never completed high school, he was enthusiastic about education and possessed an inquisitive nature. Now, working on his GED, he complained about difficulties with algebra. Who wouldn't complain? After his goal of obtaining a diploma was realized Tolby planned on rewarding himself with a motorcycle trip to the Rocky Mountains. He was envious of my trip but didn't think he'd enjoy the hitchhiking part.

We had just driven through a torrential downpour when our pleasant ride together ended in Staunton, Virginia, at the junction of I-80 and I-64. Fortunately the bad weather was localized and it was very nice when I hit the road heading east on I-64, to Richmond.

I hadn't walked five minutes when T.C. pulled over. While he was slowing down I noticed the front fender on the passenger side was slightly mangled. I didn't think anything about it because beat up cars giving me a lift is the rule rather than the exception. I get so used to climbing into cars with scrapes and dents I don't even pay attention. If I had an overly nervous disposition the driving skills of every driver would be in question. Unfortunately, the hitchhiker can't just pick and choose his ride. It would be great if all I had to do was point at a car and the driver would immediately pull over. Until that fantasy became reality, I would be taking my chances with the next vehicle, whatever its appearance.

The funny thing about T.C.'s battered vehicle was that it was practically brand new. It was a van that had been converted into a luxury cruiser. Estimating its worth at around $30,000, this thing had a TV and VCR, in addition to a powerful sound system. There was a bed, table, and ice box, and frilly curtains framed the windows.

The previous night, on an icy road, halfway through a fifth of Jack Daniels whiskey, he had taken out a couple of highway signs and went for a slide along a guard rail. I was so pleased the road here was clear and dry. He was pretty paranoid after his inadvertent, late night stunt driving and kept his speed below 65 mph. You could see his brain stretching to the limits of its attentiveness as he concentrated on the road. The pain of a hangover never looked so hideous. It was the sort of pain T.C. and other serious alcoholics must be very familiar with.

He was heading to his former hometown of Virginia Beach, Virginia. He had a date with the court there on a driving under the influence of alcohol charge. What? Did you expect me to be surprised? It made sense to me to arrive at the court drunk. What would they do, give him another DUI? Big deal! That wasn't going to keep him off the road.

T.C. had begun his trip the day before from his new home in upper Michigan. He'd been driving all night. Somewhere along the way, while celebrating with his old friend Jack Daniels, he missed an exit and ended up 200 miles off course. Back on course and so close to Virginia Beach, he was getting anxious. He was dying to hang out with his buddies and have a few drinks, maybe watch a dog fight.

Having to go to court turned out to be the perfect excuse for T.C. He wanted to get away from Michigan, away from his new wife. Without further explanation he claimed she really bugged him. What was so sad about T.C.'s life, as it unfolded before me, was that his wife was expecting a baby in a couple of months. With T.C.'s drinking and potentially abusive attitude toward his wife I doubted the child would have a happy life.

Physically, T.C. looked like the victim of a chain saw massacre. His neck, ears, cheeks, forehead, nose and mouth had been cut and sewed up, the scars plainly visible. He was missing at least one finger, and his hands contained other scars. The scars that remained on face and hands were glaring testimony to a horrible accident, or possibly, attack. Not wanting to delve into the potentially sensitive subject of his appearance I didn't ask too many questions. Whatever had happened to T.C. must have left him financially secure. The expensive rig was the product of a court decision in his favor. The settlement was large enough for him to buy his father an expensive new truck, in addition to the van we rode in. At that rate of spending I guessed the money wouldn't last long. It seemed a shame for the money to be squandered on shiny new vehicles, alcohol, games of chance, and lawyers to bail him out of future scrapes with the law.

T.C. had one of my favorite music tapes in his collection. Although I wasn't much of a rapper I loved Tone Loc's "Loc'ed After Dark." T.C. put it in and I asked him to turn up the volume a little. Big mistake! He let me have $1200 worth of car stereo wallop, when I only wanted a little $300 punch. I expected that many decibels to knock the framed picture of his treasured pit bull "Butch," off the back wall of the van. It didn't. The tribute to Butch remained, swaying precariously.

T.C. was in another world when I yelled at him to turn it back down after ending Tone Loc's, "Funky Cold Medina." I couldn't handle any more without my brain melting. That stereo system belonged in an auditorium, not a van! He snapped out of it agreeing that it was pretty loud. Hard on his nerves. Said he needed a drink. I poured him a whiskey and cut it with plenty of orange juice. I didn't want him to mix drinks and drive at the same time. Saying no to a drunk can make them mean. I did what I could to assuage him.

The seriousness of the alcohol and driving problem became very obvious to me on this trip. I have definitely become a hard liner on any question of responsibility and penalties for drunken driving violations. I hope they all get long, dry, uncomfortable jail terms. I'm sick of laws with no teeth. There are too many innocent lives at stake out there.

T.C. dropped me off so he could bypass the city of Richmond. He had that much sense left. Where I'd lost my sense I couldn't say.

James Bowen and his one year old son Christopher stopped immediately. We drove straight into town on I-64.

Back in the late 70s, while still in his teens, James hitched from North Carolina to Montana and Colorado. Unable to afford another mode of transportation, yet determined to see the mountains, he stuck out his thumb. It turned out to be an excellent journey. I too, had experienced the pull of the Rocky Mountain west as a youth and had hitchhiked it extensively. At thirty, driving his own mini-van, James was now a student in Richmond, while his wife worked in their nearby hometown of Gum Spring.

JAMES BOWEN
Richmond, Virginia

Little Christopher was destined to become a Dead Head. He had attended his first Grateful Dead concert a few months earlier, in Washington, D.C. He was happy as a clam in his car seat and very colorful in his tie-dyed tee shirt. It's such a treat to get a ride with a family. Kids can make you feel right at home. They don't seem surprised when a stranger suddenly piles into their car. It's like you've known the family a long time and they just picked you up to share some errands in town. If their parents seem to think there's no problem with the situation, the kids don't get worried.

James left me in a nice section of town called the Fan. It was a comfortable merging of commercial and residential neighborhoods. The friend Lisa had contacted lived in the vicinity. As I walked the few sun-drenched blocks to her house, I started feeling slightly embarrassed at the ease of my trip thus far. I had expected far more difficulty in getting rides. I had been especially worried about my approach to the east coast. It was a skate so far! Some days were slow, but in general things couldn't have gone much better. Between the signs I fabricated, where I stood on corners, and an endless smile, I must have been doing something right!

After a couple of relaxing days in Richmond, my approach to Washington D.C. began with some stress. My latest new-found friend dropped me at a lonely entrance ramp, north of Richmond, on I-95. There was no traffic entering the freeway there, so, I took a chance and walked down to the freeway shoulder. It was nuts down there! Even though it was early on a Saturday morning, the road was packed with cars travelling at least 70 to 75 mph. Not good conditions for a driver to look me over and have a chance to stop. After watching that frenzied race for about forty-five minutes, a highway patrol car zipped past. The state trooper gave me a nasty look and pointed back up the entrance ramp. I got the message. I wasn't about to press my luck with him, so started walking off the interstate. I'm NEVER looking for trouble. Besides, the speed of the traffic down there was nerve wracking. Things would be deadly slow, but peaceful, at the top of the entrance ramp.

I never found out how peaceful. The first car down the ramp stopped. Andy Strobel, of Virginia Beach, was headed to Mt. Vernon, Virginia. Along for the ride was his black labrador cross, Libby. A very affectionate dog. Most labs are.

Andy was a teacher by training, but had given it up for economic reasons. He now sold copiers and other office equipment. He found the money more acceptable in that line of work than the poverty wages served up by the education industry. Of course, he'd rather do neither of the above, and stick to fishing. His bumper sticker read, "Work is for those who don't know how to fish." He was kind enough to offer me a place to stay in Virginia Beach, but I never did get to his city.

After driving along through wetlands and forested areas, we were suddenly in the middle of suburbia. Andy left me along the city bus line, about twelve miles from the Capitol. The traffic here was slow, heavy, city traffic. At least I wasn't on a roaring freeway, like back in the outskirts of Richmond. Almost anything is preferable to that scene. Despite my proximity to the bus line I didn't feel like dealing with the bus system quite yet. It is such a drag searching for the correct change, figuring routes and trying to haul all my gear onto a crowded bus. I would definitely save that option as the last resort.

I started strolling toward downtown Washington. I was in no hurry and it was a gorgeous day. I was resigned to the fact that being so close to the city, I'd never get a ride. Not really even paying attention while walking and holding out my D.C. sign, I quickly got a ride.

I can imagine what you're thinking. This guy is walking along the road in the "Murder Capital" of the U.S. and gets a ride inside of five minutes, right to the doorstep of the Capitol building. Nobody could be that lucky. But it's true, and I am that lucky! Even more astonishing was the lone woman driving the car that took me there.

Jytte Atkinson claimed that she never gave people rides. For some unknown reason she made this exception. She was on her way to Penn Station, in central D.C., to pick up her daughter who was coming in on the train. My sign told her where I was going and she felt obliged to take me there.

Jytte was a native of Denmark. I told her about a small town near my parent's place in Minnesota, called Askov. In addition to being a "Little Denmark," it proudly carried the banner of being the "Rutabaga Capital" of America. Think of Askov the next time you sink your teeth into a bitter, yellow rutabaga. You'll wonder why it is considered food and why on earth a town would claim its production for fame. Scandinavians! You can never tell what's going on in our little minds.

Jytte worked as a loading dock foreman. She bemoaned the fact that there were so few Danes in the area. While living in the States, she hadn't had the opportunity to travel west. She was hoping to see that part of her adopted country someday. Before leaving Scandinavia, she had travelled to Norway and fell in love with the scenic beauty of the mountains and fjords that decorated its coastline. Having been there myself, I told her of my love for the misty fjords. Shortly thereafter Jytte left me right in front of the United States Capitol.

I always feel conspicuous on city sidewalks wearing a large back-pack and carrying a duffel. There's no blending in. People probably did it all the time, but I still felt self-conscious wearing my backpack while tak-ing in the sights and sounds of the Capitol Mall. I roamed around a bit and saw people camped in various places and hauling all sorts of possessions on their backs or in grocery carts. I began to get the feeling that Washing-ton had seen it all and I started to relax. After all, Washington D.C. was my city as much as it was anyone elses!

In my preconceived image of the Murder Capital I expected Wash-ington to resemble a bombed out Beirut. Instead, it was clean, grassy, busy, and the monumental architecture was splendid! Nobody had even tried to kill me up to that point so I began to feel right at home. I found another of Lisa's friends without incident and settled in for a couple of days of sight-seeing. Washington intrigued me because of the dichotomy of its exist-ence. It spawns so much of what is right, while conversely breeding terrible wrongs. It is a place that should be experienced by all Americans.

Washington is the heart of the first, and largest modern democracy. We expect many great things from the men and women who reside here. They come to serve and lead, representing the diverse voices of United States citizens. The halls of power and influence can induce many people to noble accomplishments for the greater good of humanity.

Of course, the flip side of those glowing ideals is the corruption and abuse of power. Political struggles for power can leave a wasteland not unlike the face of the moon. Excellent programs designed to benefit our country or others can wind up as a bargaining chip in a battle for some other politically selfish motive. Washington becomes the home for rats in an absurd race, orchestrated by political, economic and criminal machin-ery.

It was easy to see how legislative residents might get swept up in the wave of power, media attention, and influence of the D.C. environment. It must be difficult to step back and look at the world with an untainted per-spective. I think the world would be better off if our elected representa-tives traveled more frequently to visit their constituents, in an effort to keep their view less obscured by the politics of Capitol Hill. Perspective is important when your decision can affect matters on a global scale.

At the top of my Washington list of things to do was to hear a case being argued at the Supreme Court. My timing was perfect. I sat in the audience and listened to the rather solemn proceedings. With a mere half hour to argue their case both parties involved were wasting their time. The justices would decide the outcome based upon the thousands of pages of documents generated by the trials in lower courts and their own constitutional interpretations.

Departing from the Court, with all its plush trappings, I had to remind myself that the people occupying these buildings were simply American citizens. They performed the tasks that other citizens, equal in their freedom and rights, asked them to perform. I expected a lot from those people. The sacrifices of previous generations demanded constitutional compliance from those now holding the reins of power. When we forget that the vagabond has the same right to all the freedoms and opportunities as the Wall Street executive and Washington elite we will witness the failure of democracy.

My new friends and hosts, Mimi and Gerry, invited some people over for dinner. Two of them were D.C. residents who had a friend in midtown Manhattan. They were driving up for a quick visit to play tourist and invited me along for the ride. I couldn't pass up the opportunity.

The overnight trip was brief, but eye-opening. Central Park, Greenwich Village music, a 2:00 am subway ride through the tough Bedford-Stuyvesant neighborhood and, of course, a sampling of the food that can only be obtained in a New York City restaurant, were all part of the tour.

We were up until 4:00 am. Unused to those hours and so wound up from all the activity, I didn't sleep well when finally given the chance. The household began waking up at around 10:00 am. By then I was frazzled and crabby. In this state of mind we went to Central Park. Under gray skies and a cold drizzle we strolled around the Strawberry Fields section of the park. Surrounding this muddy monument to the way Manhattan must have appeared a few hundred years ago, were glass, steel, and brick edifices, the collection of new monuments to our capitalist economy.

Strawberry Fields was only a few steps away from the entrance to the Dakota Apartments. We made the ghoulish pilgrimage to see for ourselves the site of the heinous crime against the life of John Lennon and the rest of the world. Shot down by a killer with ice in his veins, we lost an artist who asked us to imagine a world so peaceful there was "nothing to kill or die for, a brotherhood of man." So many of the peacemakers and dreamers of a world filled with common cause, have met an untimely demise. It is a high price to pay for promoting such an admirable goal.

Freedom, to me, means the freedom from fear. Whenever we hesitate to go anyplace or involve ourselves in some activity because of a threat to our safety, we become prisoners. All the money and power in the world mean nothing if we surround ourselves with shields of protection. The shields become the very walls of our own prison. Through the use of intimidation, people around us attempt to control us. If they succeed, we seek refuge behind the sheltering walls of prisons of our own design, oft mistaken as home, and sentenced to live lives of fear.

In seeking an element of trust among the drivers who would stop, I also took the chance of meeting people with ice in their veins. I had to have complete trust as I opened every new passenger door. In my stubbornness, or hopefulness, I refused to allow fear to imprison me. Were it demanded of me, I was willing to pay a high price for my freedom. Were I to meet an untimely demise, it would be as a free man. As car after car rolled up and opened its doors to me, I met another freedom fighter. In the truest sense of the phrase, they fought with the weapons of trust and cooperation to tear down existing barriers of fear, America's greatest enemy.

Tired and somber from the last busy twenty-four hours, the return trip to Washington was a quiet one. The dark, wet clouds so close to the ground acted like a cold, clammy compress. The grim industrial wasteland along the New Jersey Turnpike, and heavy traffic, did little to buoy our spirits. I sat curled up in the tiny back seat and considered the thousands of miles which remained for me. I hoped the barriers of fear in our country weren't as high as the skyscrapers that were disappearing from view at 70 mph.

Getting out of Washington two days later turned out to be a trick. I took the METRO as far east as it went. One of the transit employees suggested catching a bus that went all the way to Annapolis for one dollar. It turned out to be very convenient and well within my budget!

I wouldn't be using any more public transportation now that I was in Annapolis. It seemed like getting out of town was going to be a tricky hitch. There was road construction everywhere. What really slowed me down was the construction at important intersections along U.S. 50. Drivers are especially stressed when passing through areas with unfamiliar turns, millions of signs, piles of dirt, partially completed bridges and heavy equipment whizzing past. A hitchhiker is simply another distraction to avoid! There was no way to walk out, because everything seemed to be surrounded by water. The long, narrow bridge across the Severn River was not open to pedestrian traffic. Besides, it only led to another long bridge across Chesapeake Bay. I needed a ride.

In addition to my camping gear, I was armed with several pieces of cardboard and three large felt tip pens. With this stash of sign material I could conjure up messages for passing motorists at a moment's notice. After showing "DEL," meaning Delaware as my next destination, with no success, I made a new one that asked the burning question, "ACROSS BRIDGE?," meaning the Severn River. At this point I just needed to work my way over one hurdle at a time. Hitching had to be better across the bridge, because it wasn't any good here.

It worked! John Barbo was a salesman at the Chevrolet dealership, just across the Severn River. He took me to a great spot. It was one of my shortest rides, and one of the most helpful. Chesapeake Bay was the only remaining hurdle before getting into the series of small towns and pastoral landscapes on the way to the Delaware coast.

Tom Leonard thought nothing of getting me across the Bay. He was in a great mood, having just landed a new job. Cause enough for an invite to a pizza and beer celebration at his home on Kent Island. He also insisted I spend the night on his fold out couch instead of the ground. What could I say? You do NOT pass up invitations like that when you're on a four month road trip!

I had only gotten two rides hitching that day, for a total of thirteen lousy miles. I've set a faster pace walking in the woods without a trail! Even so, I was exhausted and looked forward to the company of a high energy man like Tom. He was a serious board sailer. The walls of his house were littered with photos, posters, maps and assorted memorabilia, regarding his sailing exploits. All tastefully done, to be sure. We had a great time watching a couple of movies and polishing off our Italian/American fare.

Interestingly the two movies we watched involved escapes from tyranny: the Bruce Willis shoot 'em up Die Hard, and Runaway Train, which starred Jon Voight. The powerful message of Runaway Train was one of unceasing allegiance to freedom. Voight, playing the anti-hero, was a convict escaping from a cruel, vicious warden. The sacrifices made to obtain his freedom seemed far worse than the abusiveness of the warden. The escapee paid the highest price, his own life, to finally gain the freedom he craved. It was a fascinating study.

Even though I'd only travelled a few miles that day, I went to sleep excited about my good luck. It seemed as if the bleakest waits on the toughest corners became the springboard for exceptionally positive experiences. I was ecstatic about moving along at any pace. People like Tom gave me far greater gifts than they could have imagined.

The next morning, my spirits weren't quite so high. I awoke with a stiff neck. The paralyzing kind. I must have done some cumulative damage over the past twenty-four days on the highway. Hauling my heavy gear in and out of awkward storage compartments, standing in one place for hours on end, and the occasional gymnastics vault must have finally caught up with me.

As I grabbed my pack off the road and started running to my first ride of the morning, the sensation of a white, hot stiletto pierced my neck and shoulder. Doubled over in pain, I nearly blacked out. I rested a few moments, trying to catch my breath and clear my head, as the stiletto withdrew, ever so slowly. It was enough of a warning. My body was giving me notice to quit beating it up. Constant standing, walking, riding, carrying, lifting, and sleeping in a different place every night was wearing me out. No wonder I was exhausted after thirteen agonizing miles the previous day! I promised myself to take it a bit easier.

Chris Young would have waited all day for me to walk the thirty yards to where he was. He had made a prior commitment to pick up all hitchhikers. No exceptions. He believed it was his responsibility to help someone so easily helped. This was not some burdensome penance he assigned himself. He found it spiritually uplifting and necessary for making the world a better place. The ride with Chris was disappointingly short. I had more to learn from him!

After another short ride, with Mike Fortner, I found myself walking across Denton, Maryland. The weather was mild considering the fact it was January 18th. I had come east at the perfect latitude. The weather had been cloudy and gray quite often, but at least I didn't get hammered by cold rain or snow on a daily basis!

Kenny Piaskowski, in his bottled water delivery truck, took me up to U.S. 13. He was a real character. The first thing he did was give me grief about using a sign to catch rides. I had been flashing a sign which read "REHOBOTH BEACH." He didn't like hitchhikers using signs. He liked to see the thumbs up. To him, that meant someone wanted a ride, not a job or something.

Despite his gruff greeting we became fast friends. Kenny lived in Berlin, Maryland. He invited me to stay there if I got close. I didn't think I'd make it that night but thanked him for the offer. I was wrong. I'd be seeing Kenny again.

Stanley Ferguson took me on yet another painfully short ride, as far as Georgetown, Delaware. All of my rides since Annapolis averaged ten or fifteen miles. Of course, it wasn't Stanley's fault. He envied my trip, except for the travel method. His choice would have been a recreational vehicle. Stanley taught wood shop for disabled students, ranging in age from six to twenty-three. He found the work very satisfying. The compassion he held for his students was reflected at the roadside as he lent a hand to this stranger.

Judson Bennet took me another fifteen miles to where the road east dead-ended at the Atlantic Ocean. Judson and I must have looked pretty funny; two large men crammed into a tiny Datsun. I was fortunate to have such knowledgeable company as we arrived at the Atlantic Ocean. He knew his way around the water. He worked as a river pilot on the Delaware River, going as far north as Philadelphia. In addition to working, he was a pre-law student at a local community college. Besides saving for his own education, he was financing the college educations of his three children.

Judson was a man capable of focusing his energy on several targets at once. Between work, school, and family he lived in a world of timetables, tests, deadlines, and paychecks too small to cover the bills. The important things he had on his mind weren't enough to stand in the way of an interesting distraction like a hitchhiker. Judson went out of his way to deliver me to the beach. Some people can handle a busy schedule and still take time out of their day to pick up hitchhikers.

JUDSON BENNET
Rehoboth, Beach

I suppose we all have our special abilities and tolerances for stressful situations. My life wasn't completely devoid of stress. Eliminating stress was, however, one of my more important goals. While Judson had a schedule and established routine, I dealt with the physical and mental challenge of continual movement. Although not on any sort of official schedule I often found myself hurrying. I was always worried about getting that next good ride. It took a conscious effort to slow myself down and back off the road. I would have rather been standing around unconcerned, looking at scenery, waiting for someone to pick me up and take me to the next view. Not having achieved that state of mental calm yet, I stood on the beach trying to keep from running back to the road for the next ride.

The weather was warm and sunny. I had never experienced a January day as sweet. I gazed out across the ocean for a while trying to see Europe. I guess the Atlantic is just too big to see from Delaware to Portugal! So. The ocean is the ocean. It always seems the same to me. Lots of water. A person can drown in water. In Minnesota if a lake is too big to see across I don't like going out on it. As a resident of the center of the continent, one would think I'd be truly impressed with the vastness and complexity of the ocean ecosystem. I am. I just don't relish the thought of getting wet to explore its secrets. I'm not ashamed to admit that I didn't even take my shoes and socks off and stick my toes in!

Hard to believe I'm from the hearty, seafaring stock of Norway. I wouldn't have lasted long on a viking ship struggling toward Greenland through a storm on the North Sea. Marco Polo's overland trip to the Far East would have been more my style.

Fortunately, the boardwalk in Rehoboth Beach had comfortable benches to sit on. It allowed me to get a well deserved rest before hauling my miniature travelling circus down the road again. It was a lot easier to slow my pace with a nice spot to remove my burden and just sit. While my legs and back took a break my mind kept reaching ahead. A quick look at my atlas showed Kenny Piaskowski's hometown of Berlin to be a mere thirty miles south. If I had any luck at all it looked as if I would be taking advantage of his offer of lodging for the night.

After hanging out for about an hour the clock was approaching 5:00 pm. This left me an hour of daylight to get to Berlin. While walking out of Rehoboth Beach, I flagged down a little pick-up truck. I rode in the back, enjoying the scenery, to Bethany Beach, Delaware. From there, a building inspector got me to the north end of Ocean City, Maryland. I walked twelve long, commercial blocks before stopping for some groceries. With the aid of darkness I stashed my backpack in some decorative shrubbery. I didn't want to deal with my pack in a super market. Sometimes I have to bring it in with me, but avoided it if at all possible.

I had a snack on the dark, deserted beach, enjoying the calm weather, quiet, and loneliness of the moment. It was me and the ocean again. The waves tumbled gently onto the beach. The breeze was so gentle I turned my head to various angles in an attempt to catch it. I listened carefully for the sound of air, suddenly becoming turbulent, as it moved across the rugged terrain of my outer ear. The breeze I had captured brought with it the earthy smells of a slight saltiness and the decay of plants. As the stars began filling in the black portions of the eastern sky I began to understand why so many people loved this interface of earth and water. Perhaps the ocean has some attributes I neglected to mention in my earlier soliloquy of the high seas.

Kenny Piaskowski had given me his phone number earlier in the day. I gave him a call. Ocean City was still about 15 miles from his home. He was willing to drive up to the north edge of town to get me. I sat on a bench in front of Duffey's Tavern writing in my journal, waiting for him to show up. The view from Duffey's wasn't as nice as that from the beach. There were all the fast food restaurants known to modern science within two miles of here. A person could eat, but aside from that, could not find any other redeeming attribute along the Ocean City strip.

When I had met Kenny earlier, he was driving his delivery van. He arrived to take me home in something completely different. It was a 1965 Rambler American, with questionable brakes. It was a neat, old car. The brakes apparently functioned reasonably well but produced some hair-raising noises. We cruised the ten mile long Ocean City commercial strip. Kenny referred to it as "McBeach." That aptly described it.

Kenny lived seven miles out of town, with a nice, quiet bay in his back yard. He loved living next to the water. He claimed herons and ducks made better neighbors than humans. I certainly enjoyed the company of waterfowl, but not necessarily more than humans!

Kenny's business was delivering bottled water to residents and businesses throughout Delaware, eastern Maryland, and water-locked northeastern Virginia. He'd begun the company back in 1985. To keep overhead costs as low as possible, he managed the entire operation by himself. After five years, the business was finally turning a slight profit. Even so, it was still a struggle to keep the wolves away from the door. He was so upbeat about life, I figured he could get by on enthusiasm alone!

Kenny's housekeeping was virtually nonexistent. His entire living space was cluttered with stuff. Old lamps, trunks, boxes, magazines, newspapers, books, dirty ashtrays, drinking glasses, and clothes. There wasn't much room to walk around. How could he keep up with domestic stuff when he was always on the road? His hospitality, however, was as enormous as his laugh. It was a hearty laugh that was so free spirited, it somehow seemed old fashioned. It was so loud and robust it was like being yelled at. It made me laugh. I realized that people never laughed enough. How long has it been since you've split your sides laughing? If it's been a long time, you forget how good it feels.

Even though his business kept him occupied most of the time, he had other priorities. Nothing motivated Kenny like literacy. Promoting literacy was his passion. Arguing at length, and loudly, he claimed illiteracy was the real enemy of the United States. How could our society reach its full potential unless every member could unlock the secrets of education by reading? There can be no learning from past mistakes recorded in history unless the words could be deciphered.

Kenny wasn't all talk and no action. In developing his own literacy promotion project he wrote songs, printed up tee shirts with a message, wrote a video screenplay with a literacy theme, and organized read-a-thons on the beach. At one such event there were 100 participants practicing oral reading for twelve hours. It was one of Kenny's most satisfying moments.

Another important effort was the establishment of the Ocean City Friends of the Library. Throughout his reign as president, the role of the Friends was twofold. Of primary importance was the gathering of funds for maintenance of the facility and expansion of its book collection. Nearly as important was maintaining a program that assisted anyone who wanted to learn to read.

One of Kenny's most disillusioning moments came when the new president of the Friends of the Library exclaimed, "Libraries are for people who already know how to read and we have no business doing anything concerning literacy." The new president had a less dynamic view of libraries than Kenny did. She seemed to think of the library as a mere book repository. If you didn't know how to use the materials within the repository, tough luck. Learn how to read somewhere else so we who already read won't be soiled by your presence. That had infuriated him to fits!

As we talked and talked, Kenny prepared dinner. Linguini was his gastronomic specialty, and he whipped it up in a short time. I was amazed at its exquisite taste. It was one of the most delightful meals I'd ever eaten. Over dinner, we talked about some of Kenny's own writing projects. An unpublished novelist, he'd also written a few short stories. He kept hoping to find a publisher. He couldn't afford to publish his novel himself so continued waiting for that acceptance letter in the mail.

We had both had long days and retired shortly after dinner.

The next morning broke clear and warm. The ducks were happily swimming around in the bay, searching for breakfast. It was so pleasant and peaceful I hated to leave.

Kenny had deliveries all day. On the way to his first delivery, he took me to Salisbury, Maryland. I was sad to say goodbye to this thoughtful man. As we shook hands I hoped the wolves would find another door to haunt, for a while. That way Kenny could get on with the important stuff. It's rare to find someone so willing to share his personal gifts for the benefit of the community.

Chapter Four

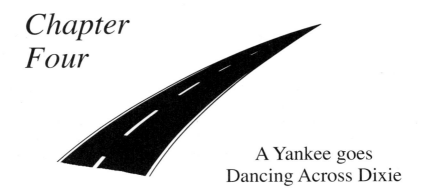

A Yankee goes Dancing Across Dixie

Although the morning at Kenny's house started out warm, by the time he dropped me off in Salisbury, on U.S. 13 south, the wind was cold, out of the north.

My first hitch of the morning pulled over after a brief fifteen minute wait. There was a twelve pack of beer on the passenger seat and an open can in the driver's grasp. Before getting in I asked the grizzled old-timer how many beers he'd already had that morning. Such an obvious display of alcohol use that early in the day made even a hardcore hitchhiker like me cautious. A quick assessment of the situation made me seriously consider turning down this ride. Though the reason was obvious to me, he wondered why I would be asking a question like that. I told him it seemed a bit early to be drinking. He spoke slowly, with a slight southern twang, claiming the one in his hand was his first. I was convinced. I climbed in and we slowly accelerated down the road.

For Clyde Cutlip (yes, Clyde Cutlip!) 9:00 am was Happy Hour. He was heading home after working night maintenance at the chicken factory. My imagination went to work. Pictures of Clyde slogging around the factory floor with chicken guts to the tops of his boots seemed too real. I imagined millions of chickens per year, mechanically killed, plucked, and gutted, whirring around on hooks on their way to the next step in processing. These twisted images were probably inspired by memories of the Black Death and The Car from Hell. Guess what Clyde was driving. Of course! He was sprawled in the driver's seat of a Monte Carlo. Perhaps that was another reason for my initial hesitation at entering the car.

This ride was quite different from the other Monte Carlos. It was in nice condition, quiet, and slow. Clyde was driving so slowly that I was worried he might get pulled over for driving less than a minimum safe speed.

CLYDE CUTLIP
Princess Anne, Maryland

Clyde was nothing if not generous. I declined the whiskey and beer he offered. I never start on whiskey before 11:00 am. Hitchhiking offers a limitless potential for self-destructive behavior. Drinkers always want someone to join them on their path to numbness. You could be wasted all the time, if you kept getting hooked up with the kind of rides I'd been getting.

Clyde safely dropped me in Princess Anne, Maryland, after a ten mile trip. The sun was shining brilliantly but didn't do the trick warming me up. The wind worked at keeping me cold and I was suddenly impatient. The real reason for my chill and impatience was that I had to pee! I hate it when that happens.

Going to the toilet can be complicated business for a hitchhiker. It's tough enough for people travelling in their own cars. Unfortunately your body requires attention more often than your car needs gas and filling stations frown upon non-customers using their restrooms. Often, there are no stores at corners where hitchhikers get dropped off, anyway. If you're with a driver who needs gas or is willing to stop at a rest area, your comfort is no problem. Unfortunately, only interstate highways have an established system of rest areas, and I spent most of my time on the smaller U.S. highways. No matter where you are, when you gotta go, you gotta go. All you can do is look for cover and take care of business.

The thing I hate most about having to answer nature's call while standing along the road is the fact that you have to leave the road. You never know who might have passed by while you're gone. It could be the ride of your dreams; possibly even the woman of your dreams. Knowing the chances of missing that awesome ride increase with every second you're away, you hurry. I hurried that morning to decrease those chances and because I was ready to pop.

I quickly stashed my pack off the roadside and ran across the highway to some cover. Thank goodness for cover. You know what I mean. Often, on the treeless plain or in the urban jungle, discretion is impossible. With only the slimmest margin of privacy you will find yourself far less modest than you thought possible.

Upon my return to the highway, patience had also returned. I stood there admiring the lush pine forest until Ralph and Norma Jean Drumbore stopped. I had noticed them pass by about three minutes earlier and was now pleasantly surprised to see their big, warm, Buick Riviera idling beside me. Like Eric Schumacher, the Drumbores had looked me over and came back to get me. This series of events had transpired within ten minutes of returning from my quick, but mandatory, trip to the woods. I was lucky this time. I often wonder how many rides I've missed over the years, due simply to poor timing.

It may seem hard to believe that I actually remembered seeing them as they passed by the first time. The reason for my recall is a direct result of my concentration on each vehicle that approached me. I look each driver in the eye and as I do I also retain an image of the vehicle they're in and often its color. When someone comes back to get me soon after their original pass, it is deja vu. The image I see is an exact copy of what existed minutes earlier. The car, color, background, the driver's eyes and face and even the sound of the vehicle, flip recognition switches in my memory.

Ralph and Norma Jean were serious square dancers, on their way to Ft. Monroe, near Norfolk, Virginia, to perform. We had a bit of a technical problem to overcome before we could take off. They had to find a way to squeeze me in. Unlike my very roadworthy gear, they had suits and huge crinoline petticoats, which essentially served as costumes for their dance. We eventually crammed my pack in the trunk with some of their less delicate clothing. I occupied the back seat along with four sets of petticoats, stacked to the ceiling.

They were an exceptionally friendly, forty-something couple, and took a trip similar to this one every year. Their square dancing excursion was fun, social, and served as an extra little vacation from their jobs at a manufacturing plant. On the way to Norfolk, they acted as tour guides and made a couple of stops which provided me with some good photo opportunities. I particularly wanted pictures during our Chesapeake Bay Bridge-Tunnel crossing.

What a concept! Completed on April 15, 1964, after 3 1/2 years of work, the 17.6 mile Chesapeake Bay Bridge-Tunnel consisted of a series of bridges and tunnels spanning the entrance to Chesapeake Bay. The roadway left the land as a bridge that ended on a little, man-made island. There it disappeared into a tunnel approximately a mile long. It emerged onto another bridge and continued until the next tunnel, also about a mile in length. Not blessed with the sensual capabilities of a mole, I had a difficult time judging the lengths of the tunnels without the aid of an odometer. It's hard to judge distances where there are no landmarks, only thousands of little, white, wall tiles. We came out of the second tunnel and onto a third bridge before it finally terminated on solid ground again in Norfolk.

Piloting an aircraft carrier between bridge abutments under stormy conditions has got to be a terrifying business. This engineering masterpiece was designed to accommodate giant Navy ships and super-tankers entering or leaving the bay. The tunnels made for fewer navigation obstacles.

I found it interesting how easterners are always going under rivers, bays, and ocean stretches, to get around. Even though it probably made engineering and economic sense, I still worried about leaks. I have a similar neurosis when standing on the down side of the big dams out west!

The Drumbores had given me the opportunity to see some stuff of interest to me. Now it was their turn to pursue their interests. As we entered Norfolk they said they wanted to check out the latest square dancing attire. We stopped at a western clothing store where they did some window shopping.

Ralph and Norma Jean were kind enough to invite me to their home in Delaware. Their hometown was already behind me so my visit would have to wait until another trip. We said our goodbyes amongst the heavy traffic and construction at the junction of I-64 and U.S. 13.

That intersection was terribly confusing. I stood at an entrance ramp, unsure if it would put me on a highway toward Nags Head, North Carolina. Beckoning drivers with my Nags Head sign, I was hoping somebody would have pity on me and at least point me in the right direction, even if they didn't give me a ride!

Jonathan Sable claimed to have been moved by the Holy Spirit, as he sped by. Jonathan hit the brakes and pulled off the busy entrance ramp onto the grass. The Holy Spirit must have been working pretty fast that day because I was concealed from drivers' views until they were nearly upon me. I must assume that He, She or It, was looking out for my best interest that day.

Jonathan's nice, late model car was running fine while I loaded up. As we accelerated down the entrance ramp, the fuel pump that his mechanic had replaced earlier that day, started cutting out. Jerking and stuttering down the road creates a nauseating feeling in me. Driving down a large, urban interstate is not a good time to be experiencing fuel problems. The crappy cars I have owned in the past have given me that sinking feeling before.

JONATHAN SABLE
Norfolk, Virginia

We went south on I-64, creeping along the shoulder for about a mile, desperately seeking an exit ramp off this eight lane freeway. Personally, I'd rather be stalled ten miles away from the nearest phone, in a rural area, than get stalled on a busy urban interstate. All I experience is a fear of sudden impact and my life going up in a plume of dirty black smoke. Rational thought or relaxation is impossible, even though I've stood along the shoulder of many a busy freeway.

Jonathan's car sputtered off of the interstate and onto another heavily travelled, limited access highway. No improvement resulted from this maneuver in either the traffic, or fuel pump situation. After a few more desperate turns to escape the main flow of traffic, my head was spinning from this circuitous route. All I knew was that his car was still running and he assured me he would get me on the proper road.

I was completely disoriented as we wound our way down unknown streets. The farther we went, however, the better his car ran. It was soon running perfectly. With the car running well and his assurance to me of being on the correct route to Nags Head, he mentioned his quick discussion with God before he picked me up. As soon as he had seen me

Jonathan sought advice from God to help him overcome his fear of this hitchhiker. Jonathan had been immediately directed to carry God's message to me.

A slender, handsome, clean cut young man in his early thirties, he was interested in my spiritual beliefs and wanted to share his with me. As a charismatic Christian he believed that the ability, or gift, to speak in tongues, was the only sure sign of heavenly salvation. He was sympathetic toward born again Christians who felt they were saved, yet couldn't speak in tongues. He firmly believed those neo-Christians would face the wrath of God on judgement day.

Jonathan asked if I had ever experienced, or seen a believer speaking in tongues. I replied no to both. He then offered an example and tried to get me to recognize any of the words or sounds he emitted. It's hard enough for me to recognize bits of a common foreign language, much less an incomprehensible, divine dialect. I was at a loss. He was very patient with me. All the while, the miles kept going by. I asked if he was taking me out of his way and shouldn't he be getting back to work. He said not to worry. I didn't. It was fascinating talking with him.

Questions I asked, like, "Why would God try gathering new members into his flock by using unintelligible sounds?," and "Why would an all knowing, benevolent God condemn billions of people over thousands of generations to the miseries of Hell because they made a poor decision that was based primarily on guesswork?" were left unsatisfactorily answered. That's not surprising. I'm a pretty hard sell when it comes to sectarian spirituality. What was clear was Jonathan's sincere concern for my day of reckoning with the Lord. I thanked him for his concern and advice and his twenty mile detour on my behalf. He said the time was well spent when talking about the Lord. Then he was off.

I found myself standing along some little country road headed south, trying to sort out reality from spirituality.

It was time for a walk. I turned away from the traffic and started off toward North Carolina. Good to stretch the legs out a bit. Shut the brain down and concentrate on the weight of the pack, sweat rolling down my belly, and where to place my foot after picking it up and swinging it forward. Just the basics for now. Despite the calendar being stuck in the middle of January, the weather refused to believe it. It was as fine as a mild day in June.

After a mile of relaxing walking and unenthusiastic hitchhiking, Mark Pillsbury, of Virginia Beach, Virginia, took me to tiny Sligo, North Carolina. From there he was turning toward Wilmington to do some fishing with his dad. The fishing would probably do him good. Young Mark and his wife were calling it quits and separating soon. I wondered why that happened so often. Sitting in a boat would give Mark some time to contemplate that very question.

Ken McDougal, from Chesapeake, Virginia, watched Mark drop me off and was waiting for me across the intersection. He had seen me during my walk following Jonathan's spiritually infused ride, but couldn't stop then because he had errands to run. Having completed them, he was now on the road to Nags Head.

Ken was a contractor specializing in sprinkler and other fire suppression systems. He had a job in the little town of Manteo. Manteo was past Nags Head which was fine with me. I hadn't really planned on stopping there, it was simply a target town to put on my sign. Ken was willing to make a short tourist stop on my behalf. He drove past the Wright Monument, at Kitty Hawk, commemorating the first manned flight. That little knoll where the monument stood was the site of one of man's greatest technological achievements. It took a giant leap of faith for the Wright brothers to rely on the combination of physics and their own skills to accomplish their dream of flight. The leap of faith I was making on this trip would prove no scientific theory. It sought to prove a hypothesis based upon human trust.

When Ken dropped me at the entrance to the Cape Hatteras National Seashore it was starting to get dark. Once again, before I could even cross the street, my next ride was patiently waiting.

Arthur Fuller had been out and about all day shopping for a new vehicle. I was his new truck's first passenger. Quite a distinction for a hitchhiker! Although he was excited about his latest purchase, his excitement was tempered by a blow he had recently suffered. Arthur had been working as a carpenter on a nearby island. A couple of nights earlier, there had been a fire at the work site and all of his tools were lost. Not exactly the end of the world but it did require a reinvestment.

Because Arthur lived on a North Carolina barrier island, I naturally assumed he was a surfer or board sailer. Wrong! He was a skateboarder who loved to sail pavement and concrete seas.

Arthur really liked the area and there was plenty of construction work to keep him busy. All the construction work available was an indication of the latest influx of people. In Arthur's mind that influx was the bad that came with the good. In addition to the tourist trade, many people remained to live in the area. This stressed the civic infrastructure and caused somewhat of a blight on the once quaint, little seaside towns.

That evening we rode down the uncrowded highway through undeveloped, federally designated park land. It was the off season now, so I simply pushed images of traffic jams and backed up sewers out of my mind and enjoyed the island splendor, with the Atlantic Ocean on my left and Pamlico Sound on my right. The island was so narrow, it seemed as though I could throw a rock into either body of water from the road.

The sun had almost set as we arrived in Avon, North Carolina. Immediately after Arthur dropped me off, Scott Wilkinson stopped and took me seven miles to the east edge of Buxton, the next town. I was ready for bed, even though it was only about seven o'clock. I found a reasonable spot amongst the thorny vines that inhabited the sandy ground. There was no threat of rain that night so I didn't bother setting up my tent. I didn't even think about what sort of critters spent their evenings roaming around the beach. I was too exhausted to worry about them. Ignorance was bliss.

Hitting the sack early would make getting up at sunrise that much easier. My plan was to catch the ferry at Hatteras the following morning. Just in case the hitchhiking was bad I was prepared to walk the ten miles to the ferry terminal.

Fifteen minutes of walking the next morning was all that was necessary. William Maxton Peele, Jr., a lifelong barrier island resident and fisherman, took me right to the ferry terminal.

On the ferry ride I met Donny Griffin, a social studies teacher from Virginia Beach. He agreed to take me the length of the island to the next ferry, at Ocracoke. When you have an opportunity to actually visit with someone and talk about what you're up to, most people would never deny you a ride. Out on the road a hitchhiker appears far more threatening. The personal touch of conversation makes a real difference. Every chance to strike a chord of recognition or of positive association makes a driver more likely to offer a lift.

Things had gone so smoothly that morning I had travelled 20 miles by car and a couple more by ferry boat, by 9:00 am. The ferry that would leave Ocracoke for Cedar Island at 9:30 had broken down. The next one to depart was at noon which left me in Ocracoke with three hours to kill. The weather was warm with partly cloudy skies. I spent the remainder of that peaceful morning walking around the little town, watching birds, and exploring the Cape Hatteras National Seashore Visitor Center.

The 12:00 pm ferry was in good working order and the two hour trip to Cedar Island began on schedule.

It was a wonderful ride across the calm waters of Pamlico Sound. Standing in the bow of the vessel I enjoyed watching the ocean birds that inhabited the Sound. The wind hitting my face was warm and moist. A substantial, and welcome change from the bitterly cold wind I had found along Minnesota and Iowa highways.

I returned inside to catch up on some journal entries and visit with other passengers. My next ride, with Dion (say die-on) Beveridge, also came about through a ferry conversation. Conversation came easily with Dion. He managed the hardware store back in Ocracoke. Taking a couple of days off, he was on his way to visit his girlfriend Rebecca, in Topsail Beach, North Carolina.

Dion had lived in Ocracoke for about two years. He was much happier dealing hardware there than he had been in Annapolis, selling expensive Mercedes-Benz automobiles. I told him, with a grin, that he was wise to leave his former position. I'd never been picked up by a Mercedes driver and felt Dion was better off associating with a different class of people. This certainly did not imply a lower class. Some of the classiest people I've ever met couldn't even afford the hood ornament off of a fancy car. I'm sorry to say that the pretty people driving those luxurious automobiles misunderstood the concept of class.

Dion dreamed of being free of the things that kept him attached to land. He was the proud owner of a fixer-upper sailboat. When it was refurbished, he hoped to begin an island hopping trip through the Virgin Islands. Awaiting the completion of that inaugural voyage was a world nearly covered with water highways. Not being from a family of shipwrights, he was at a slight disadvantage. His project was strictly learn as you go. I would venture to guess his liberal two year completion estimate might be more reasonably set at about three to four years. Inexperience and lack of money always contributes to delays in larger home-spun projects like Dion's.

While driving toward Topsail Beach, Dion made me a tentative invitation to stay at Rebecca's beachfront abode with them. Tentative because he needed to ask her first. I was hoping to stay for a couple of reasons. First was the excellent company. Second was the chance to take a shower. It had been three warm days since my last shower, on Kent Island, at Tom Leonard's.

Dion went in to greet Rebecca while I waited in the car. She welcomed this unusual guest and made me feel right at home. After a great spaghetti dinner we hit a bar in Wilmington to catch a hot reggae band. We faced a jam packed, writhing, sweaty mob of dancers. We jumped right in and danced until the band quit. Yahoo!

We arrived home safely, after driving through dense fog. Still reeling from energetic dancing, and unable to fall asleep, with my ears ringing from loud music, I kept thinking about how crowded the world was becoming and our ability to get along; or, was it our inability?

Some of those thoughts were prompted by recent events in Rebecca's life. After the death of her mother, she had taken on the responsibility of maintaining a couple of beach front apartments her mother had owned. Sadly, the last tenants left with unpaid rent and a messy place. Sometimes, for business reasons, we are forced to trust those we must deal with. We expect them to deal in good faith. When we are wronged in a situation like that, it is nearly impossible to regain our untainted trust. So it is, in our personal lives. Once our trust is abused, we automatically hesitate at giving it so readily, if we're willing to give it at all. I'm sure many people have been burned and have never regained that original trust. It is because of reasons like this I've had some long waits on the side of the road!

Our continually expanding population makes it imperative that cooperative efforts expand with it. The less cooperation existing in a confined population, the more dangerous it becomes. Dangerous to itself, newcomers, and to the environment.

America looks and feels crowded to me. One example of why can be found here on the North Carolina coast. Seeing the rapidly developing commercial coastline makes me wonder what people are after. Wonderful places to live are quickly subdivided and the natural beauty that drew residents there originally is soon lost. They instantly despoil the very beauty they seek. It's not at all surprising to see our national parks and wildlands receiving so much visitor pressure. The claustrophobic life of the suburbs and cities, in addition to our stressful daily lives, sends us searching for some sort of peace and quiet. Instead we are faced with overcrowded campgrounds, trails, and thousands of rules, and enforcers to insure our cooperation. Unfortunately, pilgrims to our natural sanctuaries are met by millions of others seeking the same relief.

Our needs as humans require places where we can stretch our minds and imaginations for personal growth. We need to feel tired on the trail, dirty and bug-bitten, cold and wet, and to glory in our ability to face nature on its own terms. Over the years, since Yellowstone was established as our first National Park, people of foresight have continued to press for more and more areas of natural beauty and resources to be set aside for future generations. Our descendants will surely need those areas as an escape from an advancing urban front. It is sad to see foolish political appointees, under the guise of national interest, or security, selling and leasing away our most cherished preserves for some short-sighted, selfish purpose. What do we, as a society, become when we sell the soul of the earth? The very essence of what we depend upon for our spiritual and economic well being is lost as we construct "McBeach." Often, it's a drag to look into the American mirror.

I tired of such thoughts as the adrenalin, generated by frenzied dancing, began to leave my system. I was comfortably tucked into bed with a sea breeze blowing through the screened windows. As I closed my eyes, seeking sheep, I listened to the roar of waves crashing on the beach. One wave. Two waves. Three wavzzzzz...

The following morning Rebecca and Dion insisted on taking me to the west edge of Jacksonville, North Carolina. They were worried about me and asked if there was anything else they could do. I exclaimed that they had been more than generous and didn't need to feel any further responsibility for my well-being. I appreciated their concern and felt that a real camaraderie existed between us. Enjoying each other's company as long as possible, we knew that in a few moments we would possibly never see one another again. Laughing at our predicament, we hugged our good-byes. They drove off while I stood alone, along the side of some unfamiliar road, just like hundreds of times before. Untrue. I had become closer to Rebecca and Dion than I normally would have with those hundreds of other rides.

Traffic wasn't moving around much that Sunday morning in Jacksonville. Sunday mornings are notoriously slow for hitchhiking. After a long, boring, two hour wait I decided to start walking. Two hours is about all I can handle in one spot. I wasn't complaining. It was a warm, sunny day. Exquisite weather for being out and about. Not what I'd been expecting for the 21st of January. I shouldn't have been too surprised because I was heading into the deep south.

The walk out of Jacksonville turned out to be a hot one. The sun never quit. In less than a mile, relief came in the form of Phil Ferguson. Being in such close proximity to Camp LeJeune Marine Corps Base, I wasn't surprised to learn that Phil was a Marine. He was a recruiting sergeant stationed in Danville, Virginia.

Phil was thirty-two years old and had been in the Corps for fifteen years. Originally from Lynchburg, Virginia, he had joined right out of high school. He liked the Corps, in general. He was proud of its unwritten code of ethics and felt it set high personal standards of honor, integrity and loyalty. This understanding between fellow Marines created a kinship that was unique to the Corps.

A couple of things did bother him, though. One was that there were too many servicemen in the vicinity. He got tired of working with marines all day long and then going home to his apartment where all of his neighbors were also marines. He theorized that the surrounding states had finally reached the limit of their carrying capacity. There wasn't enough room left in any of them for a single additional marine!

Phil's other gripe was the rank structure. Not because he wasn't a general or something, but because at certain levels there could be no social activity with members of another rank. Essentially, he couldn't date service women outside rank. Unmarried at 32, this would obviously be a negative aspect of the service. If I couldn't socialize with women I worked with, I wouldn't even have a social life!

Phil was a friendly, articulate man who was genuinely concerned with the human condition. He hoped to spend some time travelling like a homeless person. Sort of a prince and the pauper scenario. Only through such an experiment could he get a true understanding of their plight. I agreed. Unless your perspective changes, sometimes it doesn't matter how long you contemplate a problem. Only by experiencing a similar situation can you obtain a clear understanding of the obstacles others face. That becomes the first step toward a workable solution, no matter the scale of the problem.

I had been facing a barrier since leaving Willow River. The barrier was race. Over the course of nearly a month and 72 different rides I had only been picked up by caucasians. Phil was the African-American who finally ended the white streak. I felt it had been too long of a wait, and was happy that this imaginary racial barrier had finally fallen. Wouldn't you know it took a marine to make it happen! Thanks Phil. Thanks Marines.

My target for the day was an acquaintance who lived in suburban Fayetteville. Beulaville, about 70 miles east of Fayetteville, was where Phil left me and I waited for my next ride. Everybody in Beulaville must have been in church. There was hardly a soul in sight as I walked down the road toward the west edge of town. Ahead, on the right side of the road, I noticed a couple of little girls playing in the front yard. As I slowly approached their yard, they moved closer and closer to the front door. Finally, as I walked past their house, they were peering at me from behind the security of a safely locked screen door.

Walking along the quiet road, with two pairs of children's eyes staring at me, I felt a deep sense of loneliness. I'm sure the girls did as they were instructed during their ten, or so, years of growing up. I was disappointed because they didn't come running up and ask a thousand kid questions. Instead they left me to my own thoughts and stared accusingly.

If we all weren't wrapped in the bonds of fear, kids and adults alike would be more interested in unusual travellers passing through their town. If we run away from strangers every time, our lives will become small islands. We can no longer have an integrated society because the strangers we once shunned are now ignoring us. Through isolation our spirits wither. We all become the lonely strangers.

As I stood there, thinking about how scary the world must be for millions of people, Cecil Nixon, of Fayetteville, pulled up. He was dressed in his camouflage outfit as he returned home from a weekend with his National Guard unit. He admitted to never picking up hitchhikers. My sign caught his attention and he had decided to make this one exception.

It was unusual that he rarely gave rides to people. He had a long history of hitchhiking in his younger years. He used to hitch to his grandma's house all the time. On one cross-country trip the drivers were so generous, he started and ended his trip with seven dollars in his pocket. There was even a time in the army when he went absent-without-leave and hitched home to be with his pregnant wife. Without the generosity of those drivers in his past, Cecil would have been immobile. Its just good karma to return some of the good will of drivers by picking up hitchhikers when you have the chance. I was glad he could finally pay back at least one of his rides by helping me out. He was going to a town north of Fayetteville, so dropped me off at a junction in Stedman.

Young Breck Dunham, 18, was on his way to Oak Ridge Military Academy, in Greensboro, North Carolina. His curiosity about hitchhikers won out over fear. Breck had no intention of becoming an island. I was his first hitchhiker, ever. He was excited and nervous. Unsure of how to act he just started asking the thousand "kid questions." What, where, who, when, why, how, if, did, should, etc. It was a glorious break from the doldrums of the Beulaville experience. I answered his questions with stories of past trips and gave him the details of my present adventure. He was amazed at just about everything.

Breck may have been finishing up at prep school, but dreaded the thought of continuing on to college. Appearing to be from an upper middle class family, he was no doubt under considerable pressure to do so. In his innocence he was out to conquer the world with health and good looks. He was in excellent physical condition and enjoyed facing challenges that tested his strength and endurance rather than intellect. Even though he was only eighteen, he had trained seriously in the martial arts for many years. The most significant test of his abilities was an Outward Bound course. During the twenty-three days the group was out hiking and climbing, it had rained sixteen of them. A nature experience like that demands a certain physical, and mental toughness. Breck had that toughness.

Breck was willing to take me anywhere in Fayetteville I needed to go. He had been raised in town and knew his way around. We stopped at a phone booth, as close to my friend's house as I could have guessed. While I made contact, Breck waited until he was sure that my ride was coming. It had been another uplifting, satisfying experience with a young American.

After a full day's rest in Fayetteville, I was off to visit more friends in the little town of Waxhaw, North Carolina, just south of Charlotte.

Rides from people with a military affiliation continued with Allen Sandefur. Allen was a paratrooper with the 82nd Airborne, stationed at Ft. Bragg, just northwest of Fayetteville. With 44 parachute jumps to his credit he had recently returned from Panama after participating in the Noriega coup.

While serving in Panama he had seen plenty of action. Snipers posed a serious threat to the U.S. troops and two of his friends were killed. With that sad experience behind him he expressed his relief at being home. As the 82nd returned from their victorious campaign, there had been a large celebration to welcome them home. They all parachuted into Ft. Bragg. Apparently it was quite a sight for the local citizens.

The Airborne's proud motto is that they'll be anywhere in the world, on the ground, in eighteen hours. With a reputation like that, Allen could be on his way to foreign shores again at any minute. His enlistment was nearly over and he had no intention of reenlisting. Being safe at home was an important factor for this twenty-four year old father of two.

He left me in the little town of Raeford, where a trucker named Glen brought me into Laurinburg. Glen was a big, burly guy with black eyes, long black hair, beard, and a beat up, black suede cowboy hat. He wasn't very vocal but I did find out he was hauling livestock feed. What was so cool about Glen was that the truck he was driving had a "No Riders" sticker in the passenger window. Yes! We had won a minor skirmish in the fight against authority! In Laurinburg, U.S. 74 was a divided highway that carried plenty of traffic toward Charlotte. What surprised me about Laurinburg was the length of time it took me to get a ride. My luck in North Carolina had been very good, until that point.

Although the weather was splendid, my patience had worn quite thin when Sammy Cummings pulled over. It had taken over two-and-a-half hours for me to be on my way.

Sammy was driving a strange rig, with several used cars positioned on top of it. I'm at a loss to explain it any better than that. Anyway, with the help of this contraption, he delivered used cars all over the state of North Carolina. The year before he had put on 97,000 miles. He'd owned the truck and trailer for about a year now. It got really boring on the road day in and day out, and he was glad to have somebody to talk to.

Sammy had been a Christian for about three years. He used to run a bar and made lots of money. Upon his conversion, he gave up the bar business to do something more compatible with his beliefs. His new hauling business required long lonely hours, but he preferred it to his former lifestyle. Now he witnesses his faith to whoever will listen and keeps on driving down the road.

He was proud of his success in business, despite his lack of formal education. Eighth grade was as far as it went. It certainly wasn't evident in his conversation. He was an articulate man.

Sammy felt lucky to be alive after a trucking incident in his recent past. He had lost the brakes on his truck while in a series of hairpin turns on a steep grade. Had there been any oncoming traffic he wouldn't have made it. I was unsure if this incident led directly to his conversion. He did feel that surviving the brake failure was a great gift from God. He encouraged me to accept some religious tracts as we said goodbye in Monroe, North Carolina.

Unable to get a ride I walked the three miles across Monroe. My destination was a friend's house in a rural area near Waxhaw. I knew the approximate mileage to the intersection where I had to turn west. I quickly pulled out a piece of cardboard from my stash of sign material and made a sign that read, "15 MILES." I wanted people to know that I was going someplace near their home and not just a drifter. My friend was their neighbor. It worked like a charm. Jimmy Peale lived in my friend's neighborhood.

Even though Jimmy and I both spoke English, we had a tough time communicating; or rather, I had a difficult time understanding him. Jimmy's southern accent was so heavy that after repeating his name three times, I made him spell it for me. We laughed when I finally figured it out.

Jimmy was glad life here in rural North Carolina was settling back down to its normal, slow pace. In the aftermath of hurricane Hugo, people had been frantically scrambling to put lives and property back together again. As Hugo tore through people's backyards nobody could believe it had come so far inland. It would have been impossible to be prepared for the devastation. Utility lines ripped down, ancient trees exploded into splinters, houses flattened, flooding; in other words, chaos. Most of the clean up work was finished. The rebuilding would take more time. Perhaps for the most unfortunate, it would never even get started.

I was glad at the prospect of spending a couple of nights indoors and sharing the company of friends. I spent two days eating Chuck and Betty Fought's great food and enjoyed walking in the surrounding woodlands. The air was cool, fresh, and carried the scent of evergreen. It was a beautiful place to recharge my substantially drained energy.

Unfortunately, my restless spirit wouldn't allow me to hang around relaxing for long. I had the urge to continue my route south. I left North Carolina as rested and ready as I could be for what lay ahead, in South Carolina.

On the morning of January 26, Chuck brought me to the eastern edge of Lancaster, South Carolina, on U.S. 521. The spot where I stood was cold and windy, despite the bright sunshine.

After about an hour wait, ex-marine Greg Morgan took me a few miles to the little town of Elgin. Here, I was at a disadvantage. The road had narrowed considerably and there was no shoulder available for drivers to safely pull over. The cold wind was still nagging at me. I was forced to dig into my pack and pull out another layer of clothing. That is really a hassle because it takes your attention away from the traffic. Besides, not many people want to stop for a big ugly guy who's changing clothes on the side of the road. After another hour of waiting I decided to start walking. It was ten miles to the next town of Kershaw.

Twenty minutes of walking went by before Bill Myers, Jr., stopped to say hello. He was super friendly and thought nothing of taking me down the road. He was only going as far as Kershaw, where he needed to service some equipment. We spent almost as much time chatting outside his van when he left me in Kershaw, as we did during the short drive. Too bad he needed to hustle off to work. If we'd have wasted about two more minutes I wouldn't have had to face my next ride.

Since things had been going relatively slowly that morning, I wasn't about to let the guy in the green station wagon, who had stopped right in the middle of the road, go. After quickly piling in, to keep from slowing up traffic, I immediately recognized a potentially dangerous situation. The man driving had long, greasy, black hair, a heavy southern accent and a very limited vocabulary. His equally greasy girlfriend/wife/sister? was slouched down in the passenger seat up front. She looked comfortable, but wasted.

The first question he asked, as he turned around to look at me with dark, wild eyes, was if I had any crack cocaine. I replied in the negative and he was thoroughly and intensely disappointed. Staring at me with accusing eyes, he paid little attention to the road as he launched into a diatribe about my not having any crack, cocaine, speed or pot on me. Not even a lousy goddamn beer! What kind of a self-respecting, hippie hitchhiker was I, not having any drugs to pass around? What could I say? Even if I'd had any, I sure wouldn't have given him any. He was already at the edge, conversing with himself and laughing at all the wrong times with a demonical howl.

I wasn't about to take the chance of annoying or angering him further by asking him to let me out. I was nervous but saw no evidence of weapons. The possibility existed of a hidden firearm or knife and I had no doubt this maniac was capable of using either. This was one time when I felt my own imposing appearance was advantageous. With my size and strength I was confident of either avoiding, or warding off any attack, except one involving a gun.

As those thoughts entered and exited my mind, the woman began to express some visible life signs. She peered over the top of the front seat, looking like Kilroy, and sort of chirped, "Ain'cha scart a gettin' kilt?" Well, at that point I actually was; but, not from a gunshot wound. The driver was now practicing the procedure of opening and closing his door at speeds of 55 mph on a narrow two-lane highway. I didn't see much need for more practice, he already seemed quite proficient.

In the midst of gnashing his teeth, gripping and re-gripping the steering wheel, he suddenly declared that he hated "niggers." In fact, he would take me all the way to Camden, just so one of "them damn niggers out there" wouldn't get me. Stunned by these derogatory, racial slurs I found myself completely repulsed by these creatures. I'm one who's been known to put up an argument on occasion, but this moron was not to be reasoned with. White supremacy must be stuck in the genetic material of those in-bred geeks.

Much to my surprise, he hit the brakes, made a left turn and came to a complete stop. It was the end of the line for me. Not my life, just the ride. We had gone a mere seven miles to Westville, where they apparently lived. In my ultimate relief, I rejoiced inside but tried not to appear too eager to get out of the car.

When I did get all of my stuff out, I immediately felt like taking a shower. My skin was crawling. Those people were so foul. They had few brains left from the substance abuse and no souls. I was glad I wasn't black, or their next door neighbor. They probably had friends who got together dressed in white sheets and played with matches. My lawn would undoubtedly have been a target for a good old cross burning. Slime bags.

When people ask me if I'd had any bad experiences on my trip, I automatically relate that ride. Other drivers may have been drunk or stoned, but none were in a drug induced, racial hate, state of mind. That was beyond weirdness. It left me uneasy about my excursion into the back-woods of South Carolina. I hoped this case would be an isolated incident.

The Westville intersection where I stood was slow. It didn't matter much, my brain was moving slowly, too. It was a beautiful wooded area, drenched in warm sunshine and I was just happy to be on the roadside again.

I've never thought of myself as a drunk magnet, but drunks were undeniably following me. That's the only possible explanation for the high percentage of drunk drivers I encountered. There couldn't possibly be that many of them across the country. If there really are, we're all in great danger every day of our lives, as drivers and pedestrians. How stupid can our judicial system be if violators are out of jail after their third or fourth driving-while-intoxicated offense? They shouldn't get that many chances. The victim in their path doesn't get that many chances.

This guy coming at me would not be driving me anywhere! I saw him come weaving down the road toward me. Yes, weaving. Like running a slalom course with the centerline stripes as pylons. So, I stood there wondering if I were going to have to drag this guy out of his old Pontiac after he hit the ditch. It took a long time for him to get to my intersection because he was only going about 20 mph, where the speed limit was 55. Instead of pulling up next to me, or plowing into the ditch, he turned onto the crossroad in front of me and stopped.

He sat there while his engine idled and waved me over. I didn't have anything else to do and thought it would be a good chance to give this guy some grief, so I walked over. He was unable to communicate. I honestly couldn't understand a word he said. He had to struggle to keep his head up to speak to me. Good grief. This poor, middle-aged black man must have had the misfortune of being our cocaine grubbing friend's neighbor. I encouraged him to go home and get some sleep. This was not Mr. Rogers' Neighborhood!

As the beat up old Pontiac crept away, the weirdness of this place had finally gotten to me. I was getting out of there. I walked back up the road to try and figure out exactly where I was and the distance to the next town. A little post office was the nearest structure. I walked in and was greeted by a friendly post mistress. She told me the next "real" town was fifteen miles away. She was kind and offered me a handful of hard candy to make my walk (if I had to) more pleasant. I thanked her and headed back down the road with a slightly better attitude towards South Carolina.

Good feelings continued to pile up when, after a half mile, Dennis Belue stopped for me. He normally didn't pick people up but thought I displayed "something good" that separated me from other hitchhikers. I was thrilled that whatever essence I possessed had enabled me to quickly leave Westville!

Army sergeant first class Dennis Belue was a nursing supervisor at Ft. Jackson in Columbia, South Carolina. During our short ride together he communicated a strong sense of duty to his country. As a member of the armed forces he believed in serving the American people to the best of his ability. By staffing the military with decent, hard working people we could properly maintain and defend our democratic nation. To emphasize the point we stopped briefly at the site of one of his heros. The American Legion Post in Camden had a memorial rose garden dedicated to local Medal of Honor recipient, D.L. Truesdell.

At this time of the year the roses were nothing but twisted, thorny sticks surrounded by brown grass, but appearance mattered little. What made it so special was the meaning it held for Dennis and his willingness to share it with me. The memorial acted as a symbol of the sacrifice and dedication one man was willing to make in service to his country. It was an inspiration to future servicemen and women to take their duty seriously.

As Dennis approached retirement he was formulating plans for when he finally finished his service career. His dream was to get a sailboat and follow the intracoastal waterway of the east coast. Winding its way through islands, bays, backwaters, rivers and canals, the waterway would take him from New York City to Key West. The entire route was essentially protected from the potentially hazardous effects of the Atlantic Ocean. It made for a simply navigated, relatively relaxing tour.

While Dennis related his idyllic future I considered my good fortune at hearing his, and many other's hopes and dreams. One of the most fulfilling things about conversations with new acquaintances is the amount of personal ground you can cover in a short period of time. People used me as a listening post. I was benign, agreeable, and encouraging of openness. I found out what was important to them. Not only hopes, but fears, too. As the recipient of those revelations, I was constantly provided with new ideas, possibilities, inspiration, and motivation. Important things, not to be squandered. All of those drivers gave me stars to shoot for and pitfalls to avoid.

Dennis went out of his way to get me across Camden to adjacent Lugoff. He left me where U.S. 601 was a straight shot south.

Dean McGaha took me the fifty-five miles from Lugoff to Orangeburg, South Carolina. As we sailed down the road for about an hour, Dean bombarded me with his Christian message. He was very well meaning and articulate, but I just wasn't into the message any more. I almost felt harassed about the existence, or lack of my Christian spirituality. I had run out of words, questions, and graciousness, and grudgingly sat there and took it. I felt that I at least owed him a tolerant hearing. It felt like a long ride. He turned off at the near edge of Orangeburg. Of course, I was continuing across town, so started walking.

I walked at least two miles along a very busy street. The people passing by looked mean. Plain old, ordinary, couldn't-give-a-damn mean! Orangeburg felt hopelessly locked into a latent, hostile funk. Nobody smiled. Even the guy that picked me up wasn't smiling. He did have a good reason to be crabby, though.

Thomas Darby's poor, old Toyota truck was barely running. Since there was no shoulder on this four lane road through town, he had to stop in the busy traffic lane. It took a half block for him to stop because the Toyota's brakes weren't too good. When he down-shifted, to help slow the vehicle, the tailpipe spewed billows of wet, blue smoke. Seemed he had an engine problem as well. He told me he rarely drove it because it went through three gallons of oil per day. I felt sorry for the guy. Anybody who drives a car in even worse condition than mine, deserved my sympathy!

Thomas was out looking for a cheap fuel pump for the truck. He was travelling in my direction, more or less, via some off the road junk yard.

He confirmed my initial impressions of Orangeburg. He started telling me bizarre stories. He claimed the "establishment" was bringing drugs into the city and were trying to subjugate the black youth. He said prostitution was on the increase and it was turning into a rough place. He also mentioned the existence of a black, underground army, guided and maintained by whites. His theory was that those whites were trying to gather power from a white backlash toward blacks, after their little army stirred up trouble. Of course, the black army would be sealing their own fates, as well as that of their black brothers and sisters, by this ruse. The problem was that the young black men saw their mission as revolutionary and didn't see the manipulation by the controllers and financiers that doomed their struggle to certain failure.

THOMAS DARBY
Bamberg, S. C.

That's all I can tell you about his theory. I didn't really understand it very well. If I had, I could have written a dissertation on it. I couldn't just pass it off as paranoia because it seemed just convoluted enough to be feasible. There must have been some grain of truth to his conjecture. In this strange neighborhood, I deemed anything possible. The weirdness was creeping back into my psyche. I wanted out of South Carolina!

Thomas couldn't even get me to the next town. It took about an hour to go less than fifteen miles. I wound up walking into, and then across, Bamberg, South Carolina.

I was tired of walking. I sat down on some steps, off the sidewalk, for a rest. It was getting dark, so as I rested, I glanced around looking for a place to sleep. Just seconds after I sat down and put out my sign, saying "301 SOUTH," Bill Johnson pulled up. I wasn't supposed to be getting rides when I was sitting down! He said that he was only going about two miles down the road. I piled into the back of his pick-up truck and was soon stunned to find myself two miles out of town and into nowhere. I guess his mileage estimate was disappointingly accurate. As Bill turned into his driveway, I desperately asked if I could camp in his yard for the night. The temperature was dropping fast and it was completely dark. He said yes and I was relieved to have obtained a good camp spot for the night. I was far too tired to roam around in the dark looking for a camp site.

It had been a long, hard day, and it had taken nearly twelve hours to travel 110 miles. As I prepared my camp I felt like an alien. I wasn't even thinking. I was disconnected from the real world. All my motions were instinctual. Put the tent up, unroll the insulated pad, lay out the sleeping bag, drink some water.

Bill and his wife Joanne probably thought all of this was pretty strange, too. Nonetheless, they invited me in for some soup and a sandwich. They brought me back to planet earth! We had a pleasant visit. Joanne kept worrying about whether I'd be warm enough outside. She offered me an extra quilt. I thanked her but declined, saying I had a very warm sleeping bag. I told them that a flat grassy lawn, access to a toilet, a yard light, and a late night snack, were deluxe accommodations. As good as they come.

Bill had worked at a local factory for twenty years and had to get to work early the next morning. Joanne had worked with social services for over nineteen years. She had dealt with many needy people over the years. She incorrectly identified me as destitute and was very concerned. I had to assure her that I had enough money to get to my cousin's house in Florida. Just to make sure, she packed a good lunch and offered some money. I thanked her, but declined the money. I did enjoy the lunch, though.

South Carolina confused me. It was full of the good, the bad, the ugly, and the incredibly sweet!

The morning of Saturday, January 27, saw almost no traffic. What I did see were birds. Cardinals, jays, flickers, and even a pileated woodpecker were active in the tall trees. After an hour of throwing rocks at random targets and watching flickers trying to tear down the pine forests in their search for bugs, I decided to find another road.

My local strategy was failing. I had been trying all along to avoid freeway travel. I wanted to enjoy the scenery along the smaller highways and meet a more diverse cross-section of people. In Bamberg, my intent was to split from U.S. 601 and take U.S. 301 across Georgia, to Jacksonville, Florida. From there I'd cross over to Tampa, where my cousin lived. It would have worked out great, except that nobody drove highway 301. Why would they when I-95 was only twenty-five miles away? It would take them to Jacksonville far faster than the highway I was planning to take. Of course, I didn't learn about the 301 traffic deficit until Bill had told me the night before. My wait with the woodpeckers finally convinced me to find another way.

I walked the couple miles back into Bamberg, then out to its eastern edge. I'd had enough of crabby faces. That alien feeling was creeping back. I chose U.S. 78 east. It was the shortest route to I-95. Once on it, I hoped I would be one quick ride out of South Carolina. But, just because I wanted out didn't mean a Rolls Royce was going to appear out of nowhere and be my deliverance! I expected something more like a black Monte Carlo to take me to a landfill to shoot at rats.

It was about fifteen miles to the next town of Branchville, halfway to I-95. I didn't feel like walking there so I set my backpack down and decided to wait it out on the east edge of Bamberg. It took two more hours. At least it was a warm, sunny day despite the cold dispositions of the drivers.

Joseph Dobson and Mark Morris passed me by but came back. They were only going about five miles down the road and figured they'd save me from walking a few miles. I thought it was a good plan. Momentum is the hitchhiker's best friend.

In their mid-thirties, Joseph and Mark were from tiny Sycamore, South Carolina, in Allendale County. They were in the area to visit an elderly friend who was recovering from a heart attack. Understanding my predicament, knowing from experience how tough it was to get rides in the vicinity, they volunteered to take me the ten extra miles to Branchville. We all agreed my best bet for going south was on the interstate. Branchville was halfway there. I was very appreciative.

Robert Johnson came by after a half hour wait. He lived near Branchville and worked in Orangeburg. He used to hitch a great deal when he lived in Indiana. He said it was useless to hitchhike in this area and was very surprised to see me. I asked if he wouldn't mind taking me an extra ten miles to I-95. He said he'd be glad to help get me out of there. I was relieved. The weather was holding warm and sunny and I had finally made it someplace. At least it felt like someplace.

It had taken five hours to go twenty-eight miles and both drivers had taken me a total of twenty miles out of their way. If my progress kept to that pace, I calculated the remainder of the trip would take 300 days. Oh, brother!

The scenery had changed in an instant. I was suddenly reminded why I kept to backroads as much as possible. There was nothing quaint, scenic, or friendly about the St. George, I-95 interchange. I was surrounded by strip development, busy intersections and very fast, heavy traffic. The entrance ramp was poorly designed for a hitchhiker, so I walked down onto the freeway shoulder. Locating what I thought was the best place to stand, I set my pack down and mentally prepared myself for a long wait. My freshly constructed sign proclaimed a hopeful, "TAMPA."

I got fooled. In a few minutes a couple of pick-up trucks stopped. The two guys driving them, Brett and Denny, worked together and were heading home to watch the Super Bowl. I climbed into Brett's truck and our little caravan was on its way. After the usual small talk I finally asked the dreaded question, "How far are you going?"

I thought if I were really lucky, Brett would be going the one hundred miles to Savannah, Georgia. When he replied Sarasota, Florida, I had to shake the cobwebs of long waits and short rides out of my head, and rethink my Florida geography. I carefully asked the name of the town again and gently asked for its location in relation to Tampa. I was tip-toeing around all these questions because I didn't want to appear too eager, hear incorrectly, or make him change his residence through some time warp, trans-universe slip.

Brett reiterated his Sarasota hometown. There it was! He had said it again! He was so flippant about it. Almost as though going to Sarasota, 470 (FOUR HUNDRED AND SEVENTY!) miles away and 50 miles SOUTH of Tampa, was no big deal! So far it was real; no geographical time warp transformation had occurred. I nearly wet my pants. I sat there with a big, stupid grin on my face while the mileposts flashed by. I couldn't tell you what Georgia looked like but life was good anyway.

I changed out of my long-johns as soon as we stopped for gas. Florida. The sunshine state. I wanted to be ready!

Brett was married and had two kids. He worked with a telephone company subcontractor, splicing wires. There was work in all sorts of unusual places. He'd worked up in Vermont and more recently, South

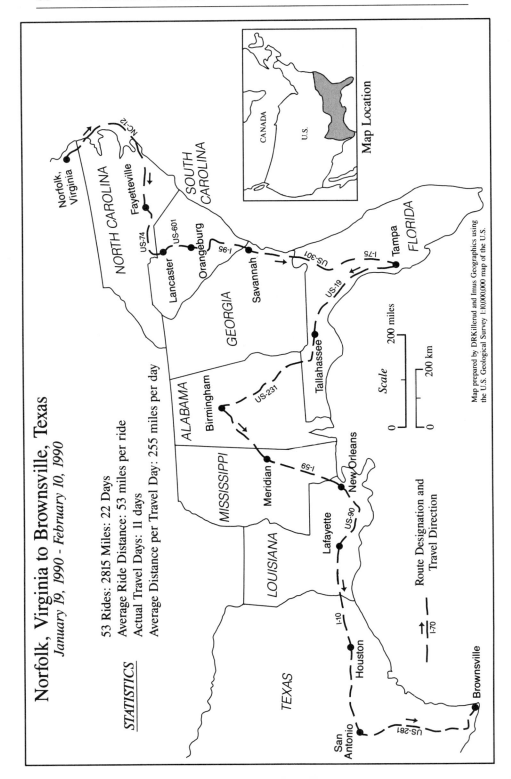

Norfolk, Virginia to Brownsville, Texas
January 19, 1990 - February 10, 1990

STATISTICS

53 Rides: 2815 Miles: 22 Days
Average Ride Distance: 53 miles per ride
Actual Travel Days: 11 days
Average Distance per Travel Day: 255 miles per day

Scale

0   200 miles
0   200 km

Map prepared by DRKillerud and Imus Geographics using
the U.S. Geological Survey 1:10,000,000 map of the U.S.

Map Location

CANADA

U.S.

Route Designation and
Travel Direction

I-70

Carolina, reconnecting portions of the state to the outside world after hurricane Hugo did its dirty work.

The day before, Brett and Denny had finished up their work and hit the bars. It had been a late night with little sleep. Brett was tired and made sure I had a driver's license. I would be having driving duty sometime before we hit Tampa. It was a rattle-trap truck with poor steering and I wasn't looking forward to my driving task but didn't complain.

All went well because I only drove about 100 miles. I was tired, too! It had been my longest ride of the trip so far, and it came at the perfect moment.

Along the way I had telephoned my cousin Morton, and we made arrangements to meet at a Tampa exit ramp around midnight. Somehow, the timing worked out, we hooked up, and I was ready to relax for a couple of warm, Florida days.

Being from the cold, north country, I wasn't used to roaches. They made quite an impression on me. They seemed to be taking over and some of them were big enough to be mistaken for small birds. Speaking of birds, I went bird watching at Lettuce Lake Park and saw at least ten different species I'd never seen before. It was the highlight of my Florida visit.

Tampa didn't exactly strike me as a real gem. It seemed crowded and dirty. There was garbage strewn everywhere. Nobody seemed to care or felt any sort of community pride. Perhaps the folks who had once cared simply gave up and moved away.

There were many new subdivision communities and apartment complexes springing up. Wherever there was a bare patch of ground there was construction equipment. Each new complex that went up was built with a wall around it. I suppose that's one way to keep the litter out of their neighborhood. Barriers like that undoubtedly helped keep the resident's lives more secure, but it would get to feeling like jail to me. It was in my desire of true freedom for those residents that I wished the walls didn't have to exist.

Each wall that went up made cross cultural and economic contacts even more difficult to achieve. Education and cooperation, instead of segregation, is the only thing that can deflect serious racial or economic turmoil. Under that sort of turmoil the walls will tumble down overnight, just like the Berlin Wall did. The site planners were getting rich, designing for the wrong kind of future.

The dictionary calls people like me vagabonds. I move around constantly. Not just on trips. Residences, too. That doesn't necessarily imply irresponsibility. I'm no vagrant. I always pay my bills. I don't have to rob 7-11s to pay them either. I'm a good citizen, pay taxes, don't litter, give to the Salvation Army, and even work occasionally. Something resides in my bones that makes it impossible to sit still, or settle down, for any length of time. I always feel like getting the hell out of Dodge, no matter where I am. The thrill of the unknown keeps pulling. Where will I be; who will I meet out there? Singer/songwriter Joni Mitchell called hitchhikers, like me, prisoners of the fine white lines of the freeway. She was as right as she could be. The jailer used only the dome of the sky as my prison cell. I couldn't have cared if he'd thrown away the key.

Five days of hanging out with my cousin was just what the doctor ordered. On February 2, it was time to continue my prison sentence.

My sights were turned to the north and west. I began my 39th day on the road by blowing 75 cents on a city bus. I deemed it was far more worthwhile than standing at a stop light in suburban Tampa while people in business suits drove by and delivery vans hustled about their business. Taking the earliest bus out, it was still before dawn when I arrived in the village of Lutz. It was only a five mile ride north but was better than walking!

Lutz was on U.S. 41, but I wanted to be fifteen miles west, on U.S. 19. I would have to do the hated zig-zag route finding to get there.

It was an hour and a half wait before Bruce Kiper stopped. Bruce was only going a couple of miles down the road, to Land O' Lakes. He invited me to breakfast at his favorite coffee and donut shop. Despite the long wait already that morning, I wasn't in enough of a hurry to turn down an apple fritter. We spent about thirty minutes talking, non-stop.

He was my age, 34, and had recently opened an antique motorcycle shop: Ancient Age Motors. Bruce's first motor scooter ride was at ten. It was terrifying, yet thrilling. He was hooked. As the years went by the scooters kept getting bigger. By the time he reached 16, he had his beloved Harley. He drove it for fifteen years. True, mechanical love!

Bruce had a number of old cycles in his shop, in various stages of completion. The shop had done well so far but the supply was drying up. European collectors and investors were buying everything in sight. With no further explanation he claimed European interest in collectible motorcycles was much higher than in the United States. His operation was doomed without old cycles to rebuild and sell.

BRUCE KIPER
Land O' Lakes, Florida

Bruce didn't seem like the violent type, but he owned a pit bull. (Rightly or wrongly, I automatically associate pit bulls with maiming, mangling, death, and destruction.) He used the dog for publicity purposes to promote U.S. made motorbikes. He had "trained" it to "attack" Japanese made bikes. He hoped to get the dog on David Letterman's "Stupid Pet Tricks" segment. As far as I know the dog had never been on national television. Bruce did show me a photo and article on the dog in one of those ubiquitous, special interest biker magazines.

After giving me the tour of his little shop, he brought me back out to the road.

I was unsure about the best strategy in choosing my route north from there. I could have stayed on the smaller U.S. 41, but finally decided to go west a few miles to the Gulf coast, then turn north when I reached four lane U.S. 19. It had been an interesting morning but I found myself at an in-between hitchhiking spot. You never know if you should start walking or try waiting it out. I thought I'd give waiting a try.

Luck was with me that time. Donald Smith, of Land O' Lakes, brought me to Elfers, at the junction of U.S. 19. He was going to some huge flea market site to get a booth for the coming weekend. He made and sold engraved and airbrushed personalized license plates for the front of Florida cars.

Donald told me that the Tampa area had a higher per capita crime rate than Miami. What he was getting at was not to be surprised if I had some long waits ahead of me. He never used to pick people up until a couple of years ago when, out of the blue, he gave a ride to a hitchhiker from a middle-eastern country. Don enjoyed meeting the man so much he invited the guy to stay with his family for a couple of days. Now, Don normally picks up people with backpacks. The backpack strikes that ever important chord of recognition for Don.

I was left in one of my least favorite situations. U.S. 19, at this intersection in Elfers, was a busy, four lane, urban highway jammed with local traffic hitting the shopping centers which were placed at two mile intervals. Of course, between the shopping centers were fast food restaurants, car dealerships, motels, etc. You know, strip development. Florida is truly the ultimate example. Florida's Atlantic and Gulf coasts set the shining standard, providing credit card shoppers with everything plastic can buy!

I figured it was probably hopeless, but I made getting out of there a personal challenge. I was in a stubborn mood and refused to take the city bus that cruised by. I was determined to either hitch, or walk my way out of it.

I stood at a stop light with a sign that read, "NORTH 19." While waiting for the light to turn green I examined the cars that would come my way when the signal changed. A semi-truck was sitting in the right turn lane, preparing to head east down the road I'd just come over on, from Land O' Lakes. Before the truck made its turn someone opened the passenger door and jumped out, waving to the driver. It was a young woman.

When the light turned green the traffic took off past me like dragsters at the strip on Saturday afternoon. They had shopping to do. The woman who had jumped out of the truck came strolling across the intersection toward me on the same signal. She was poured into a black mini-dress and her walk was liquid. I was suddenly enjoying my place on the road. We greeted one another and began chatting. She had worked all night at a club featuring exotic dancers and was hitching to her other morning job, like she did every day. She was young, tough, attractive and clearly didn't take any grief from anybody. She didn't give hitchhiking a second thought. It's just how she got around.

After our short conversation, she continued down the road with her thumb, and legs, in plain view. She had no trouble attracting a ride. The first three cars passed me by. Then it was a race to see which car could stop first for my gorgeous, leggy friend. She chose her ride, waved back at me, and was gone.

Depressed, I turned back to face the traffic approaching me. It was obvious she was instant ride material. It was at that moment I realized what a super-human effort I had before me, as a plain old, ordinary guy. I was good at getting rides, but what I had just witnessed was ridiculous! It was my thirty-ninth day on the road and my tentative plan showed about eighty days remaining. If I'd possessed that woman's charms I could have cut my travel time in half.

Man! Birmingham, Alabama, my next destination, seemed like a long way away.

The sun was frying the pavement and I didn't feel like walking yet. Sixty-seven year old Fred Avis of Hudson saved me the trouble. A handsome, white-haired gentleman with wire rimmed glasses, he was soft-spoken and acted just like a grandpa. Though bashful, I did find out that he'd retired from his teamster job seventeen years earlier. As an ex-teamster he tried to support American industry when he could. He complained that department stores no longer even stocked American made products. He was going to hold off on the purchase of new shoes for his wife until he found a pair made in America. It was proof that his union roots ran deep.

Fred brought me to the junction of Florida 52, about ten miles ahead. Even there, I was still surrounded by the same commercial scenery. It was time to start walking. Young Jim Buda was out running an errand. He honked at me from a parking lot as I walked by and waved me over. He told me he could get me a few more miles north.

Jim was recently transplanted from Rochester, New York. He did mechanical work for a local trucking company, which was where he dropped me off. It was a tough spot. Finally out of the suburban sprawl there was nothing to slow cars down. I couldn't say which was the worse of two evils! By the time vehicles had reached my position on the road their engines were roaring as they sped by me in the 75 mph range. I continued my slow walk along the shoulder of the divided highway while the sun cauterized my face.

When it got hot, my pack became extremely heavy. Remember, I had enough gear to withstand temperatures below 0°F. When I wasn't wearing it, or sleeping in it, or eating it, I was carrying it. Along that Florida highway, clad only in sweat drenched shorts and tee shirt, everything else was packed into or hanging from my pack. My tennis shoes provided little foot support for the weight I was hauling. Five miles of walking at a stretch was my limit. By then my feet would turn to hamburger!

The scenery was terribly boring along this part of U.S. 19. The terrain was completely flat. I was too far away from the Gulf of Mexico to watch waves or boats or to enjoy a cool breeze. Off the highway right of way was nothing but brush and shrubs. Covered with spines and thorns, the tangled brush wasn't very inviting. I wasn't desperate enough for shade to crawl into that evil patch. Yet. There was nothing to do but walk and wonder why nobody would stop.

I had walked for two very tough hours (my feet were turning into jumbo burgers with BBQ sauce) when a guy driving a pick-up truck in the left lane hit the brakes, dipped into the center median for a few seconds, to avoid being rear-ended, then cut back across two lanes of traffic and wound up on the shoulder a hundred yards ahead of me. That was my cue! I hustled up to where the truck waited, impressed by the effort the driver had made on my behalf.

He had noticed me walking along about an hour earlier when he was going south. Now, on his return trip north, he couldn't believe I was still walking. Pure sympathy got me that ride. I had no pride, I took them any way I could get them! The man, in his late twenties, told me he was an ex-cocaine addict. He was glad to finally be clean. That guy was so energetic straight, I couldn't imagine what he would have been like, buzzing around on coke. Yikes!

At 2:00 pm I had finally arrived at the northern Pasco county line. It wasn't anyplace special and I wasn't all that excited about being there. It had been a tough morning. The total distance I had travelled since getting off the bus in Lutz, at dawn, was thirty-five miles. I was really dragging. I had a splitting headache, my feet were killing me, and my shoulders were chafed and sore from carrying all of my excess gear. Seven hours of Florida sunshine was making me a tad giddy. I was starting to think about ducking into the thorny brush for some shade relief.

A five miles per hour average was extremely slow, even for Florida. I'd tried hitching out of Miami, back in 1979, but had given up after two days without even making it out of the state. I eventually contacted an automobile transport (drive away) company. I got a car that was to be delivered to Corbin, Kentucky. I was lucky. South Florida is one of the toughest places in the United States to get rides. Even though I knew, from past hitchhiking experiences, that there would be times like this, it was still difficult to deal with the pain and frustration.

At 2:15 my knight in shining, red armor, pulled his four-wheel-drive Toyota truck to a stop. The first thing he did was offer me an ice cold beer. It was the best tasting brew I'd ever had!

Raised in a re-modeled 120 year old church in Sopchoppy, Florida, just south of Tallahassee, Pete Williams now lived with his aunt and uncle and worked in St. Petersburg. Pete was not particularly fond of Tampa/ St. Petersburg, nor the rest of south Florida. He referred to it in general as a "hell hole." He clearly preferred the north but needed the work to earn money for school.

It was a Friday afternoon and he was off work and headed for Talla-hassee to party with his old friends. I was ready and willing to lend him a hand by driving and helping him drink a few beers. I wound up drinking very little and driving a lot. It was safer that way as he was starting the party immediately!

We'd be rolling into Tallahassee after dark and he assured me I'd have a place to stay that night. However, when we got there he apologized, saying he wasn't all that sure where he was going to stay that night. It didn't matter to me, I was a walking motel. I thanked him for the long ride and grabbed my gear.

Refreshed after the long rest and cold drinks in Pete's rig, I decided it wasn't time for bed, yet. Besides, some interesting miles remained for me that night.

Pete had left me at an in-between place. I was east of the city center and five miles south of I-10. The sun had been down for over a half hour and the sky was completely dark. The intersection had a couple of busi-nesses, which created waves of heavy traffic and enough incidental light to keep me visible. My sign said, "WEST I-10." In an effort to get out of that in-between spot, I just wanted to get to the interstate.

As I hitched northbound, a guy in a pick-up truck waiting at the stop light southbound, started yelling at me. Nothing bad. He was trying to get my attention. Shouting across a lane of busy traffic he said to watch out for him, as he'd be returning north in about fifteen minutes. I'd be able to rec-ognize him because he would be hauling a boat and if I was still there, he would slow down enough to allow me to jump into the back of his pick-up truck. He was willing to take me to I-10. The light changed and he was gone.

I stood there wondering if I would have to run to catch him, or what. Communication hadn't been easy, shouting across traffic in the near lane. Perhaps I had misunderstood. Wasn't he going to pull over and stop? There really wasn't much room where I stood, especially for a full-sized truck and boat trailer. If this guy was for real, I'd have to be strong and fast. Strong to throw my gear into the truck and quick to climb in behind it.

I kept a sharp eye out. I did not want to stand there any longer, and walking in the dark down this narrow road was no option. Suddenly, he was coming down the road, boat in tow, beeping his horn and slowing down in the traffic lane. I was ready. The truck stood tall on big tires and four-wheel drive suspension. The top of the rear fender was nearly shoulder high on me. With both hands underneath my pack I military pressed it over my head and threw it in. My second parcel, a nylon duffel bag, hung securely around my neck. I gripped the edge of the fender and swung one leg up and over. Following the lead of my backpack I rolled and flopped into the back.

We were on our way. Nobody behind us honked. They probably laughed, though. It must have looked pretty silly, but walking five more miles on my already sore feet, would not have been a laughing matter. A few minutes later we were stopped at a light in the left traffic lane when I made my exit. The driver pointed to the westbound ramp on I-10. I jumped out and walked through the stopped traffic to reach the roadside.

I was impressed by that guy. He could have easily driven by and not bothered with me at all. It was nice that he shared the back of his roomy truck. Accommodations like that were always a welcome sight when you've stood and watched empty trucks go by for hours.

I started walking up the freeway entrance ramp onto I-10 and a huge semi-truck stopped immediately. I was amazed. It was dark and busy and a trucker pulled over. Life was looking good!

Normally, with a truck ride, the only limiting distance factor is how far the hitchhiker is going. The trucker is almost always going farther.

This situation was no exception. Gary Lee was happy to take me a mere 62 miles to the junction of U.S. 231 on his way back home to Dallas. If I would have actually been going to Dallas I could have had an 800 mile ride!

Gary was friendly and easygoing. He had been raised in Birmingham, Alabama. He had married at a young age and now, at only 38 years old, had been a grandfather for three weeks. He was worried about the possibility of becoming a great-grandfather before the age of 55!

We pulled off of I-10 an hour later at U.S. 231. I was going north from there to Birmingham. There wasn't much traffic at 8:30 pm but I figured I might catch someone heading to a bar, or something. The cool air gave me a little shot of energy so I had to at least try. It's irresistible! Florida had been pretty good to me upon closer examination, but I still wanted to wake up in Alabama.

A van exited off the freeway. It dropped off a passenger who I assumed was a hitchhiker continuing west on I-10. If the van driver was dropping off one guy, chances were good that he'd pick me up. I had my ride to Alabama when Jim pulled up next to me.

A quiet man, Jim was heading home to Dothan. Even after suffering a heart attack and being diagnosed with cancer, he continued chain smoking cigarettes. Assuming he'd die soon anyway, he had apparently given up on life. Divorced, he seemed confused, unhappy, and lonely. He sat there in the dark, smoked, didn't say much, and drove home.

Jim was nice enough to take me close to the edge of town on the road to Montgomery. It was already past 10:00 pm. That was late for me and my energy was gone. I had to muster enough strength to walk for fifteen more minutes before finding a nice wooded spot for the night. It was suburban camping at its best.

It had been a long, productive day. Once the momentum had started that afternoon, the rides just kept rolling. Thank goodness it was finally over and rest was at hand. The night was damp and foggy, but I slept well in my warm, dry cocoon.

The next day began gloomy and wet. I packed up my gear, even though it was completely soaked. I fully expected to make it the 195 miles to Birmingham that day and sleep under the roof of a friend's house. I started out early, just after dawn, to make sure.

Ellis Rogers was quick to stop in Dothan and took me the fifteen miles to the next town of Ozark. He was an ex-marine working now as a pilot for a small corporation out of Dothan. He was friendly and talkative. Whenever he didn't hear exactly what I said as we conversed, he would ask, "Sir?!" It was kind of fun being called sir. I lowered the volume on my voice once in a while just to revel in the sharp interrogative, "Sir?!"

My second ride of the day was with Tyrone Taylor and Sharon Boyd. Tyrone was surprised to see me on the road. Apparently, hitchhikers didn't use U.S. 231 too often. Although he was in a big hurry, he felt compelled to stop. He was driving a nice, little rental car. It had a good stereo and we bopped on down the road at 85 mph. His own car had been stolen. Fortunately, it had been recovered, but was still in the repair shop with minor damage. Sharon didn't say much during the ride and mostly napped. I got the feeling I was the third that made a crowd.

Tyrone was a student at Southern Technical College in Montgomery. He was in a technical drawing curriculum. To help pay for school, he worked for a civil engineering firm. He seemed like a great young man, even if he did drive a trifle fast. Despite being pressed for time, he took me to the northern edge of Troy. Originally from the area, he knew the perfect spot to drop me off. Then he was gone in a whirl of rainy mist.

I turned down my first ride there in Troy. A pick-up truck stopped immediately and was going all the way to Birmingham. The problem was that there wasn't any room for me. Hard to believe, but true. The truck bed was full of ladders, tools, building materials, and assorted other stuff. The pile was slick from the steady drizzle falling from a brooding gray sky. I could not safely ride back there for ten minutes, much less the 100 miles to Birmingham. I was forced to say, "No thanks," a very heart-wrenching thing to say as I stood in a cold rain.

Sure. I turn down one lousy ride and suddenly all the rides dry up. There was quite a bit of traffic going past me in Troy. I was in a perfect spot, just past an intersection with a stop light to slow traffic down. My sign read "B'HAM," so everyone knew where I was going. It didn't make sense, but I stood there in my rain gear, forcing a soggy smile at unenthusiastic drivers, for over two hours.

Something finally clicked and I was in the unlikely position of having to deal with two drivers who had stopped one after the other. The famine was over and I had my pick! Thanking the driver of the first vehicle, I turned him down because I'd be riding in the back of his small pick-up. It was just as full as the truck I'd turned down earlier.

The passenger seat of the other little truck was jammed with possessions Mike Canfield was protecting from the bad weather. He was more than willing to garbage bag them up and throw them in back, allowing me to ride in dry comfort. It took about ten minutes to suitably adjust everything before we were on our way, all the way to Birmingham!

I'm not exactly sure where to begin Mike's story. Vietnam perhaps. He spent three years there, while serving in the Army. His tour of duty seemed like forever. When he finally got out, he struggled with the personal horrors of war for another ten years. The emotional pain was very enduring although outwardly he seemed to have recovered reasonably well.

MIKE CANFIELD
Birmingham, Alabama

The devastation of the minds and spirits of so many young American men during the war years, should leave future war planners considering tolls more subjective than simply calculating potential fatalities. The mental scars left on the American psyche can be far more debilitating than flesh wounds. Every effort to find a peaceful solution to conflicts will avoid the most senseless waste of life imaginable; trading our children's lives, not for freedom, but for convenience and economic gain. It's too bad coming generations of leaders will selectively forget that war is hell.

Over the years, Mike had done a considerable amount of travelling. He'd been as far as Japan and Australia, in addition to southeast Asia. This trip he was on may have turned out to be his least favorite. He didn't think too much of Florida, claiming people there had a bad attitude. That might not have been a fair assessment. His perspective was certainly biased, due to recent personal events.

With most of his belongings along for the ride, he had left his home in Mulvane, Kansas, only three days earlier, and had driven to New Port Richey, Florida, where he intended to marry his girlfriend, now his ex-girlfriend. She apparently had serious second thoughts about this marriage thing, serious enough to send Mike back home to Mulvane, only moments after his arrival on her doorstep. He hadn't even been in New Port Richey long enough to catch a nap. It's no wonder he wasn't thrilled about his short stay in Florida!

Mike was glad for the company. After facing emotional stress of that magnitude its good to have someone to talk to. The road can be the loneliest place in the world and if I hadn't been standing in Troy, waiting for Mike to pick me up, it would have been as lonely as the North Pole for him.

When we pulled into Birmingham, the hometown of an old friend from my days as a ski bum, it was mid-afternoon. If it had been later in the day Mike and I probably would have gone and destroyed some beers. Instead, he just dropped me off near a phone. I thanked him for his generosity and wished him a safe trip as he continued northwest. I would be going southwest from Birmingham so it was definitely the end of the ride for me.

I tracked down my friend Steve and settled in to reminisce about the two years we spent as roommates in the shadow of Lone Mountain. We had both worked at the Big Sky ski resort, north of Yellowstone National Park. Things hadn't changed much. He was still a hard working, responsible adult, while I was still looking for ways to avoid hard work and adult responsibilities!

At each of my stops I enjoyed visits with old friends or new acquaintances. I would arrive tired, usually hungry and always in need of a shower to cut the road grime. They welcomed me in and took care of the basics. In addition to the basics we'd go for sightseeing walks or get involved in some activity that didn't include much driving. During my rest stops I had little interest in driving around!

It had taken 100 hitchhiked rides, across 4256 miles to arrive in Birmingham. That made for an average of about forty-two miles per ride. I felt that was a decent average considering the small highways I'd been following thus far. Were I travelling interstates to big cities the average ride distance would have been much higher.

In the forty days since leaving Willow River, I had accomplished much. Those hundred drivers had taken me to places I'd never seen before:

the dark green hills of West Virginia, our nation's capitol, the barrier islands of North Carolina, and the backwoods of South Carolina.

The most important accomplishment was the melting of deeply established cynicism toward the American people. The very fact that I had made it this far was proof of the enormous amount of trust and cooperation that existed in our communities. Given a chance, most people would take you for all you were worth. That was the message constantly heard from our news media and rumor mills. My view, however, was that given a chance, most people would be generous to a fault. We patronize the wrong people in the news because the wrong people are sensational and bizarre.

Sometimes, long waits made it hard to believe in the goodness of people in a particular place. There are so many factors affecting a hitchhiking situation it is impossible to place blame on the neighborhood. You never have prior knowledge of local events. The day before someone might have been killed at the corner where I stood. People would be especially leery about stopping for me. I couldn't blame them. It is important in the attitude of a hitchhiker to understand beyond our means. With little or no information about what goes on around us we have to maintain an exceptionally positive and patient attitude.

Standing around with a positive and patient attitude can be a very lonely business. The hitchhiker is a lonely island, surrounded by people. You stand alone, on a conspicuous corner, open for inspection to all passing traffic, or other on-lookers. As an anomaly, you get lots of attention from all kinds of eyes: sympathetic, nice, condescending, evil, fearful, trusting, young, and old eyes. In some cases it may only be a matter of a few seconds that you are in their line of sight, but still, you are on display in front of thousands of people. You can't be overly self-conscious. To survive out on the road you absolutely must be tough enough to endure the most discriminating gaze. There can be no shrinking from the necessity of facing every car that approaches, with the belief that it will be your next ride.

When people pass with scowls on their faces, honk horns to be obnoxious, yell, or make obscene gestures, your general mood naturally declines. Mine does. It's hard enough to be out there without crabby people impressing upon you how mean they can get. Sometimes the accumulation of pain brings you to tears. The tears must be brief, or invisible, because every driver that looks into your eyes can sense your mood. The driver who picks you up does not want to deal with your pain.

The longer you stand there, the more self-critical you become. You wonder what you're doing wrong. You wish you could look at yourself in a mirror, to see for yourself if you've actually grown fangs or something.

You stand alone, sometimes for hours, enduring, until someone stops. Then the loneliness, frustration, worry, and wondering, instantly evaporates. You have a companion and potential friend to share the travel experience with you. The reward for your persistence is a satisfying, peaceful feeling coupled with the thrill of the unknown.

On February 6, Steve brought me to an entrance ramp on I-59, at the very southwestern corner of Birmingham. Surrounded by lush green forests and bathed in bright sunshine, I was in an extremely positive state of mind. Two or three good rides would get me to New Orleans where I would stay with another friend. I didn't have a care in the world!

Ever so slowly, with the passing of car after car, my good mood eroded. After nearly a two hour wait, that interchange had become very lonely. I was getting into a serious self-critical mode. I had just taken a shower, my clothes were clean, and I was smiling. My cardboard sign was brand new. I was sure I was doing everything right. Jeez, I wondered, what's wrong? Maybe I had fangs now and looked like a vampire!

Raymond Price snapped me out of my introspective funk. The loneliness disappeared when he pulled over. Even though he was driving a big

RAYMOND PRICE
Tuscaloosa, Alabama

pick-up truck, there wasn't much room. I had to put my pack between us on the seat. He didn't mind. The bed of the truck was equipped with a metal grate that served as a livestock rack. I was sharing a ride with Raymond and seven hogs. Those big, fat oinkers were soon to be transformed into bacon. I think I heard him say he was hauling them for a neighbor. It was difficult to understand him because of road noise. Also, the cigar stub he spoke around obscured a virtually incomprehensible southern accent.

I did gather that he had lived in the area for about fourteen years with his wife and eight kids. He didn't work too much anymore due to a back injury he sustained in 1979 while working for Pullman railroad cars. Raymond loved farming and got around a bit, despite his bad back. It was nice of him to stop even though he didn't have much room. He turned off the freeway thirty-five miles later at Tuscaloosa.

Oddly enough, my next ride was exactly the opposite. After a short wait, an elderly man driving a white Cadillac took me a few exits farther. He seemed uncomfortable and nervous, not saying much of anything. I tried to set him at ease to no avail. Tuscaloosa wasn't a large city but that man's ride had taken me away from its busiest interchange. That was always something to be grateful for and I thanked him for the ride.

Big, Roscoe "Dub" Presnall pulled up in his Mercury Grand Marquis. I would be experiencing yet another ride in complete comfort. This time it was a long one, through thunderstorms and tornado warnings across Mississippi, all the way to New Orleans!

Dub lived a fast and furious life. Up until his recent retirement, he had been a businessman in Birmingham, owning two pool rooms and three grocery stores. They must have been reasonably profitable because he appeared to be financially secure in his retirement.

He entertained me with stories of travel adventures and misadventures around the U.S. Many of the stories involved Las Vegas gambling incidents. The most notable was the time he won $11,000 betting on a guy who was shooting craps. He admitted that even with a once-in-a-lifetime win like that, he probably still wound up in the red after tallying the wins against the losses. Las Vegas was not a town to walk away from with more money in your pockets than when you walked in. If it were, it couldn't exist for long!

Back in the early 1950's, Dub played AAA, semi-pro baseball for the Montgomery Chicks, of the Southern League. During three years of play he batted .275, hit 48 home runs, played 3rd base and catcher. Unlike the crybaby pros of today he never complained about the wages back then. Players made $100 for a win and $75 for a loss. It was enough just to be paid for playing a kid's game! One of his most memorable moments came when Jimmy Piersall hit a triple off the outfield wall while he was catching.

As a baseball lover, he gets a big thrill out of attending games in the old, classic stadiums of major league baseball. His favorites include Wrigley Field in Chicago and Fenway Park in Boston.

Baseball wasn't his only sports love. Football, especially the big games, were dear to his heart. He went to the 1975 Superbowl in New Orleans to watch Pittsburgh beat my hometown favorite(?), Minnesota Vikings. He was supposed to have gone to the 1990 Superbowl, but claimed the postal service ripped off his tickets. He guessed some backroom mail clerk had enjoyed the game from seats he had paid for.

For Dub, trips to New Orleans were commonplace. He loved the food and atmosphere. One time he sat down to a plate full of raw oysters and wound up eating five dozen. This talk of massive amounts of food served to whet our appetites. We stopped at a fast food joint and Dub kindly bought my lunch.

There is one last anecdote of Roscoe Presnall's life that revealed what a tough scrapper and survivor he was. In twenty-three years of the grocery business, his stores had been robbed thirty times. Once, when he was behind the counter, three men held him up. When they demanded the till, he told them off. They replied with gunshots to his belly. They then grabbed the money and left him for dead.

Although the hospital staff said he had shown no life signs, they miraculously revived him, shoved his guts back in and sewed him up. He said his body was so full of scars, it looked like he'd been drawn and quartered.

It was a real thrill to share a ride with a man who'd experienced so much of life, and had even received the benefit of a second chance at living. For Roscoe, the world was his big toy and he intended to play on. After he dropped me off downtown he went to carouse. I assumed New Orleans could handle it. I knew Dub could.

I met up with Greg, a high school friend from Minneapolis. We did some pre-pre- Mardi Gras carousing of our own. The next couple of days were an exercise in consumption. We ate crawfish pie, crab salad, boiled crawfish, and raw oysters. It all got washed down with cheap beer.

In a crazed search for the best Mexican food around we set off across Lake Ponchatrain for the village of Mandeville. To get there we had to negotiate the twenty-five mile long causeway that crossed the middle of the lake. Our timing left a lot to be desired. The winds on that black winter's night whipped spray from the lake surface up onto the bridge. Thunderstorms and tornados pummelled the lake, not to mention the poor idiots who were stupid enough to be out there on such a foul night!

Having safely reached Mandeville, Greg drove directly to the restaurant we sought. Our huge appetites were left to gnaw at our bellies because our plans were foiled by something as simple as a "Closed" sign! We turned around to face another wild ride through the storms that continued to rage over the lake. Hanging out with Greg was even more dangerous than hitchhiking!

Some fine street music and French Quarter debauchery rounded out the remainder of my New Orleans visit. A couple days of that foolishness was quite enough thank you very much! The night before Greg took me back to the road, he purposely tried to sow a seed of doubt in my mission in Louisiana by showing the film classic, Easy Rider. No, I'd never seen it before. And, no, I wasn't moved to extreme mistrust, even after the brutal demise of the characters on the backroads of Louisiana. I reminded myself that it was just an old movie. Besides, the victims weren't even hitchhikers. Nice try, Greg.

It was only 7:30 am when Greg dropped me off. I was taking U.S. 90 west out of New Orleans. It was a good intersection with a stoplight but most of the traffic was headed in the opposite direction, consisting of commuters heading into town for work. The sunlight that barely filtered through the morning clouds had me believing I was in a black and white movie from the 1930s. The surrounding terrain was gritty and colorless. The dirt that seemed to coat everyone's car left the original color up to the observer's imagination.

The Louisiana bayou and south Texas were next. I was stepping off into unfamiliar territory, again. My next acquaintance was in Phoenix, Arizona. I would be on my own for the next 1200 miles.

William "Eddy" Wagner took me the few miles to Paradis, far enough to get me out of the urban influence of New Orleans. Far enough away so that the colors of life began to return.

Even though our visit was brief, Eddy talked fast enough to cover a couple of important topics. After spending twenty years in the Air Force, and doing three tours in Vietnam, his biggest concern was the treatment of veterans. Any member, or former member of the armed forces who suffered from a physical or mental disability as a result of injuries or experiences involving service to their country, deserved the finest care possible. He understood it would take a substantial financial commitment from the citizenry but felt it was well worth it. Those who were willing to defend our freedom by risking their lives should be compensated and aided in every possible way. Anything less than a full effort extended to veterans would be deemed a failure of the nation. It only made sense that the beneficiaries of our servicemen's efforts be the ones to pay.

The second big subject we talked about was the environment. Louisiana has the reputation of being one of the most polluted states in the country. Lots of heavy industry and petro-chemical manufacturing contribute to air and water pollution. Eddy worked as a electrician at a chemical plant. He expressed concern about waste chemical discharge into the local water table. The worries he faced came from two directions: the threat of unemployment by the strengthening of environmental protection laws, and the terrifying prospect of serious health problems striking his family due to tainted water sources. It was a lose-lose situation. He hoped we could find a happy medium between an ecologically sound environment and slow death, either by poisoning or economically catastrophic unemployment.

Following my discussion with Eddy I got a good, fifty mile ride from Paradis to Morgan City, with Gary Smith. Although raised in Arlington, Washington, he was born in the land of hockey, Hibbing, Minnesota. His mother used to baby-sit singer Bob Dylan, when Dylan was still Bob Zimmerman. It may have been only a small brush with fame perhaps, but a brush no less!

Gary had a fascinating profession. He was a deep-sea diver. When he started diving at the tender age of 13, he salvaged old, wooden boats, just for fun. Now, after thirteen years as a commercial diver in the Gulf of Mexico oil fields, he felt he had pressed his luck far enough. Deep-sea diving is extremely hazardous, technical work, and many divers die unnecessarily each year. Gary attributed the majority of those deaths to poor training, claiming the only available training was pathetic, at best. He hoped to establish a diving school in New Orleans as soon as he could garner the financial backing.

Deep sea divers work off of boats and oil drilling platforms. Their work environment is extremely hostile. At the base of oil rigs they work with heavy equipment and electricity. Their isolation underwater is highlighted by the very isolation of their support team on the surface, hundreds of miles from land. Drilling platforms are dangerous places because of the possibility of explosions and uncontrolled fire. Life in the Gulf of Mexico is a life on the edge.

The stress of their profession promotes family problems and divers often abuse alcohol as an escape from the isolation and rigors of work. Life offshore is akin to another world. Links to friends and family on the mainland become fragile, and frequently break. I hoped stability would reenter Gary's life now that he was a creature of the land once again.

It was Simon Edwards who picked me up outside of Morgan City. He had just failed a drug test and suddenly found himself out of work. The test had exposed a small amount of THC, a chemical residue of marijuana, in his system. In their attempt to keep the Gulf drug free, the powers that be sent him on a seven hour boat ride to land, from the offshore drilling platform where he worked.

On the platform, drilling performance is everything. It is a complicated and dangerous procedure. Humans almost need to become mechanized to maintain the type of efficiency required for a well to be successfully drilled. When they're thirty miles off shore, on spindly metal legs sunk into the mud at the bottom of the Gulf, they're all alone and everything had better go right.

Simon was affable and didn't seem to be burned out from the work. As I mentioned earlier, life offshore was a different world. Death was always creeping around in the form of bad weather, heavy seas, mechanical failure, or human error. There were no second chances out there. At 36, after six years of drilling holes into the bottom of the Gulf of Mexico, Simon was worried about approaching the edge of his ability to cope with that scary world. I think he was actually relieved by his newly arrived unemployed status.

When we arrived in Lafayette, after a mellow ride, Simon surprised his girlfriend by bringing a guest in for a late breakfast. She was very accommodating and sent me off on the road again with a red rose. How thoughtful!

When Simon brought me back out to the road, he was struggling with a new situation that had come up. His employer had left a message with his girlfriend. They wanted him to come back to work as soon as possible. THC residue or not, he was a good turbo-drilling engineer and they needed him. He wasn't easily replaced and without him the drilling company was losing at least $10,000 per day. The company could not afford to be shut down because they were missing an engineer.

His emotions had been seriously jerked around. Even I was mad at the people involved, and I was only an observer. Simon hadn't yet decided what to do as we said goodbye. I hoped he'd choose a healthy life, back on land.

I was on I-10 west when Daniel LaBouve took me to Jennings, Louisiana. He worked as a foundation filler. It was an important construction job because the water table was so close to the ground surface, the ground couldn't support structures without added stability measures. Even when you're dead, the water makes life difficult in Louisiana! You need to be "buried" in above ground mausoleums. It is pretty weird, seeing a Louisiana cemetery for the first time. No tombstones or grass, just acres of inscribed, granite boxes.

Yet one more offshore oil man was to pick me up that day. I began walking down the entrance ramp in Jennings when a maniac named Byron threw open the door of his pick-up, practically hitting me with it as he skidded to a stop. He was headed home to Beaumont, Texas, after being cooped up for thirty-one days on a rig 72 miles offshore. He was ready to tear up what was left of the mainland.

I could tell Byron was a man unleashed. He couldn't talk or drink beer fast enough. He had lots to talk about and tried to get as many words into the conversation as possible. Having me to talk to was like possessing a treasure. He said that if he'd had to spend another minute talking to his fellow rig workers he would have gone crazy. He breathed in the earthy air, drank, talked and drove fast, trying to do everything at once.

Our conversation was difficult at times because we disagreed about things like littering the highway with beer cans and the value of the Emancipation Proclamation. It was his civic duty to throw trash out the window of his truck. He was trying to provide work for the poor, unfortunate bastards who were on welfare. If Lincoln hadn't freed the slaves there wouldn't be anyone on welfare and the Japanese wouldn't be taking over the U.S. economy.

Whew! When I called him on the stuff I thought was complete bullshit, he had an answer for everything. Not an answer I would exactly call logical by any stretch of the imagination, but certainly heartfelt.

Byron turned north at the east edge of Beaumont, Texas. He dropped me off in the middle of a hopelessly tangled freeway interchange. It was a bad, bad place to be on foot. So bad that I was hoping for a cop to come by and take me anyplace but here. Heavy Friday afternoon traffic, major construction activity, no way to walk out, little room to pull over, a sharp curve, no visibility beyond where I stood, and to top it off, the setting sun blinded oncoming driver's eyes.

Byron should have been my last ride. Ever. I was standing at the edge of a marginal shoulder. Marginal, but enough to keep me about six feet from where the two lanes of freeway traffic roared by. I didn't like being that close to traffic on the outside edge of a sharp curve. Things were beyond intense. My senses were being completely obliterated by the rush of steel, rubber, glass, continually changing air pressure, wind, exhaust fumes, and construction dirt constantly being flung into my eyes. I felt as helpless as a newborn baby. I stood in my place and the world around me was in complete control.

The danger came and went, unbeknownst to me. I was so out of touch with my surroundings, I didn't realize what had happened until a few minutes later.

As I stood flashing my "HOUSTON" sign, large trucks would come by at high speeds and throw dirt up into my face. In an attempt to avoid that nastiness I would hold the sign in front of my face and close my eyes until the blast had settled down. It was little protection, but better than nothing, for dirt and wind. A flatbed truck went by at a normal highway speed and I covered up as usual. All I heard was an unusual roar and clatter that sounded strangely louder and closer than the normal passage of vehicles. When the dust cleared, I peeked over my sign to again watch the oncoming traffic.

As the seconds ticked by, I began to think something had happened. Now, ignoring traffic, I stood there looking around, wondering what had transpired while my eyes were closed. About ten yards down the road I noticed a large, heavy block of wood and steel cable. It hadn't been there a few minutes ago. I was sure it hadn't because I had just walked past where it sat, looking for a way to walk out of there. I traced the trajectory from where the highway curve began and where this thing landed. Yes, it went right through me. Or, it should have. My knees started shaking and I kept replaying the event from a hundred different angles. I should have been crushed chest high, or at the very least, had my legs clipped out from underneath me. My cardboard sign, acting as a shield, provided me with a protection that could only be described in comically mythic, or miraculously biblical, proportions.

Things did not bode well for me in Texas. On the other hand, I did survive that episode without so much as a scratch. I should probably look at that event with a positive perspective. There was no denying my good fortune!

A wonderful man named Nick Breax saw my terrible predicament, and stopped. He was only crossing town, but helped me escape a very bleak and dangerous spot. Poor Nick had to suffer through my emotionally charged adulation of his timing and good natured trust. Although I was still trembling I was a happy man!

I was at a safe interchange on the western outskirts of Beaumont when Nathan Lovett, of Odessa, Texas, offered me a ride. Working for an oil field supply company, he was hauling a large section of pipe that he had salvaged from a drilling site. He paid $4,500 for it and expected its value to increase to $35,000 when it was refurbished. My technical knowledge of mechanical stuff is negligible, but my arithmetic led me to believe there was a hefty profit in that operation.

A complex young man at 23-years of age, he envisioned a 300 percent increase in his present salary, within five years. He was sure the small company he worked for would boom and he'd be riding the top of a cresting wave.

Nathan was tough. A couple of days ago in Houston he had been jumped by five guys, but was able to fight his way out of it. Despite that recent trauma he was still willing to pick up a hitchhiker. With that sort of generous spirit he seemed far more concerned with my welfare than he was with his own safety.

When he was 14 years old Nathan quit school and went to work in the oil fields. That's where he got tough. He claimed to have been in many fights over the years, but had never lost. He did lose to the oil fields though. Between the tender ages of 14 and 22 he had broken his leg, both hands, and received a concussion. He was happy to have graduated from the oil derricks and to have been assigned to the luxurious position of driving a truck.

Nathan was a thinker. He was fascinated by unexplained events and cultural mythology. UFOs and creatures like bigfoot, attracted his attention. Even though Nathan believed in such mystical phenomena, he perceived religion as superstition.

NATHAN LOVETT
Houston, Texas

He related an interesting observation regarding our justice system which I had never considered. He felt the few guilty who escaped conviction and punishment, were simply the price society paid to keep the large majority of innocent citizens from going to jail. The point seemed valid and softened my extremely cynical view of our courts, ever so slightly.

Nathan had a motel room reserved on the eastern fringe of Houston. After spending the night there he would depart early, continuing on I-10 to San Antonio, then northwesterly for Odessa. He offered to share his room and invited me to accompany him in the morning. I gratefully accepted. I welcomed the hot shower and dry floor to sleep on.

That night we experienced the most violent thunderstorm I'd ever seen. Through 360 degrees of arc the otherwise blackened horizon was lit up by an electrical storm that would have made the mighty Thor cower. Lightning crashed all around the motel. If I hadn't had the good fortune to meet up with Nathan, I would have had to take shelter under a vehicle or some kind of structure because of the lightning danger. My tent would have disintegrated in the face of the wind and hail. It wasn't quite as strong as a tornado, but I would guess that the storm spawned more than a few twisters in the region that night.

Nathan had been married for three years. He telephoned his wife and told her he had picked me up and I was staying with him that night. The side of the conversation I could hear indicated that she had flipped over that and was sure her husband would be the victim of my sharp axe or revolver, or both. I assume he made it safely back home after he dropped me off. If not, I'm sure his panic-stricken wife would have contacted the authorities, and I would have been picked up and jailed long before this!

We left Houston at 4:00 am under clear skies, by the light of a full moon. We arrived at the perimeter freeway of San Antonio by 8:30 am. Nathan continued talking the entire way. My final impression of him was that he thought most problems were less complicated than they seemed. He saw little gray area. Problems, therefore, required simpler solutions.

He appreciated having a good listener in me. He was lucky I'd had lots of practice before I'd met him. It was my pleasure.

I was getting closer, but even in San Antonio, I still felt far away from my southerly destination of Brownsville, Texas. You know you're in a big state when the next medium-sized town is almost 300 miles away! Before 9:00 on that Saturday morning, traffic was light at the outer limits of San Antonio. I made a sign that said "I-37 SOUTH" to get me going in the right direction, and started walking. I soon got a ride from a couple of nice men driving a little truck. Enjoying the view from the back of their truck, I watched the dry, wide open spaces of south Texas pass by. Seventy-five miles had rolled by when they dropped me in the town of Three Rivers. They insisted on giving me a dollar when I climbed out of the back of the truck. I thanked them and I said I didn't need the money. They insisted I take it and said it was a gift to me from the Lord and I should get myself a "sody pop." How kind!

The potential for getting a quick ride out of Three Rivers, south on U.S. 281, looked bleak, if not impossible. After about an hour wait I watched a woman drive slowly past me. She made a couple of U-turns to get back to where I stood and opened her door. Graciella Garza was a recently born-again Christian, and lived near McAllen, Texas. She worked for a car rental agency and was returning a car from Austin.

Not long ago she was compelled to pick up a hitchhiker who also happened to be from the mid-west. Her reasons for stopping this time, for me, seemed unclear. It may have been for company, guilt, or an element of Christian charity. I observed that most of the drivers who witnessed their faith to me were newly converted. It was like they were trying to make up for lost time. With their enlightenment and redemption fresh in their lives, their zealousness translated into picking up hitchhikers and sharing a Christian message. Perhaps there were other non-witnessing believers I rode with who did their preaching by example.

Graciella was somewhat ashamed of her former partying lifestyle. Now, as a Christian, her values had become considerably more conservative. Facing the challenge of raising a six-year-old daughter alone, she prayed that religious influence would make her better prepared to give her daughter the best possible advice. Maternal pride showed through as she told of her daughter's successes in school.

We rode together for almost 150 miles, to the little town of Pharr. For some unknown reason she was getting nervous by the end of the ride. Most drivers become more relaxed with hitchhikers as they get to know them. I didn't understand her tension, but when the ride was over I thanked her and wished her luck.

In Pharr I was closer, but still fifty-six miles from Brownsville. It was a beautiful, warm day. The sun was brilliant. It reflected off of windshields and shiny metal surfaces. Every car that went by blinded me with glare. The visor on my cap could not protect me from secondhand sunlight!

I was impressed by the concentration of population. There were literally dozens of little towns and a few large ones. The traffic was heavy and the road had a good shoulder. After an hour wait in high temperatures, I started walking out of sheer boredom.

Not long after I began walking, a really sleazy sort of guy saved me a six mile walk, to Donna, Texas. He looked like the kind of guy who would work at a used car lot named Lucky Louie's.

"Ah yah, laidee. Dis heeyah caa za reel cream puff, if yah know what ah mean. Best ting on da lot an' ah kin getcha innit foa $999.95. Ah'll even knock a coupla hunnerd bucks off if we play a little backseat bingo, if yah know what ah mean! BINGO! Heh heh! Whaddya say?"

My next ride, with Tony Martinez, took me the remaining distance into Brownsville. Tony had worked in education for the last thirty-eight years and was about ready to retire. As a high school industrial arts instructor, he loved teaching and enjoyed working with his students. He thought they were very bright but noted a disappointing lack of motivation in school and life.

After earning an M.A. in history from the University of Texas, in Austin, Tony moved to the Rio Grande valley in 1956. He'd been there ever since. In addition to teaching, he did some tree landscaping to supplement his income.

He was able to impart some of his cultural knowledge of the Mexican immigrants in the area. He said the Mexican community was very tight and family oriented. That was one reason there were so few elderly Mexicans in nursing homes; the extended family provided for them at home.

Tony, willing to play tour guide, exited off the main highway. We took some smaller roads, enabling me to get a closer look at the small communities. As we approached Brownsville, he invited me to camp out on some land he owned. As a greenhorn in south Texas, I figured it would be the smart thing to do and happily accepted his offer.

He told me where to set up my tent so I wouldn't be bothered by "wetbacks" passing through during the night. "Wetback" is the slang term used to describe illegal immigrants who crossed the border by swimming the Rio Grande. Just before dark, he brought a nice meal of spicy rice and pork and some water. Water was definitely a priority for me. Even though I tried hard to keep my quart water bottle refreshed, my long day in the sun had dried me out. I was carrying a small amount of food but this dinner gave me a big caloric boost.

On Sunday morning, February 12, I awoke to fog, after a restful sleep. Tony came by to pick me up and gave me a brief tour of Brownsville. At the Rio Grande River, we watched prospective illegal aliens on the opposite bank surveying routes across the river.

The human struggle often seems so sad and bitter. Watching poor families contemplating the Rio Grande swim makes us reconsider the severity of our own personal problems. The perspective I gained from the few minutes I spent on the bank of the Rio Grande hit me hard. Life suddenly seemed ridiculously easy for us Americans.

Tony recommended a trip to Port Isabel, on the gulf coast, and set me on the road toward it. I didn't really feel like going there and decided if a ride wasn't forthcoming in less than half an hour, I'd head northwest.

Felix Sauceda stopped moments after I'd made that decision and I was headed for Port Isabel. Felix worked fleet maintenance on four shrimp boats. He was only going to work, about five miles down the road, which was nowhere. He liked to help people out and said there wasn't enough of that sort of spirit around anymore. Even though there was nothing but desert surrounding me, I was happy to have met him.

Soon thereafter, Freddy Joe Mansell came skidding wildly to a stop on the shoulder. Driving a full-sized pick-up truck with dual rear wheels he exhibited the sort of confidence that implied that if he didn't already own the damn road, he could certainly buy it if he were so inclined. Larger than life, wearing a big black cowboy hat, he was a man who'd travelled the world over and was proud to call Texas home. Texas had been good to him. He was already on his third retirement. He'd been retired before at 35 and

FREDDY JOE MANSELL
Port Isabel, Texas

42 years. I don't think he was 55 yet. He was boisterous and gruff and full of advice. He said there were a lot of opportunities to make money in south Texas. However, not all of the opportunities were necessarily legal. Freddy left me at the bridge to San Padre Island.

I was at the water and comfortable and had no desire to go over the bridge to the Island. I sat and rested a bit, until this mean, fat, ugly guy chased me away. Apparently, I was sitting on the private property of their commercial charter fishing dock. There hadn't been anyone around until he got there, and I wasn't even on the dock or behind a gate. I didn't seem to be doing much damage to his non-existent business that morning. More than likely he considered me an eyesore. Maybe, if he'd been civil, I would have chartered his boat for the day. The irony of the whole situation was summed up by his t-shirt. It read, "Miss Hospitality." That was the name of the boat tied to the dock. It was a shame that her crew was unworthy of the vessel's namesake.

I had achieved my southern goal, a mere two days from New Orleans. My cultural and geographical ignorance led me to believe this area would be very harsh, cruel, and full of civil tension and strife with the clash of cultures. Except for the example cited in the previous paragraph, most of my observations proved those initial feelings groundless. There was a spirit of cooperation here that I hadn't felt anywhere else. I was very impressed with the looks on people's faces as they drove by. Everybody was smiling and talking and apparently having a great time with life. It was the complete opposite of the feelings I got in South Carolina. It was quite pleasant here. I was glad I had come this far south to connect the Brownsville dot with the rest of my journey.

I took a deep breath of the cool, salty sea breeze and hoisted my overloaded pack onto my back. I had a lot of daylight left and didn't feel like wasting it. I was aiming for Laredo, Texas. It was time to head north.

Chapter Five

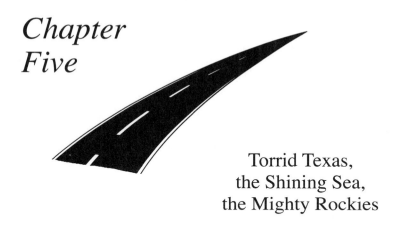

Torrid Texas,
the Shining Sea,
the Mighty Rockies

The road is a place of extremes. It is nearly impossible to find softness out there. Other than grabbing your gear for the last time and throwing it on an airplane for a flight home, there is no real escape. Even if you get a plush ride or stay in a house once in a while you usually have to struggle to make it through the day. Exhaustion from walking, riding, or standing, will get you one way or another by the time you hit the sleeping bag.

Toughness, in both attitude and physical strength, is an absolute necessity. If a hitchhiker starts out weak, the toughness will be acquired. If it isn't eventually acquired the trip will fail. A popular misconception is that hitchhiking is a free ride. Believe me, none of the miles come for free. The hitchhiker faces extremes in environment and personal emotions. Extremes like heat, frigid temperatures, glaring sun, depressing clouds, a full bladder, an empty stomach, crowded and dangerous highways, empty farmlands, frustration, exhilaration, anticipation, impatience, self-doubt, noise, and silence, are a hitchhiker's constant companions. You accept one ride out of a certain situation only to be dropped off at another place where you may face a completely different set of environmental or emotional extremes. You never know what's coming. It makes you constantly alert and drives you kind of crazy, too. You have to be at least a little crazy, otherwise you just couldn't take it.

After my little tiff with Mr. "Miss Hospitality," I began retracing my steps in the direction of Brownsville. I needed to get back through Brownsville to reach the highway that would take me toward Laredo. It was a lovely south Texas day and I was glad to be a part of it. It was one of the rare "soft" moments along the road, but I realized it would be short-lived as the temperature would be climbing to intolerable levels when the afternoon arrived. I was headed straight into the desert where there would be no relief from the heat. I just walked slowly, enjoyed the morning, and mentally prepared for what was to come.

I hadn't walked far when snowbirds Jerry and Jeannette Vaughn stopped. "Snowbird" was the term used to describe mid-westerners living in trailers or recreational vehicles who had "flown" south to escape the real winters up north. Much to my surprise, I found the entire area heavily populated by this migratory flock. Being from the mid-west, I felt right at home with Jerry and Jeannette.

During the summer the Vaughns lived in a rustic, wilderness cabin near Marquette, Michigan. Jerry was a retired corrections officer (prison guard) and Jeannette poured beer at an American Legion club near their home. Every autumn they hauled their trailer, at a leisurely pace, to Port Isabel, Texas, by December. They returned north at a similar pace, by the first of May. Ah, to be retired!

Jerry had a gun rack mounted in the rear window of his pick-up truck. It was one of the first things I noticed as they drove toward me. I had automatically assumed they wouldn't stop. I rarely get rides from people driving vehicles with gun racks. It must be against the National Rifle Association bylaws to pick up hitchhikers. He had the most intelligent use I'd ever seen for such a rack. That was where they kept their walking canes. Neither Jerry nor Jeannette moved around too quickly anymore because of worn out knee joints. Nevertheless, the Vaughns were energetic folks.

After the Vaughns dropped me off in Harlingen I experienced a long wait. Not really wanting to strike off on foot, it took two hours before I finally gave up and started walking.

There was plenty of traffic and this sudden ride drought left me wondering if my luck was turning bad. I had walked two hot, tiring miles, with my shoulders complaining from the weight of my fully loaded backpack, before Serge Pilon stopped.

Originally from France, Serge was living in south Texas after a short stint in California. He was a volunteer at a bird rehabilitation clinic. It was a non-profit organization that aided injured or abandoned birds in returning to the wild. He loved handling birds. Holding an injured, helpless bird in the palm of one's hand is sure to bring out the gentlest side of even the roughest character. Handling any injured creature exposes the vulnerability of wildlife and reveals the power and effects of the human race on nature. The very power that destroys a more delicate side of wildlife, is the same one that can destroy our human habitat. The care we extend to non-human life will ultimately be returned in the form of a higher quality of life for humans.

Unfortunately, the position Serge held at the clinic was only as a volunteer. He needed to wait tables at a restaurant to remain financially afloat. He hated working for a living and earned just enough money to pay for food and rent. Foregoing career goals, he simply maintained life goals. He had a love of boats which led him to take river tours whenever possible. This all fit neatly into his relaxed lifestyle which I admired. Apparently, we had a lot in common.

Serge had a bad attitude towards cars. Far too expensive to purchase, maintain, and insure, he considered them a necessary evil. He couldn't stand the fact that his crappy little car could drain off such a high percentage of his hard earned income. Perhaps his European experience had shown him the benefits of a good public transportation system over the inefficiencies of our one person, one vehicle system. As a hitchhiker I liked to think of myself as an ambassador out promoting car-pooling and ride sharing!

When the quick ride with Serge ended, I found myself back in Pharr, where Graciella had dropped me off the day before. I immediately began walking west, toward McAllen. I wasn't waiting around any more, not with the next town only four miles away.

Not long after, two guys in a trashy old Buick stopped. I knew this was going to be a weird ride, but after so many miles on the road I was beginning to feel invincible!

The driver of the Buick was a young kid, about sixteen-years-old. He was long gone into teenage wasteland. He was so amazed at having another passenger he kept looking back at me with wonderment in his dilated eyes. It's a good thing cars can practically drive themselves!

His partner was about twenty-five-years-old and fancied himself the king of the world. Wearing polyester pants, black shirt with the top button buttoned, and very dark lenses in his aviator sunglasses, he maintained a tacky, mysterious, Hollywood air. He leaned casually against the passenger door, his left arm draped along the top of the Buick's front seat. That position enabled him to converse with me, and at the same time, survey most of his kingdom as the kid chauffeured us along. He was out to help me and, more importantly, impress me. He hurled strict orders at the neu-rotic driver to do this or that and assured me that nothing would stop them from bringing me to the western edge of McAllen.

From my spot in the back seat I had noticed that the gas gauge needle was buried in empty. We must have been running on nothing but gas fumes when the kid tried exiting off the highway. That exit was before the intended destination and the big boss man would have none of it. He reached over, grabbed the steering wheel and swung us back onto the road, just missing the steel supports of the exit sign. The kid was whimpering about the fuel situation and was told in no uncertain terms that they were going to get me across town. The Man didn't give a damn if they did run out of gas. They were on a MISSION, goddamnit!! They had to get me to the edge of town or all hell would break loose. Not wanting to face any more hell than that which was already occurring in his brain, the driver cowered in his seat and drove on. When the kid looked back at me again, his eyes were still dilated, but the wonderment was gone. His new passen-ger was suddenly making his life extremely difficult and I noticed a genu-ine Fear rising in his eyes.

To be magnanimous the Man told the kid that everything was cool and that he'd take care of the situation. The Man then turned his attention back to me and asked if I'd tried any south Texas pot. I told him that I'd only been here a couple of days and hadn't sampled any green. At that he threw a big fat baggie of pot to me for examination. Even though I wasn't buying, I acted sufficiently impressed. He wasn't giving it away so took it back and continued expounding on the quality of the local dope. Ho hum! The conversation was boring but the last exit was coming up and these bozos had saved me from another long walk. I watched them pull away from the corner. They had had enough gas as far as I was concerned!

I quickly made a sign that said "LAREDO." I was on U.S. 83, North. There wasn't much civilization along the 142 mile stretch between McAllen and Laredo. The temperature was soaring and my pack was as heavy as it could be. My feet were raw and blistered. There would be no more walking under these conditions if at all possible. I knew that when I got a ride out of McAllen, the chances were good it would be all the way.

It was a short wait and I was pleasantly surprised when Victor Val-lero, Pedro Martinez and nine-year-old Pedro Martinez Jr. pulled over. Conversation began slowly due to a Spanish/English language barrier. Pedro spoke English fairly well but Victor spoke only Spanish. My Span-ish was limited to Taco Bell menu items so I sat ignorant when the three of them conversed together.

I shared the back seat with young Pedro Jr. In the beginning he was shy with this stranger, but soon warmed up and became very talkative. I was glad about that because junior was completely bi-lingual. Whenever his father and I ran into vocabulary difficulties the youngster helped with the translation.

I was thrilled with the company I was in, not to mention the fact that they were going the 142 miles to Laredo! I kicked back in the big old Chevy and watched the desert pass by my window.

The guys lived in Dallas where Victor worked construction and Pedro was a mechanic. As partners, they owned a hog farm in Reynosa, Mexico. They had recently begun their operation with thirty pigs. Within the coming year they hoped to expand their stock to as many as 500 head. They travelled to Reynosa every two weeks to work a few days and were presently returning to Dallas from such a work session.

They were travelling to Dallas via Laredo to pick up some friends at the Greyhound bus station but were running late. When we stopped for a bite to eat they asked me if I could phone ahead and try paging their friends at the station. They asked me because they thought the operator might not speak Spanish. There wouldn't have been a problem because anyone employed in a public service position down there was undoubtedly bi-lingual, as was the operator I talked with.

Contacting their friends was a success and Pedro told them they were not forgotten and to be patient for a short while longer. When we finally made Laredo, there were three men at the bus depot anxiously awaiting our arrival. I didn't feel at all unwelcome as we all squeezed in and rode fourteen more miles to the lonely intersection of U.S. 83 and I-35. I said goodbye to my friends in this happy carload and faced the rapidly lengthening shadows of the scrub brush all alone.

My loneliness didn't last very long. The first vehicle that approached pulled over. Tom Moss was the driver of that vehicle and appeared incredulous. Not so much because I was hitchhiking, but because I was white. The faces he typically saw along the roadside were Hispanic. The wide open spaces of the southern Texas frontier are one of the pipelines for illegal alien traffic from Central America and Mexico into the United States.

Although off duty at the moment, Tom worked as a pilot for the U.S. Customs Service and was very familiar with the area geography and human situation. In addition to the human smuggling taking place there were illicit drugs and other commercial products illegally flooding the United States. From the sound of it, mythical Sisyphus had an easier task rolling his stone burden up the side of a Hades mountain than the Customs

Service and Border Patrol had in trying to stem the tide of smuggled people and goods.

Tom dropped me at the intersection of U.S. 83 and Texas highway 44. The only thing there was a bar and an unoccupied travel trailer. I saw two people when I poked my nose into the bar. The patrons weren't in a social mood and didn't bother acknowledging my existence. It was an isolated, lonely intersection. I turned away from the neon beer lights and walked into the dark of night. I was ready for some sleep.

By the time I had walked a hundred yards away from the odd security of the beer light, I began to get an eerie feeling. It was so quiet and dark. I was completely unfamiliar with the country. I didn't know what to expect once I stepped off the roadway. Was it sandy or hardpan? Would there be a place clear enough of scrub and thorns to set up my tent? What about nasty little creatures like rattlesnakes and scorpions? In addition to those questions, I wondered about ruthless human coyotes who smuggled their living, Hispanic cargo into the country. Apparently, the human cargo often paid their toll with their own lives. What the heck would I run into out there?

With my senses tuned in at full volume, adrenalin coursing through my system and my muscles prepared for a hair trigger reaction, I started my search for a place to sleep. My eyes were accustomed to the dark and the stars were shining through clear skies so visibility wasn't a problem. A barbed wire range fence lined both sides of the highway. As I walked down the road looking for a spot to jump the fence, a car slowly approached me. I was suddenly bathed in light from a powerful fender mounted spotlight and bright headlights. "Now what?" I thought.

It turned out to be a couple of young men in Immigration and Naturalization Border Patrol uniforms. They were out looking for bad guys. Where Tom was incredulous, these guys were stupefied! They had a million questions. I told them my story. They laughed and joked that I had more balls than brains. It was a statement I certainly couldn't deny!

Worried about my safety, the patrollers went on to tell me of the use of this road junction as a major transportation route and pick up depot for illegal aliens. This was how it worked:

Near U.S. 83, there was a strobe light atop a tall microwave communications tower that could be seen as far away as Mexico. This provided potential immigrants with a directional beacon. After crossing the Rio Grande, the illegals walked east over the twenty barren miles from the river to U.S. 83. By following the light they couldn't possibly miss the highway, which ran perpendicular to their route. Once on 83, they paralleled the roadway heading for the flashing yellow caution light that marked the intersection at Los Botines, where I stood. Here they waited for a truck to haul them deeper into Texas and points north. If they made it that far, they were in, and quickly disappeared into the melting pot.

Of course, most of the overland travel occurred at night to avoid detection by the U.S. authorities. It was quite a system. I suppose circumventing the border patrol required a fairly elaborate system.

It was obvious that I was far too dorky to be a part of that smuggling scheme, so the patrollers had little professional interest in my activity. I wasn't breaking any law, except for trespassing (up to that point, I had actually only considered perpetrating that infraction), which these guys had no enforcement responsibility for anyway. They kindly directed me to a reasonably safe spot to set up my tent and wished me luck. The radio suddenly screamed for their attention with another call and they went racing off down the road.

Alone again, surrounded by silence, my imagination filled the star-studded night with all sorts of monsters, both human and non-human.

I hopped the fence where they suggested. Actually, it wasn't nearly that graceful. "Battled my way over the fence" would have provided a more accurate image of the scene. Using my flashlight sparingly to avoid attracting any attention, I made my camp. It was a clear cool night and I fell asleep as soon as my head hit the pillow. I must not have been too worried about my personal safety.

At one point in the night I heard a truck idling out on the road. I assumed it was being loaded with its human cargo. I was far too tired to worry about what went on around me. As long as I wasn't bothered, I slept.

During the entire time I spent in the vicinity of that junction I heard a cowbell clanging. It was the only thing that penetrated the otherwise silent landscape. It must have been another signal indicating the actual rendezvous location with the truck. The unobtrusive clanging never stopped. Perhaps, for some, it was like the Liberty Bell ringing out the freedom and better economic conditions of the United States. For others, however, it tolled out the fear, loneliness and continuing misery in a foreign land, far from the love of their families. As a bystander I couldn't help being moved by such a struggle. No doubt similar scenes were being played out at thousands of locations across the globe. Those few days I'd spent in south Texas revealed much that I didn't fully understand about the struggle for survival. It's one thing to hear of such trials and tribulations on the news yet quite another to actually observe them on a first hand basis.

When I returned to the road early the following morning, after a full nights rest, the bar was closed and the area was devoid of life. The place was so forsaken there weren't even buzzards drifting around overhead. Tough country. Not for the meek. When the meek eventually inherit the earth, I have a feeling they'll give this part back.

It was Monday morning, February 12. After nearly two hours at the Los Botines junction, with fewer than twenty-five vehicles passing me, Fito Casaverras stopped. I was elated! Desperation had been creeping into my psyche during that long, lonely wait. Fito and his three man crew relieved that hopeless feeling. They were all steel workers and were headed for a week's work at a construction site 100 miles away in Uvalde, Texas.

Fito spoke excellent English but his crew spoke only Spanish. Fito was very friendly and said he liked to help people whenever he could. We cruised down the road at high, back country speeds and arrived in Uvalde in no time. I had considered turning west toward Del Rio before arriving in Uvalde, but was worried about getting rides out of tiny Carrizo Springs and Eagle Pass. I ultimately opted for the sure thing by riding with Fito into Uvalde. From there I figured it would only take one more ride to reach Del Rio as opposed to the slightly more complicated route through Eagle Pass.

It was another lovely, warm spring day. Not expecting much traffic, I walked to the west edge of Uvalde and opened my pack to fix a sandwich. I hated dividing my attention between the road and distractions like lunch. Too bad a guy's gotta eat!

Sure enough, halfway through my sandwich preparation, Tim, Sally, and toddler Troy Tapp stopped, but so far down the road I wasn't even sure they were stopping for me. I hastily repacked my lunch and anything else that had been disturbed and jogged down the road toward them. As I stepped up to the car, they were still busy organizing themselves and their stuff so I could fit in. Sally and Troy had climbed into the back seat. My pack went into the back seat with them, leaving me with the front passenger seat to myself.

Their car was a complete disaster. It was an old, rusty, black Chrysler Cordoba with lousy suspension. The interior looked lived in. Old french fries, squished ketchup packets, dirt on top of grime, melted chocolate, and other assorted litter was strewn about, filling the nooks and crannies. My initial impression was one of disgust. I was determined not to let little Troy touch me for fear of the dreaded, sticky baby hand contamination. It was going to be a long ride, in more than the literal sense.

The Tapps, originally from Michigan, had moved down to Texas because of a warm weather preference. Tim worked as a welder in Sabinal, just east of Uvalde. Life for Tim hadn't been physically comfortable since 1980. While in the Army with the 101st Airborne, stationed at Ft. Hood, he broke his back. Oddly enough, the accident didn't occur during one of his fifteen parachute jumps. It happened during a training exercise while rappelling down a cliff side. His rope broke and he plummeted 60 feet to the ground. He survived the fall with a broken back and assorted other injuries. He had spent the following fifteen days in the hospital and the next nine months in a body cast.

He felt poorly treated by the Army because they had discharged him four days prior to his scheduled promotion to sergeant. By doing so, the Army had saved some money in added compensation to him for his injury. It sounded like shabby treatment of a member of the armed forces. The complaint echoed Eddy Wagner's concern of the treatment of veterans. Tim had a good attitude about it though. Life was life and sometimes things didn't go exactly as you'd like them to. He was extremely happy to have survived at all.

SALLY, TROY AND TIM TAPP
Del Rio, Texas

Tim and Sally were going to Del Rio to get a puppy. We were about 30 miles away when we came across a disabled vehicle. Tim didn't balk at checking to see if the people at the vehicle needed any assistance. He never passed anybody by. It was just a rule he lived by. I think it's called the Golden Rule, isn't it? I guess we sometimes forget about that rule amongst all of the other stupid rules we seem to abide by.

We got the stranded motorist on the road again after about fifteen minutes of fooling around with a jammed bumper jack. Tim was the kind of guy you'd want behind you in the desert, just in case. He stopped with a smile and left with a wave, not an outstretched hand expecting compensation. It seemed to be the right thing to do. He had good karma piled a mile high!

A million pretty people in pretty cars have passed me by on the road. Here were a couple of plain folks, getting by, doing what they could to help others on a personal level. They didn't just write an anonymous check to some corporate charity. They had a day to day involvement with strangers and friends alike. I was happy to be riding in their messy car and experiencing their genuinely open and generous hearts.

Down along the Mexican border, at Del Rio, I found it interesting that my next ride was from a German national. Detlef Kaluza, 25, of Furth, West Germany, was on an extended tour of the United States. Driving a rental car, he was out looking for what remained of the wild west. His intent was to drive remote back roads to secluded camping spots. Detlef figured the narrowest dirt roads down the rugged canyons of the Pecos River country would give him a taste of the frontier. He was probably right.

Following his exploratory drive through the desert country he would be heading to Austin, Texas to meet up with a friend. That friend was in Austin, cooling his heels under a medical quarantine after a trip to South America.

After discovering his intentions I suggested sharing the cost of a campsite and shower. We decided on Seminole Canyon, just north of Del Rio, as our camp. The first thing we did was stretch our legs with a six mile hike. It was a good opportunity to do some exploring in the desert and get off of the road for an afternoon. I needed the break. I was in the middle of a long stretch between friendly destinations. It was the third night out from New Orleans and I was still a couple of days away from Phoenix.

After our hike, with little remaining daylight, Detlef and I set up camp, took a wonderful sunset stroll, and then prepared a marvelous dinner. Detlef gets the credit for the delicious spaghetti entree. Why is it that meals on a camp out always taste so good? That dinner was no exception.

During our conversations I was impressed by Detlef's intelligence, English language skills, political astuteness and broad travel experience. In addition to travels around Europe and the United States, he had recently completed a nine month motorcycle tour of northern and equatorial Africa. He described his Africa trip as very tough, but fun and worth the trouble. Many of the roads were nothing more than glorified cattle trails. Some situations, with his big 1000 cc BMW motorcycle, left him struggling a mere twenty miles over the course of a ten hour day. It was exhausting work.

For Detlef, travelling was his number one priority. While at home in Germany he worked as a carpenter. He saved as much money as he needed to take a trip then simply left. His next trip would be to New Zealand. He hoped to live and work there for a year. I couldn't imagine anything slowing this highly motivated young man down.

That night we tried sleeping in my wind-whipped tent. We weren't very successful. The camp ground was on a hard, flat desert plain. There were no trees or rocks around to provide wind protection. It came screaming across southeast Texas and tried to blow us into Seminole Canyon. The tent poles flexed dangerously close to their limit. The whole structure snapped and popped all night. The sand and dust that got kicked up off the desert floor sounded like big raindrops as they struck the nylon fly. Remarkably, the tent remained standing. Even though it was a noisy place to be, our little house kept the airborne gravel in the desert where it belonged, and not inside our sleeping bags.

We broke our fast the next morning with a delightful repast of tea, bread, marmalade, and cheese. Civilization never had it so good!

The weather was surprisingly cold, dry, and windy. We were both excited at the prospect of driving on some remote back roads. After visiting Judge Roy Bean's museum in Langtry, we drove north to a wide spot in the road called Pandale, at the confluence of the Howard and Pecos Rivers. The surrounding countryside was stark and ruggedly beautiful. The rivers had cut through a couple hundred feet of plateau to reside in their present course. There was no soil structure or grass to act as an erosion buffer, and the water ran surprisingly clear. Vegetation was so sparse that the land seemed raw and naked under the glare of sunshine. The floodplain was the site of numerous flash floods. Small plants and newly formed soil had little chance in this environment. The floods would sweep away anything that wasn't bedrock. It was that type of cleansing that left the exposed, white rock, gleaming like the surface of the moon.

The road was much better than we had expected. Detlef's rental car negotiated the hills, rocks, and gravelly washes without a bit of trouble. Of course, if it had rained, even a little bit, the road would have become an impassable quagmire!

From Pandale we started heading back east and eventually north to Sonora, Texas, and I-10. Before Detlef and I parted ways we lunched on nachos and beer. When in Texas do as Texans do! We did!

When I hit the interstate after our lunch, it was scorching hot under a blazing azure sky. Over the next three hour wait I became very sad and lonely. I was dying to talk to someone who already knew me. I was tired of telling my story to strangers, time and time again. I wanted to rehash old times with someone I'd had old times with. There was no possibility of that sort of contact for three more days; even longer, if I had to spend three to four hours waiting between every ride.

The next town west on I-10 was Ozona, thirty-six miles away. I wasn't about to strike off into the desert on foot with that far to go to a town. If I didn't get a ride the rest of that day I wanted to be close to those nachos and beer!

Traffic leaving Sonora was sparse. Each car that went by provided some small amount of entertainment. There was nothing to do but bake and anticipate oncoming cars. I would try guessing whether an approaching car or truck would exit the freeway or continue on past me. It was wide open country and I could see vehicles approaching for at least two miles. I had a 50/50 chance of being right. Boring? You got that right. Each car became an adventure in psychology. I tried to look as happy and persuasive as possible, despite my misery.

When standing along the road, time becomes a wholly different dimension from what we're used to. It really isn't measured by a sweep second hand across a watch face. It always, always exists in the ticks and tocks of the traffic rhythm. One by one, at inconsistent intervals, the vehicles pass by. Sometimes you can face up to 100 cars per minute. Other times it can even be less than one car per minute. At that point along the Texas interstate it seemed as though the pendulum of time, measured in any dimension, had stopped completely.

Finally a car approached with a young man driving. I stared him down as hard as I could and he hit the brakes. YES! I had practically willed him to stop. Looking back at my situation I felt I may never have gotten out of Texas without the help of Germans. It was Frank Storz, 21, of Ludwigsburg, West Germany, who freed me from the torrid grip of Sonora.

Frank had been working in Charlotte, North Carolina over the past three months. He was now spending two months touring the U.S. taking advantage of the youth hostel system of inexpensive accommodations. Like Detlef, Frank spoke excellent English and had toured much of Europe.

Frank wanted to explore some western ghost towns and his next stop was Alpine, Texas. He didn't have a tent so I volunteered mine for the night. I was willing to take a slight detour with Frank and experience some of the beautiful mountains in southwest Texas. Not very many people know about this secret, wondrous part of the country.

The next morning I suggested we take highway 118 past the McDonald Observatory on our return to I-10. A very strange thing happened as we cruised along the winding 118. The horn on Frank's car suddenly started blowing. Man, that was so nerve wracking! We couldn't get it to stop even after the ignition was turned off. I asked where his fuse box was and started pulling fuses. I finally disconnected one that stopped the awful sonic abuse. What a scene, out in the middle of nowhere. We could have charged admission but there was no one around to buy a ticket!

After passing through the cool, pine forests of the Davis Mountains we continued into a windy and dusty El Paso, Texas. For some reason things didn't feel comfortable there. Maybe it was just the anticipation of a big storm coming, or on a more metaphysical level, a lack of connection with the people. El Paso was so far from where I came from. I expected a little town but found a big city. For some unknown reason I withdrew from it.

I could see storm clouds roiling and feel the wind changing. That was clearly visible and palatable. The spiritual side of my discomfort wasn't as easily distinguished. We saw few people and never had a chance to talk with any of the residents. They seemed to be hiding. I couldn't see into the eyes and soul of El Paso to determine if I was safe there. It's the same sort of eye contact a driver needs to make before deciding to pick someone up. I received no positive feelings from the area and was glad to have a ride into and out of town with Frank.

Our destination for the night was Silver City, New Mexico. He was hoping to spend the night at a hostel in town. I hadn't planned on going to Silver City, but was going along because it was a sure thing. I would go to Phoenix via the smaller highways through the mountains. That way I could avoid the city of Tuscon, Arizona, and freeway hitchhiking. Silver City, perched on the Rocky Mountain continental divide, was as good a starting place as any for my assault on southeastern Arizona.

When we arrived in Deming, New Mexico, the weather was getting rough. Building materials, trash, cardboard boxes, dirt, and dead brush blew by us. The wind was tearing everything apart and the temperature was dropping. We turned north on U.S. 180, straight into the teeth of a winter storm. A few miles north of Deming a couple of giant, car-eating tumbleweeds came drifting across our path. They were larger than the car and we were forced to come to a complete stop while one of them rolled right over us. Our sight was completely obscured for the few moments it took for the weed to roll by. That certainly gave Frank a taste of the old west. I was indelibly impressed as well.

As we approached Silver City, I was getting burned out on my ride. Frank was a nice guy and I had enjoyed our conversations. We had talked a lot over the past day and a half but I just felt like being quiet for a while, experiencing the tempest in silence. It was not to be. We talked about the weather.

The strong wind was suddenly accompanied by blinding snow. I was amazed at the intensity of this snowstorm, so far south. I'd seen blizzards rage in the northern mountains and midwestern plain, but this took me by surprise. We were less than 100 miles away from sunny Mexico. Things didn't look good.

Frank sought out the hostel and urged me to fork out a paltry $11 for my own warm, dry bed. Too stubborn for words, I was determined to endure the night out-of-doors, blizzard or not. He simply thought I was out of my mind. I probably was a little twisted after facing 100 degree heat in Sonora the day before. I can't handle that sort of abuse. It probably melted my brain.

Frank drove me out of town about three-fourths of a mile to a spot where I might camp. We had travelled a lot of miles together and we both had an entire continent left to cross. It was nice to have shared a portion of our journeys together.

I had to set up my camp in a hurry. I climbed up a slope to get away from the road and to find a level spot. I found a small flat circle, sheltered by low, brushy trees. It was snowing like crazy and I wanted to keep it out of the tent interior. I had no intention of sleeping cold and wet that night.

Setting up the tent under those conditions was strenuous and darkness added to the difficulty. As I hurried to erect the tent one of the poles ripped through its retaining sleeve. Oops! I felt like an idiot. But I was hurrying because my hands were freezing! By rushing things and shredding my own tent I would have to walk back into town and try to find the hostel again. Shelter here, or there, was absolutely necessary that night. What was the solution? I didn't have time to sit and figure it out. I rushed, carefully.

The tent stood despite the torn sleeve. I crawled into my dry, cozy bag at 8:00 pm and let Mother Nature howl me to sleep. I slept like a baby would, after a sweet lullaby.

When I packed up the next morning I bitched aloud about my cold hands. Yelling seemed to take some of the sting away. Despite my noisy complaints I was actually thankful for the large temperature drop of the night before. The freezing temperatures had kept everything from getting soaked. It saved me from having to deal with heavy, wet snow. My hands would have been much colder if the temperature had been 33°F instead of 20°F. That didn't mean that my hands weren't hurting at 20°F.

My original idea of going to Phoenix through the mountains had died and was buried under about 10 inches of freshly fallen snow, just like the roads. I was forced to take New Mexico 90, south to Lordsburg, where I would connect with I-10 again.

As I trudged across Silver City I noticed that things were pretty quiet. The road conditions were terrible and were reflected in the lack of traffic. I gave up standing in town and began walking south, up a long hill. Incredibly, Cheryl McGee and Margie Blaisdell, their car loaded with ski gear, pulled over halfway up the slippery hill.

I enthusiastically piled into their already crowded car and buckled up for a potentially wild ride. They told me that the road we were on had been officially closed earlier that morning. I found out why, as Cheryl fought to keep her car on the ice covered road during our climb to the continental divide.

Cheryl was a registered nurse and Margie was an M.D. They lived and worked in Ft. Defiance, Arizona, on the Navajo Indian Reservation. Both women served there in the Indian Health Service.

I told them about my stereotypical impression regarding alcoholism on the reservation. I assumed alcoholism ran rampant, destroying lives and any potential social, economic, and political opportunities in an already oppressed minority culture. They replied that alcoholism was no worse on the reservation than in other segments of the American population. It was simply far more visible due to the poverty. Middle and upper class Americans were just better at hiding the problem behind fancy clinics, treatment centers, and lawyers. They said most of the people they treated in the

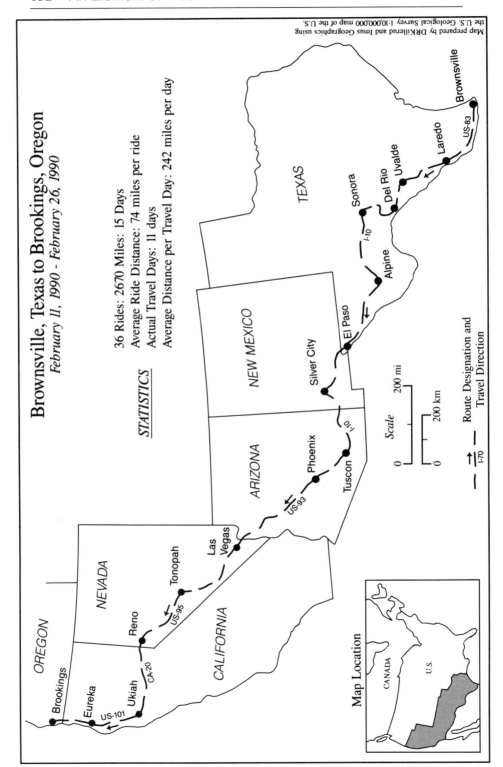

Brownsville, Texas to Brookings, Oregon
February 11, 1990 - February 26, 1990

<u>STATISTICS</u>

36 Rides: 2670 Miles: 15 Days
Average Ride Distance: 74 miles per ride
Actual Travel Days: 11 days
Average Distance per Travel Day: 242 miles per day

Map prepared by DRKillerud and Imus Geographics using
the U.S. Geological Survey 1:10,000,000 map of the U.S.

Scale

200 mi

200 km

0

0

Route Designation and
Travel Direction

Map Location

CANADA

U.S.

native American community were just normal folks with the usual ailments.

I mentioned to them that I had lived in Montana for about ten years and had worked a number of summers in Glacier National Park. Cheryl said she had been raised adjacent to the park in Browning, Montana. She had also gone to the University of Montana, which has a strong nursing program. Back in 1986 I completed a Masters degree in Geography at Montana. Not surprisingly we had common acquaintances from the park and the university. I was astonished at the coincidence. A situation like that, totally random, shows how small the world really is.

On the Blackfeet Reservation, in Browning, she was raised in an environment where you trusted nearly everyone. She theorized that the harshness of the elements in the high plains country made people more reliant on each other, thereby fostering a higher level of trust.

As she promoted her theory of trust based upon remoteness and environmental factors I began to consider my own experiences. Many times I would find myself at an intersection or stretch of road that was inhabited by nothing but the ghosts of hitchhikers past. It would be so remote I had to assume that no one would ever stop for me. Despite my consistently faltering faith, time and time again, every time in fact, someone would take me away.

In a crowded urban landscape with hundreds of cars passing by a hitchhiker every few minutes, it is easy for a driver to just let the next guy make the effort of stopping. If the driver doesn't act at that particular moment everything will be fine because he assumes that within a short period of time someone else will. On the other hand, at an insignificant, outlying intersection drivers carry a greater responsibility, whether they want to or not. Those drivers realize that it could be dangerous for someone to be stuck out there and are practically coerced into making a decision regarding a hitchhiker. Who can say when the next car will come by? It could be a very long time. A driver facing that situation may still pass by a hitchhiker, but it is much more difficult for them to do so. I've found that remote intersections and poor weather conditions, generally lead to quick rides. As recognition of the hitchhiker's plight increases, so does sensitivity, and people become more inclined to stop.

As we pulled into Lordsburg, coming down off the continental divide on highway 90, we were met by a sight I'd never beheld. Automobiles and trucks were lined up on I-10 and access roads as far as the eye could see. The unimaginable had happened. The interstate into Tuscon was closed due to hazardous snow and ice conditions. Highway closures are relatively rare even in the northern United States and I was amazed at the predicament we were suddenly faced with, now a mere forty miles from the Mexican border. Fortunately, we weren't caught in the stationary traffic. We drove into town and Cheryl and Margie were kind enough to buy my breakfast. That was sure to put a smile on my face.

As we finished eating, the highway reopened and we were soon zooming toward Tuscon. The road wasn't bad at all and I couldn't figure out why it had been closed.

Cheryl and Margie left me in the middle of Tuscon at a freeway entrance ramp. Traffic was heavy and I had no desire to walk down onto the freeway shoulder. It looked like a dangerous place to be so I remained at the top of the ramp. My sign read "PHOENIX" and it took an hour before someone finally stopped.

It was an interesting ride. The driver was a young man of Asian descent. There was no conversation. He simply pointed to the back of his little pick-up truck. I knew what he meant so I hopped in back and made myself comfortable. The weather was really warming up which made getting comfortable a pleasure, rather than a sentence. A couple of hours later, in Phoenix, I knocked on the window and signaled I wanted out at the next exit. He stopped and I jumped out. I'd never had a ride like that one before, or since.

I was finally near old friends and contacted them immediately. The long, lonely stretch between New Orleans and Phoenix was finally over. I could satisfy my need to rehash old times because I was staying with my Alaska hitchhiking buddy Chuck and his wife Suzanne. In fact I had acted as a matchmaker by setting them up on a blind date.

Chuck and I had gone to junior high and high school together. We lived a block apart in St. Louis Park, a western suburb of Minneapolis. We shared an interest in music, sports, travel, and of course, girls. We'd gone camping, canoeing and skiing together for years. When we were old enough for college our paths split. Even so, it was only natural that we would continue to keep in close contact.

Bright and talented, Chuck thrived at Stout State University in neighboring Wisconsin. Not nearly as studious in school as Chuck was, I wallowed. Struggling through the Agricultural Engineering Technology course work at the University of Minnesota, I couldn't finish fast enough. All I wanted to do was to hit the road.

During our senior years we began to hatch a plan. We would be graduating simultaneously at our respective schools and both wanted to share in a big adventure. Before either of us got a job following our graduation we would take a hitchhiking trip together, to Alaska. The impetus of our plan was enough of an emotional boost to keep me going until I had my sheepskin in hand.

A couple of days after our graduation we walked down to U.S. 12, a block away from our houses, and set off north to Alaska. We gloried in the adventure. The Dakotas, Montana, the Canadian Rockies, the coastal mountain ranges of British Columbia and finally to the Pacific coast. We rode the inside passage ferry into southeastern Alaska making our first landfall at Ketchikan. Hiking in the stands of ancient trees of the Tongass National Forest we had our first indication of how impossibly huge the state and its resources were.

In Skagway we split up to explore on our own. We met again in Denali National Park. We shared stories of the routes and adventures we had experienced alone. I was thrilled to be camped out together again. It wasn't to last.

Responsible and anxious, Chuck wanted to end his vacation in fantasyland and get a start on his professional career. He left the Mount McKinley area and headed back to Minnesota after two months of travel.

I, on the other hand, had no interest in my career and fully intended to stick around Alaska for as long as possible. I postponed my departure until the long nights of late autumn began to darken the land. It took ten days to hitchhike from Anchorage to Minneapolis. It would have taken far longer if I hadn't been lucky beyond belief.

Standing at one of those really (I am serious about this), really remote locations, I got a ride, my longest ride ever. I went from Northway Junction, Alaska, to Seattle, to Fargo, North Dakota, with one driver. Six days and 3500 miles.

Chuck fell into, and had stuck with the career track. He and his family lived in a lovely house in Phoenix. Exactly ten years later I was hitchhiking across the country to his house for a visit. For me, things had changed little over that decade!

The visit with Chuck and Suzanne was inspirational. When I left, on February 17, I was psyched to hitch the long, lonely road between Las Vegas and Reno. It was one of those places I'd wanted to hitchhike because I considered U.S. 95 a classic highway.

The transportation system of the United States and Canada is absolutely incredible. Pulling out a map of North America reveals the web. It is a thrill to put a finger on a highway at one end of the country and trace its course. One ribbon of pavement with a number on it can go on across the entire length, or breadth, of the continent. It is a fact which has enamored many a traveller. It is easy to fall in love with a highway.

As we trace the highway's route on the map we see names of towns, mountains, rivers, political boundaries, and other indications of a history worth exploring. Choose a highway, then step outside and pursue it. Follow it from beginning to end. The towns and physical geography come to life. They are no longer abstractions on two-dimensional paper. Watch the world melt from one scene to another with every passing mile. It is the beautiful continuity that can only be found in linear travel. Each tick of the odometer provides proof of the continuity, and the change in scene, our reward. The road can change in quality and condition along the traverse, but those identifying signs keep showing up as a reminder that you're not lost. Just keep holding onto the safety line of tar. It is a secure feeling to be able to follow something so simple across such a complex surface.

I found U.S. 95 to be a classic because it travelled from Mexico to Canada through some of the most beautiful, and solitary, terrain in the country. Listen to the towns: San Luis, Yuma, Needles, Las Vegas, Tonopah, Winnemucca, Rome, Jordan Valley, White Bird, Lewiston, Moscow, Coeur d'Alene and Bonners Ferry.

Here's a small sample of the geographical features it passes through: Chocolate Mountains, Colorado River, Dead Mountains, Eldorado Mountains, Amargosa Desert, Sarcobatus Flat, Monte Cristo Mountains, Humboldt Sink, Alvord Desert, Snake River, River of No Return, Gospel Hump, Lake Pend Oreille, and the Kootenai River. Finding and exploring these places is something my vagabond blood cannot resist. It is my friend the highway that takes me to each treasure.

As far as I was concerned, hitchhiking through Tonopah, Nevada rivaled the romance of standing on a corner in Winslow, Arizona, as in the rock anthem by the Eagles. I had already hitched through Winslow a number of years back and wanted to see if the Tonopah experience would be worth an anthem of its own!

From Phoenix, I was off to Las Vegas. My original plan had included a visit there with the parents of another old friend. Unfortunately, those plans fell through so my next target was Soda Springs, California, near Lake Tahoe, 500 miles away.

It took two short rides and a hot five mile walk to escape the suburban wastelands of Phoenix. I was tired and had given up walking by the time Charles Robert "Bob" Stone picked me up in Peoria.

Bob was quite a character. The first thing he asked was if I wanted to buy him some beer. He was encouraging me to cough up some compensation for the ride he was about to give. I didn't mind. I was glad to be moving under the power of an internal combustion engine, and not my weary legs. It was a hot day and he knew just the place to get some cheap beer. I picked up some pretzels, too. I didn't want to appear ungrateful. He seemed to know about beer. He informed me about an unknown ingredient in Budweiser beer that was addictive. That didn't sound so unusual to me. I thought alcohol was the addictive ingredient. As far as I knew, all beers had alcohol and were equally addictive!

Bob had been a World War II pilot. He had made it through the war years without mishap but crashed his plane in 1947 without even been fired upon. He never did say what had actually gone wrong to cause the crash. Anyway, he had obviously survived a deadly miscue.

Some thirty years later Bob met the man who had pulled his unconscious carcass out of the plane wreckage. The man was leaving a janitorial position and Bob was replacing him. They had never met until Bob went in to work to receive some training. The man identified himself after hearing the story of Bob's mishap. Both were amazed at the coincidence of finally meeting after 30 years!

Moments after Bob left me in Wickenburg, Arizona, Henry Rohmer stopped. Henry was a man on top of the world. He was married, owned his own semi-truck, loved to travel and loved to drive. He had it all. He was hauling concrete reinforcing bar into Las Vegas but couldn't unload it for two days. That gave him more than enough time to gamble away his $200 self-imposed limit.

Henry expressed a concern about the truck driver's image. He said most truckers were good drivers and didn't deserve their bad reputation. He had driven 142,000 miles over the past year without an incident. After so many miles, one would think there would be no time for a life outside of driving. He claimed to take plenty of time off for fun and relaxation.

Out on the open desert highway we cruised along at 80 mph and enjoyed the lovely scenery. Everywhere we looked there was red and buff colored sand and rocks, highlighted by stark shadows, courtesy of the rugged rock outcrops. The most notable vegetation along that stretch of road was the Joshua tree and saguaro cactus. It was a true wilderness, although unlike the tree covered mountain slopes of Montana I normally associated with wilderness.

As we passed through the Colorado River gorge, over Hoover Dam, we were met by a narrow road with terrifying cliffs surrounding us. It didn't seem as though Henry could possibly thread the truck through such a challenging obstacle course. All went well and we eventually rolled into the Sam's Town casino complex, just south of Las Vegas proper. Henry would be going no farther into town that night. Apparently Sam's Town would be the recipient of his $200!

It was rainy, chilly, and dark. It looked like I would be spending the night somewhere in Las Vegas. Amongst all the flashing lights of the casinos, I wondered where I'd be setting up my tent.

I started strolling toward downtown. After a couple of miles I took refuge from the rain under an overhang. I made a sandwich and watched the traffic whiz by. I was taking it easy. My luck getting out of Phoenix and into Las Vegas had been good and I was enjoying the slow pace of walking into town.

Upon finally reaching Main Street, in the center of town, I was exhausted. Only then did I begin to realize that the center of town was a dumb place to start looking for a place to camp! I was also confused about what road to take north. My map showed two different highway 95s. One was a business route while the other appeared to be a freeway. The business route said Tonopah Highway, and seemed the most direct route through town. Most of the traffic seemed to be on the freeway, however.

Under the influence of fatigue, my judgement was turning bad. I was really tired and should have just bedded down in somebody's back yard. Instead, I started walking down the rain slickened freeway shoulder. It was the beginning of a nightmare of my own concoction.

After walking a quarter mile in fast, heavy traffic, the shoulder narrowed, bounded by a high concrete retaining wall. To stay off the dangerous roadway I climbed onto the wall ledge. What a bunch of foolishness. I found myself in no better position and perhaps faced an even more dangerous situation.

The slope above the wall edge was covered with all kinds of landscape shrubbery. Fearful of slipping down the slope and over the retaining wall, I bushwhacked my way through the shrubbery for a while. Recognizing the futility of this course of action I eventually decided to escape the highway right-of-way. I hacked my way to the top of the landscaped slope and slithered down the other side of the embankment. That too was covered with dense vegetation. I had nearly reached my goal when I was met by your typical ten foot high chain link fence with three nice strands of barbed wire across the top. All along the other side of this fence were houses with their own chain link fences enclosing their yards. This was all clearly designed to keep the likes of me from passing through their property. I was in no condition to try climbing such a series of obstacles with my large pack and duffel. Those planners were so competent!

My map showed a park a few blocks north. Because of my fatigue I wanted to limit walking distances as much as possible. Rather than backtracking, I chose to continue struggling along the retaining wall to the next exit ramp, which was now finally in sight. I was feeling pretty stupid by this time. It was dark and rainy and there I was, locked into mortal combat with a quarter mile of decorative shrubbery, feet and hands desperately clinging onto man-made soil created out of the bark and wood chips of some extinct forest. That was what stood between me and the relative safety of a residential street. The endless stream of traffic below me continued to speed by, throwing even more water into the air. What in the hell!? I was not a happy camper.

Of course, much to my dismay, upon reaching the exit I found I needed to backtrack about six blocks to the park. My strategy was not working well at all. I got to the park, practically in tears, and faced yet another fence. Having no other choice, and realizing that standing there crying probably wouldn't make the fence go away, I patiently began a zombie-like walk of the park's perimeter until I found an open gate and entered. The park was huge and muddy. I wound up sleeping in the outfield of a ball diamond. It was the only place that wasn't torn up or covered with mud. The rain had finally stopped so I didn't bother setting up my tent.

It had been quite a Saturday night. While the city plunged into another night of stealing from the incompetent and giving to the criminally rich, I slept in peace.

The next morning I quickly packed up and left the park. Rumors of the past led me to believe the Las Vegas police force didn't take too kindly to vagabond types. Their job was to make sure the tourist trade didn't have to deal with any distractions outside of the bright lights of the casinos. I had no desire to call their attention to me until I got on the road. I could deal with just about anything on the street, but not while crawling out of my sleeping bag. A vulnerable position to be in, no matter where you are.

Remembering my terrible freeway experience of the previous night, I decided to follow business route 95 which made a diagonal to the northwest corner of town. I figured traffic would be slower and I'd be generally safer. I was right. It was not only slow, traffic was practically nonexistent. The few people out driving that Sunday morning of February 18 were in no mood to invite me along for a ride. Their mood was probably tainted by the amount of money they'd lost the night before.

My mood was also tainted. Unsure of my route I walked and walked. I wanted to find a shortcut to the freeway that would take me north. I would eventually hook up with it but hoped for a cutoff road that would get me there sooner. Rides were not forthcoming on the business route. There were a couple pedestrians I talked to but they weren't at all helpful with directions.

Angered and frustrated I walked at least eight miles to the junction of the 95 bypass and the 95 business route I'd been following. I refused to take another step. It just didn't make sense that people wouldn't stop. I was depressed and worried that after so many miles and 132 good rides, I wouldn't get the one ride it took to get out of Las Vegas. I didn't want to fail here on the edge of Sin City.

My heart was broken. At that point I really felt like calling a taxi, buying a plane ticket and taking the easy way home. Had I done that, the failure would have been complete. That would have been the twist of the knife in my broken heart. I wrestled with myself and the trip, which had developed all the complexities of a love affair. The trip had become my worst enemy and my greatest joy. I definitely wanted to go home, but wanted more than anything to continue the trip. There were still so many towns left to pass through. It was a matter of gathering my wits, settling down into a patient frame of mind, and waiting. The problem that needed to be solved simply required patience. I was good at waiting. The best. The ride would come eventually. It had to.

There was a pay phone at a nearby convenience store. It was my only link to a friendly voice and encouragement. I dialed my brother, back in Willow River, to vent my frustration. My brother, Scott, cheered me right up with the type of wacky humor that could make me forget what I was depressed about in the first place. Grateful for his encouraging pep talk I returned to my wait site with renewed optimism.

Scott's phone conversation acted like a booster shot. After a couple more hours of waiting, its protective effects started wearing off. Needing another dose, I began to remember why I had been unhappy.

I had been sweating profusely throughout my sixteen mile walk across Las Vegas, leaving me wet, clammy, and uncomfortable as I stood in one place trying to get a ride. Soon a cold wind slipped down from the mile high peaks surrounding Las Vegas, giving me one more thing to worry about; fighting off a chill.

Jim Tuey finally pulled up and offered me a sip from his flask of Canadian Mist whiskey. An excellent weapon in the fight against a deep chill. Now, that was more like it! Perhaps I wouldn't have to fly out of town after all.

JIM TUEY
Indian Springs, Nevada

Jim lived in tiny Indian Springs, Nevada, about 30 miles north. There is an Air Force base nearby and the giant, Nevada Test Site is adjacent, to the north. Jim had worked at the test site until a couple of days before. He'd quit because there was too much weird stuff going on. He didn't really elaborate but seemed a trifle nervous about the weapons they experimented with. As a sheet metal worker he hadn't been directly involved in weapons research but was happy enough to be unemployed. He had decided that his health and genetic well being were more important than his paychecks.

On the way to Indian Springs I mentioned my surprise at having experienced so much cold and damp weather in a supposed desert climate. Jim took my confused expression as a hint of my misery and invited me to have a hot shower and lunch at his mobile home. After the shower and a change into what remained of my dry clothes, I watched about a half hour of television. I needed to relax and my host had made me feel right at home.

After a lunch of ham, eggs, and toast, Jim took me a few more miles down the road to a place called Cactus Springs. It was a wide spot in the road with a gas station and a bar. It was typical of most American wide spots. What made it atypical was the trouble I had trying to get beyond it. I waited for over two hours before darkness, cold, and fatigue drove me to my tent for the night. Despite the lack of vegetation nearby I found a protected spot that was fairly well hidden from view.

It had taken me nine hours to get one ride and advance a mere 30 miles toward Reno. My romantic visions of hitchhiking the classic U.S. 95 were suddenly tempered by the reality of actually doing it. I didn't think it would be easy but this was ridiculous. Worried about my endurance, I knew I couldn't take too many more days like the past two.

My camp was assembled by 6:00 pm. Inside my cozy sleeping bag I fell instantly asleep and didn't stir until 6:00 the next morning. It had been a frustrating couple of days. I was struggling to maintain good spirits in the face of more cold and snowy weather. There were a lot of cold, empty miles between Cactus Springs and Reno.

Surely, one of the most important psychological enticements for a driver to consider picking up a hitchhiker is the hitcher's appearance as a friendly and enthusiastic person. Nobody wants to pick up a deadbeat. For the hitchhiker to lure a driver he must constantly devote his attention to the traffic. Acting lazy or obnoxious, smoking, drinking, sitting or lying down, or scowling at drivers will add up to some long waits. It's hard enough to get rides when you're being perfectly pleasant. Every little negative aspect of your disposition will be sensed and further decrease your chances with the already small percentage of potential drivers. Maintaining a positive disposition was particularly difficult over the course of the next day in Cactus Springs.

February 19 started out as an exquisite day to be on the road. The weather was cold, clear and windy. Every breath I drew was crisp and clean. The surrounding mountains blushed rouge under a white negligee of fresh snow. The jets from Indian Springs Air Force Base played tag amongst the shimmering crags of the Spotted Mountain range. The scenery couldn't be beat.

I could see at least three miles back up the road and as each car approached I would be standing and smiling, trying to attract their attention with either my thumb or sign. There was an unexpectedly large amount of traffic passing by. Unfortunately, I could do nothing to make them stop. I must have gone through my routine of standing up and smiling, followed by sitting down and resting, a couple thousand times. Somehow I maintained my patience. I had no choice in Cactus Springs. There was no other way out.

I was really sick of waiting but wasn't stupid enough to strike off into the desert on foot. Almost all of the cars blowing by me sported Nevada plates. That meant the locals were clearly ignoring me. After waiting two hours the day before and nearly seven hours already that day, I finally decided to change my strategy. I switched to the "ACROSS BRIDGE?" sign method, hoping to express my willingness to take a short ride.

The map showed Lathrop Wells as the next town. It was forty miles away but the relative distances there, in the desert southwest, were comparable to going across a bridge on the east coast. I drew up a Lathrop Wells sign hoping to attract a local driver to get the momentum started. I felt so dead in the water at this point I was considering hitching my pant leg up and showing a bit of calf. Is that desperate, or what?

No matter how long the wait, a hitchhiker must be completely tuned into the traffic. Our senses strive to detect the first indication of a car stopping. We watch for them to signal and slow down in front of us. If a driver hasn't made up his mind by the time he reaches us, it's not too late. Look him in the eye. Convince him that its the right thing to do. Search for that ray of hope. It may still be found.

The sweetest sound in the world to a hitchhiker is the decrease of engine rpms as the driver releases the throttle, then hits the brakes. Your heart skips a beat as you spin around to watch the brake lights come on as they head for the shoulder. The feeling is magical and addictive. It is impossible not to smile and think, "All right! It worked again!" The rush is powerful and inexplicable.

I finally got my chance to experience that rush again, after a wretched nine hour wait over the course of two days in Cactus Springs.

A big, noisy, old Mercury sled went blazing past me at about 75 mph when I heard the familiar throttle down. I spun around to witness the illuminated brake lights confirming my number one wish. The lights did come on but the driver did not pull onto the shoulder. Instead, he made a quick U-turn across the highway median, came back down the other side, then crossed the median again in front of me and drove up with a screeching halt.

Five minutes after changing my bait I had a local driver hooked, one who was headed to Lathrop Wells. Too bad I didn't think of making a sign for the next town nine hours earlier.

John Collins could get me there and was in a big hurry. He was late for work. He was a miner of bentonite and hectorite and had lived in the Amargosa Valley for about eleven years. He was from a family of fourteen kids and was raised mostly in Washington and Oregon. John enjoyed his life in the arid mountains of Nevada and California. The only problem was the 115 miles, round trip, to Vegas to get groceries. His misfortune; my benefit!

Lathrop Wells was damn near a metropolis compared to Cactus Springs. It must have boasted a population of 50. I could have used a break from the roadside with a stop at a store or restaurant but there wasn't any-place like that around. Besides, the momentum for rides had finally begun. Getting the next ride was always the most important thing.

I immediately made a sign for Beatty, only 28 miles away. The first car that approached stopped. Chuck Buswell, driving a white Cadillac Eldorado, was on his way to Tonopah. He planned on sleeping in Beatty before continuing 93 more miles to Tonopah in the morning. He was tired after a long night in Las Vegas and wanted to rest before making it to work the next day. As we conversed, Chuck woke up enough to drive all the way home. My luck had apparently returned.

We rolled into town just as darkness fell. At an elevation of 6000 feet Tonopah was freezing cold and buried under snow. As I started my walk across town, I assumed I'd never get out of there that night. The prospect of setting up my tent under those conditions was not my idea of a good time. I was not in the mood. Still angry about my Las Vegas debacle I wanted to make a few more miles if possible. The momentum was in my blood and I wasn't willing to stop, yet. I would have been very crabby the following morning if I'd spent that night in a bitterly cold Tonopah.

I know, it sounds like I was sulking. I was really sick of the road and wanted to go home. I knew it was just a phase, but recognizing that fact didn't make the cold and fatigue go away. Shivering some of the cold out of my bones, I smiled at the blinding headlights that approached. I hoped the drivers wouldn't notice that the smile I managed to muster was through clenched teeth.

A young couple passed me by and pulled into a service station. When they returned to the road they immediately stopped to pick me up. It was Jack Green and Holly Wilbanks riding in their tiny Honda Prelude jammed with luggage. Incredibly, I managed to squeeze in. I wanted out of Tonopah so badly that night I would have strapped myself onto the roof if I hadn't been able to fit inside.

While at the station, they had planned on offering me a ride and had purchased a cup of coffee to help warm me up. They were very considerate and thoughtful. It was a pleasure being in their company.

Jack, at age 23, understood my feelings about getting out of this town. He'd hitched this road a few times himself. When he had gone out onto the road he sought an education. His goal was to see and feel the world around him. He wanted to experience the harshness and softness that existed hand in hand in the real world.

Jack and Holly were heading to Reno where they both attended the University of Nevada. Jack was a senior in education, what he termed "the imagination science." His intent was to identify the process that most effectively educates the human mind. He was very self aware and spoke his thoughts and ideas from firm intellectual ground. From an extensive literature background in the humanities and personal observations of different teaching and learning methods, he believed most school systems lacked the vitality to properly present a subject. It all boiled down to a paper chase. The spirits and sensibilities of students and instructors were mediocre in the dogmatic pursuit of a diploma. The diploma simply became an employment ticket, not a reflection of the love of learning and comprehension.

In an environment where a pure love of learning was the central ambition, universities would become less competitive and more free thinking. Jack wondered what attendance would be like at a college that offered no paper credentials. Although critical of present educational practices, he recognized them as a mere phase in a dynamic, evolutionary process that began with the first thoughts of mankind. He was excited to be entering the field with a desire to take the next evolutionary step. He hoped to establish a school, in a rural setting, where instructors would teach free thinking in an environment devoid of authority, competition, or fear. Impressive aspirations for such a young man.

When we spoke about trust, Jack said trust, peace, love, and understanding should be commonplace, instead of exceptional. He spoke softly but carried a big intellectual stick. Thank goodness he didn't use it as a weapon. He was content to use it as a tool for building a better educational institution.

We talked a steady stream of ideas, impressions, and observations. The 220 miles to Reno went by quickly. The Prelude may have been bursting at the seams with its load but zipped along at speeds as high as 75 mph the entire distance. My perseverance earlier in the day had finally paid off.

I stayed at Jack's apartment that night. The next morning he took me on a brief tour of the University before bringing me to I-80. We thanked each other for the opportunity to share thoughts and ideas. I must say it was one of the most gratifying experiences of my life to have met Jack. Refreshed and revitalized, I hit the road to Soda Springs, California. My Nevada hitching blues were gone.

We are all faced with opportunities, chances to make the world a better place. Our chances come daily. Some of us respond because we are sensitive enough to recognize the opportunities and have the desire to make the most of them.

On the contrary, my ride out of Reno, provides an example of an ugly and selfish incident. I had become the culprit in a missed chance at understanding and cooperation. An incident that shows how much one can become what they hate. My sensibilities had shut down.

The I-80 entrance ramp, west out of Reno was under construction. I walked down to the freeway and continued along what remained of the shoulder. Adding to the confusion of the construction was a big pick-up truck on the shoulder with a flat tire. The man changing it seemed to have everything under control. There was another car sitting about twenty yards ahead, without any occupants. It was a short, busy, complicated stretch of road.

After a few minutes of walking through this obstacle course, an old timer pulled his double cab pick-up truck over. I threw my stuff on top of a bunch of junk he had in back. When I climbed into the front seat I was essentially entering his home. The old guy slept and ate in there. Everything he owned was on that truck, including his little dog. He must have been about 75, and he reminded me of Jed Clampett on the Beverly Hillbillies, driving to California to take advantage of everything the west had to offer. The main difference was that this man was flat broke and only had enough gas to get to the next exit. He had sold some stuff at the last truck stop and used the few bucks to put gas in his truck. He was coming from somewhere around Kansas and seeking relatives in Stockton, California. It would be a long, slow drive for him, going from exit to exit for the next couple hundred miles, to his destination.

I was thinking about giving him some gas money out of my own tight budget but became holier-than-thou when he said he was dying for a cigarette. If I did give him some money I figured he'd spend it on smokes and wine. I became judge, jury, and prosecution for this man. I made my decision to cut him loose from my good graces, leaving him at the mercy of the cold, snowy road at the next exit. Ebeneezer Scrooge and Silas Marner would have been proud. I had neatly succeeded in hurting my soul and stood waiting for my next ride with my head hung low.

Perhaps I did make the right decision. Maybe he would have squandered the money. It was too late now. He'd never get the chance to prove me wrong. I was very disappointed with myself. Conceivably, the world will be better off now that I'll be trying to overcompensate for my insensitivities of the past.

Being blind to the larger picture, my mind went back to the task at hand; getting a ride to my friend's house in Soda Springs, California, still thirty-five miles away.

Mike Werner, driving a semi-truck loaded with steel mill rolls, was on his way to the San Francisco Bay area. He'd been driving truck coast to coast for three years and loved it. He was probably about 25 and thrifty enough to stash his money in bank CDs. He was serious about retiring on the interest after only a few more years of jamming gears.

Mike was really generous with his time. Not only did he pick me up, he stopped his rig for a stranded motorist as we climbed up Donner Pass. All he could do for her was send for a tow truck because the poor woman's engine had blown. The point was that he had pulled his big, fully loaded rig over, on a steep grade, to offer his assistance. He was living Jack Green's theory of love and cooperation as the rule rather than the exception. I watched his exemplary actions and brooded about my own selfishness during my ride with the old man.

I spent three days skiing and enjoying the winter wonderland of the Donner Pass area. One day, while sitting around collecting dust, I calculated my rides and mileage. On February 23, after sixty days on the road, 128 drivers had taken me 7550 miles. I wasn't even halfway! I studied the map and realized that if I were going to go the complete distance by my a self-imposed May 1st deadline, I needed to quicken my pace a bit.

February 24, was a splendid day to be in the Sierra Nevada. I stood at the base of the Soda Springs I-80 entrance ramp in blinding sunshine. Although the Donner Pass vicinity is the site of many deadly snowstorms, there was no chance of inclement weather that day. It was like being on the beach. The snow lined the freeway like a frozen wave, towering eight feet above the shore. The roadway was dry but dirty from the accumulation of four months of traction sand, salt, and gravel applied by highway maintenance trucks. As vehicles sped by the finest particles would be cast into the air creating a slight haze. It hung over the roadway, the only flaw in the otherwise pristine mountain air.

Having no interest in a visit to Sacramento or San Francisco, I decided to head toward the northern California coast. That decision made for a tricky little move to hook up with California highway 20. The exit for highway 20, off of I-80, was only two exits away, but walking that far along the freeway shoulder was too dangerous. I made up a sign which read, "Grass Valley." This was to discourage long distance travellers but encourage locals who would immediately recognize my intent to shift roads in a couple of miles.

It worked like a charm and after a mere half hour wait I had a ride with Kevin Oliver. With an empty horse trailer in tow we were off to Grass Valley and beyond!

Working out of nearby Nevada City, he was a snowplow operator for the California highway department. He was responsible for keeping the steep, narrow, and winding highway 20 from becoming snowbound. As the plow operator, Kevin knew the road better than anyone. The challenge of staying on the road while working at night in blizzard conditions, must have been formidable.

As a highway department employee, Kevin was called to San Francisco the day after the big earthquake in October, 1989. That was the quake which caused the collapse of a segment of the Oakland Bay Bridge. He, and other employees throughout the state, were called in to help with cleanup efforts there and elsewhere in the metropolis.

When I hopped out of Kevin's rig in warm, snow-free Penn Valley, I pulled out a new piece of cardboard. I continued to make signs for cities that weren't so far away. After my struggle to get across Nevada I had learned my lesson. The short ride strategy was working fine and Ralph Garcia took me to the next town, Yuba City.

In his late 20s, Ralph had lived in Yuba City all of his life. In fact, he had never even been out of the valley! He was impressed with my far ranging travels. I, in turn, was impressed with his patience at remaining in one place for so long.

A quick ride with Terry Lovelady brought me to Sutter junction, and then Jeff Brooks took me a few more miles to Colusa. Jeff's parents owned a nearby orange grove and he gave me a couple of the sweetest, juiciest oranges I'd ever tasted. It was a glorious day. The weather was cooperating nicely, the country was covered with farm fields and lush orchards, and I was enjoying short rides and meeting lots of people. It turned out that Jeff was my last short ride of the day.

It was a man named Manuel who stopped for me in Colusa. I rode with him for 85 miles, all the way to the junction of 20 and U.S. 101, near Ukiah. It was a good ride with a fascinating man. Manuel worked as a reporter for a California newspaper. His professional and personal life were intimately linked in the world of journalism. Trying to make sense out of politics, economics, the environment, and cultural events were all a part of his daily efforts to present the world to his readers.

The miles fell like dominos that day. Minutes after Manuel dropped me off, just north of Ukiah, William Baptiste pulled his truck over. He was thrilled to have some company for the 160 mile ride to Eureka, California. Tip.....crash. Another big domino hit the road!

The drive was a beautiful one. Dotted with small towns, U.S. 101 winds its way along steep river corridors and through the few remaining old growth redwood forests. William used to be a logger in those forests until he finally said "NO!" to the continuing destruction of an important part of our national heritage. Now he drives a truck, occasionally stopping along the road to savor what's left of the sweet, lush forest.

As a Vietnam veteran, like our old friend Mike Canfield of Kansas, William struggled with life in the aftermath of the war. In addition to continuing mental stresses, many of the physical injuries he sustained began creeping back as aches and pains. He told me that when he makes his fortune he'll spend the money on some northern California land. Then, if he chooses to work, it will be to tend his grove of trees and hillside of wildflowers.

We arrived in Eureka as night began to fall. William left me downtown. It was a nice, mild evening. I found a picnic table on the front lawn of the Humboldt County Courthouse and put it to good use. Enjoying cheese and crackers for dinner I watched the traffic go by on U.S. 101. It was a pastime I never tired of. It had been a long, successful day and I wasn't motivated to pursue many more miles. In Eureka I had the satisfaction of finishing another leg of my journey by reaching the west coast of the United States.

Finishing my meal, I walked slowly north down the sidewalk with my back to traffic. It was dark and I wasn't paying any attention to drivers as I held out my sign saying Arcata, which was only six miles away. It was the same sign I had used in Ukiah when William picked me up.

I was astonished when Ted Romo stopped. When I had finished loading my gear and fastening my seatbelt, a guy knocked on Ted's window. Ted rolled it down and the guy asked if he could get a ride with us to Arcata. He had seen my sign and was essentially riding on my coattails. It was a weird situation, one that had never happened to me before. Ted was cool about it and agreed to give him a ride.

Our unwelcome guest had just spent 14 days in jail for beating up his wife. Although not a threat to us, neither Ted nor I were thrilled about having this guy along for the ride. Fortunately, Arcata was only about 10 minutes away.

When we dropped our other passenger, Ted asked me what I was up to. I told him that my immediate concern was finding a place to camp that night. He had done a lot of hitchhiking during his younger years and knew my needs. He immediately invited me to his home for dinner, shower, and shelter. Even though he lived back in Eureka, what could I say? It was like manna from heaven. While Ted ran his errand in Arcata he contacted his wife Joan to warn her of a surprise guest that night.

At the Romo's dinner table that evening we talked about trips and geography. Their family took a big trip every summer to give their kids a taste of what North America had to offer. As they travelled they would pick up hitchhikers on occasion. While on their vacation during the previous summer they picked up a couple of people and hauled them all over northern Canada. I guess having me around wasn't that much of a novelty for them. I had an enjoyable time and a restful night.

Ted brought me to a good spot in Eureka. I found myself on the road to Arcata, again. It was early Sunday morning, that notoriously bad time to be hitchhiking. After a long wait I got a short ride in the back of a pick-up truck.

As I clambered in, the guy in the passenger seat stuck his head out the window and asked if I had any bud. In Humboldt County, California, and elsewhere I suppose, bud is a slang term for marijuana. Growing bud was one of the biggest money making propositions in Humboldt County. Farmers grew so much of it around there I expected the locals to harvest their own supply, like picking cherries. The guys in the truck must have been too lazy to bother and figured that by giving me a lift I'd pay them back with a joint. I wasn't packing any so had none to share. I rode to Arcata for free.

In Arcata, U.S. 101 was designed as a limited access freeway. I remained on the freeway shoulder despite warnings prohibiting pedestrians. I didn't really want to be there but felt I had no choice because there was almost no traffic coming down the entrance ramp where I stood. I feared reprisals from the California Highway Patrol for standing on the highway shoulder. During my wait there and additional walking, two patrolmen passed me by. One of them even smiled and waved. I was glad their strict reputation didn't hold true in every case.

It was a long wait and walk before Richard Gilliam stopped and brought me the ten miles to Trinidad. He bummed some gas money and I gave him a couple of dollars. He was extremely surprised at my generosity. He was expecting more like fifty cents. I was still reeling from my self-ishness outside of Reno and was trying to make up for it.

RICHARD GILLIAM
Trinidad, California

Two bucks was a bargain. Getting past Arcata was very tough, with a hitchhiker on every entrance ramp. There is nothing worse than a road-way littered with hitchhiking competition. People become desensitized at the sight, like when faced with dozens of panhandlers on a city street. They get sick of seeing them and simply start ignoring them.

While I was looking through the camera lens to snap Richard's photograph, I noticed a lit cigarette dangling from his lips as he dispensed gasoline into the tank. It's a wonder we're all not dead from explosions and conflagrations due to general stupidity and thoughtlessness. If I'd been torched at that gas station, my two bucks wouldn't have been such a bargain after all! My luck did continue though and we both made it to Trinidad.

Trinidad wasn't all that great of a place to stand. When Richard dropped me off there was already a man at the bottom of the entrance ramp trying to get a ride. I proceeded to walk down the ramp and along the highway until I was 150 yards past him. Not wanting to interfere with him getting a ride, I gave him plenty of room. The quicker he got a ride the sooner I'd be on my way, too. As we both stood there waiting, another man got dropped off on our crowded little corner of the world. I wondered why everybody was ending up here. Perhaps I had reached the legendary "ends of the earth!"

The newest hitchhiker walked up to me. We talked for a couple of minutes and he accepted some food I offered. He was a migrant worker of Hispanic origin, headed north to work in the fruit and berry farms of Oregon. All he had was a plastic garbage bag with a few clothes in it. He was all smiles and had a very positive attitude. We were all on the road, just doing what we had to do. When we finished chatting he moved on down the road past me as a courteous hitchhiker would normally do.

The guy in front of me finally gave up and disappeared on the road back into Trinidad. I grabbed my gear and moved into a better position closer to the base of the entrance ramp. I replaced him quickly so no one could swipe that prime spot. I had waited him out and was smug about my tenacity.

It was still a long time before Rich McLaughlin stopped. Rich was an archeology student at Humboldt State University in Arcata. He had noticed me a while ago as he headed south to run an errand. Surprised to see me still standing in Trinidad and sympathetic to the long waits I'd experienced that day, he offered to take me ten miles past the turn off to his house on Patrick Point. For that, I was thankful. He dropped me off in the small town of Orick.

In Orick, I found out what can happen if you don't have contingency plans for contingency plans. Rich's picture was the last exposure on the roll. As I went to load another roll of film, I was aghast when I couldn't find my stash. I tore everything apart. It wasn't there. I freaked! I frantically searched my memory for places I could have left it. The only possible place it could have been was at the Romo's. I called them back in Eureka and, sure enough, they found it in the room where I had slept. I had lucked out by taking their address and phone number with me when I had left that morning. They agreed to send it ahead to friends in Eugene, Oregon. I was not about to hitch the 40 miles back to Eureka. It had taken me six hours to get to Orick. Redoing those painstaking miles would have driven me mad!

I figured everything would be fine because I could use the remaining film in my other camera to get me to Eugene. Good assumption; bad reality. Later, when I sent that film off for developing, it was sucked into the black hole of the Postal Service, never again to be seen by human eyes. It was very disappointing to have missed recording photographs for some of the characters you'll be reading about in the next few pages.

After my search, panic, long distance phone call, and reassembly, I returned to U.S. 101 in Orick. There were no other hitchhikers around which saved me any competition for rides. It was a short wait.

Carl Miller picked me up but didn't say anything. He nodded his hello and I thought it was kind of strange, his being so quiet. I tried asking a few questions in an attempt to initiate a conversation on a topic of his interest. Eventually he loosened up and I learned he was a published author. He wrote fantasy books. His first novel was called Dragonbound. His most recent work was The Warrior and the Witch.

I think he had been so quiet earlier because he was busy designing fanciful worlds of monsters, sword masters, and voluptuous female warriors mounted upon faithful, winged white steeds. Carl seemed spacey or absent minded until you realized his intellectual capacity for organizing enough chimerical thoughts to fabricate the lives and lands which existed in his books.

Although he used to pick up hitchhikers quite often, he normally refuses to now. He didn't appreciate destitute riders hitting him up for cash. Usually happy to share a ride, he felt harassed when asked for a handout. I could sympathize. I hated it, too.

Carl got me to a great place just north of Crescent City, California, at the junction of U.S. 101 and U.S. 199. A couple of tough looking brothers stopped immediately. They were towing an old truck home to Brookings, Oregon. They were good old boys who did what they pleased and did what they could to avoid getting caught. The driver didn't even have a driver's license. Insurance? Who knew? Who cared? My luck was holding out. I had made it to Oregon without busting.

I got one more ride that day with another anonymous driver. He took me to a good spot a couple of miles north of Brookings. I was exhausted by then and didn't want to continue any farther that night. At 5:30 pm I went to bed in a patch of trees along the road. I was hoping to reach Eugene, Oregon, the following day. I lay awake for a little while anxiously anticipating seeing close friends who lived there. Content with my progress and confident about tomorrow, I drifted into a long, deep sleep.

If the morning of February 26 hadn't been so foggy and chilly, perhaps my muscles would have loosened up a little. My long sleep had practically paralyzed me. My stiff neck and back had turned all the normal movements of breaking camp and hitting the road into tortuous tasks. The physical stress of continual movement was beginning to accumulate once again.

Fortunately, I didn't have long to wait before Ron Callahan pulled up in his Datsun recreational vehicle. It's always a surprise when any kind of mobile home, RV, or camper stops. It happened less often than with any other type of vehicle or driver. I anticipated rides from Cadillacs long before I'd expect an RV to stop. Taking a stab at explaining why that was true led to the peer identity argument. Nearly all RV owners fall into the category of retired, conservative, upper-middle class people who liked to play bridge. My peers they are not, and none of them are willing to share a chat about their grandkids with me. That was unfortunate, for everyone.

Ron was not your stereotypical RV owner. Living in Medford, Oregon, he had recently landed a full time nursing job in Brookings. The reason he was on the road that morning, north out of Brookings, was to help out the hospital staff in little Bandon, Oregon, where they were short of qualified nurses. If he had had the energy, he could have easily found enough work for every minute of every day. Medical staff were hard to come by in southwest Oregon. His reward came, not through salary, but through the satisfaction of aiding people. His words had the ring of a platitude, but I believed it was an honest statement.

Ron was raised in Saginaw, Michigan, at the northern fringe of the industrial, midwestern "rust belt." In his younger days, he had always wanted to do a trip similar to mine but found himself trapped in a boring, factory job. When he finally realized his creative energy was being completely sapped and wasted, he quit his job to pursue painting, wood carving, hiking, carpentry, fishing, and his new career in nursing. Having escaped from the factory and the paycheck junkie syndrome, creativity was now the biggest motivating factor in his life.

We talked long on many subjects. There was a time in his nursing career when he had worked in a ghetto trauma center. The violence he witnessed there was incomprehensible to him. There, he found no end to the injustice of man against man. His move to Oregon was an attempt to distance himself from the tragedy of inner-city decay.

I mentioned the unusual negative feelings I had while travelling across South Carolina. He had been there too and shared my impressions of its racial tension and deep rooted mistrust.

We had a fundamental disagreement about how much room there was in the United States. Ron felt our country was still huge and uncrowded, while I felt slightly claustrophobic. Even in the western states, the population seemed to be increasing out of control. More and more farms were being paved over for parking lots. Semi-arid and desert lands with a low carrying capacity for a human population were being stampeded by easterners flooding the sun belt. That influx puts major stresses on the water, power, and wildlife resources. Those stresses can have wide ranging effects. Home and business air conditioning, excessive automobile use, gardening, and golf courses are but a few examples of activities that promote pollution and over-consumption of limited natural resources. As the population moves west to get away from the crowded cities back east, the countryside will become more and more like that which they are trying to escape from. Crowded, polluted, strife ridden, wildland free, urban areas wherefrom there will be nowhere left to escape to.

Ron's good nature led him to pick up more than hitchhikers. He did his best to aid abandoned animals. While travelling to different towns for work, he slept in his RV at state parks. While staying at them he discovered an interesting pattern. People would abandon their household pets "in the woods." Apparently people considered state parks "the woods." Assuming that their pets were wild animals the owners thought they would be able to survive without human care. Of course, Fido could do no such thing. Ron did what he could to find new owners for the unwanted pets he had rescued. In the vehicle with us was an abandoned beagle he was bringing to a friend. I thought it was great that he didn't wait around for someone else to take care of things. He was willing to just do what had to be done.

The excellent ride with Ron ended 80 miles north of Brookings in Bandon, Oregon.

Benji was the name of the man who took me into North Bend. He had some interesting thoughts on alcohol and drug abuse. Benji thought there should be a designated reservation where addictive substances were available in any amount, at no charge. That would enable all within the boundary fence a chance to destroy their lives, minds, or bodies as they, or the drug, dictated. Also available would be counseling services and medical help for those who had finally reached their limit and decided to dump their habit. With all treatment centralized in a few locations across the country, the expense would be far less than the present societal burden of addiction. He theorized it would save countless innocent lives on roads and in homes. The substance abusers would be out of the way, destroying their own lives without harming others.

Benji was on his way to an Alcoholics Anonymous meeting. He was well aware of the self-destructive nature of substance abuse and its effects on family. He wanted to help rid the country of its worst enemy, irresponsible use of addictive substances. It couldn't happen too soon for Benji His dream was for it to happen within his lifetime.

Benji dropped me off in the center of North Bend. It was a nice, warm day. I needed to stretch my legs a little so I walked north toward the edge of town. I had been making good time that day and was certain I'd be in Eugene by that evening.

I walked through the nice village to the beginning of a long bridge over the bay. With water behind me and tall fir trees on both sides of the road, I stood on a good shoulder to await my next ride.

In less than an hour I was riding out of North Bend with a young educator. Although he loved teaching, Paul Barthol of Walterville, Oregon, was getting burned out on education. Teachers were running scared and fleeing the profession. They couldn't do anything honest with students for fear of being sued, or otherwise harmed. "Education is a messy little business. There must be a better way to make a living and still help people." The sad words of a young, enthusiastic, unemployed teacher.

His present job search revealed a ridiculous priority within school systems; coaching. He'd been ruled ineligible for a number of high school positions because he lacked coaching experience. Apparently, a degree in education, worthless paper credentials piled on top of more credentials, extra classes to remain on top of things, attending mandatory continuing education courses where they beat the same dead horses over and over again, mean nothing to a potential employer. If an instructor couldn't show a high school baseball pitcher how to throw a curve ball, in addition to teaching him history, the instructor was rendered obsolete. Our school children become the big losers when people like Paul are forced out of the system.

All of this fascinating, but depressing talk brought me to the doorstep of Jim and Lynn Meacham in Eugene. Temporarily, home sweet home. For five days I basked in the luxury of intimate friends, while awaiting the arrival of the film I'd left at the Romo's, in Eureka.

By the time it arrived I was getting anxious to hit the road again. My back wasn't too sore, I had eaten as much food as I could take, and shared so many of my adventures with my friends that they would be glad to get rid of me.

After feeding me a big farewell breakfast and packing a lunch, friends Jim, Lynn, Paula and Dave brought me to the very eastern edge of Springfield, a town across the Willamette River from Eugene. It was Sunday morning, the 4th of March, day 69 since leaving Willow River. Hoping the worst of what winter had to offer was over, I was ready to head east, across the Oregon desert and into the northern Rocky Mountains.

March in the Willamette Valley of Oregon is a beautiful time of year. The winter rains and mild temperatures turn lawns and pastureland a brilliant green. Plants that were dormant during the short winter were starting to sprout or bud out. On state highway 126 I stood at the entrance to a cemetery. The skies were mostly gray and sent a gentle drizzle to earth. The long, lush grass of the cemetery lawn consumed the moisture with an unquenchable thirst. After an hour wait at this quiet spot on the edge of the city, the 145th ride of the trip approached. It promised to be the start of a big mileage day.

Wayne pulled his El Camino to a stop and opened up. An El Camino is one of those things that can't decide if its a pick-up truck or a car. It had a small interior for people and a small bed in back for hauling. My nylon pack cover was protecting my pack from the rain so I just threw it in back.

At 5'8", 240 pounds, Wayne was a big, burly guy. He had long, wavy white hair, dark rimmed glasses, and a thick white moustache. He claimed to have stood at that cemetery intersection himself a few times, waiting for a ride. I wasn't surprised. He looked as though he'd been on a lot of roads. Tough roads. He told me that he had spent two years as a "mission tramp." It was a great life, not having any worries or responsibilities, just travelling from one rescue mission to another to obtain food and shelter. He had spent so much time at the Eugene Mission he eventually became a staff member there and had to work for his keep!

Now retired and living in Moses Lake, Washington, he had recently won a court case with the Veteran's Administration. He had enlisted in the Army just after World War II. During his service career he had done a tour in Korea. While there he claimed to have gotten all busted up. Many years later he had gone to court to obtain a medical discharge and associated benefits. His case was successfully fought and he had fewer financial worries as a result.

Wayne was a slow moving character. He loved taking scenic drives and drove them well below the speed limit. Whenever there was someone behind him, anxious to get by, he pulled over to give them plenty of room to pass. He didn't drive any faster than 45 mph during the 100 mile trip to Sisters. That was quite a switch from the typical drivers I had experienced. A high percentage of drivers that picked me up liked to go fast. We were on a steep, wet, mountain road over Santiam Pass and I was secure in the knowledge that we wouldn't go flying off a cliff into oblivion due to a manic lust for speed.

The mountains surrounding Santiam Pass are a treasure trove of wonder. Wilderness areas abound along the summit of the Cascade Range. Millions of acres of old growth forest, pristine mountain lakes, glacier covered volcanic peaks, and ancient lava flows provide the backdrop for hiking, climbing, fishing, skiing, bird-watching or any of a thousand other recreational activities. Having lived in nearby Salem, I had taken advantage of those opportunities and feel qualified to say that this part of the country has a great deal to offer someone seeking nature at its finest!

As we slowly wound our way up and over the Cascade Range, Wayne related a hitchhiking incident he'd experienced in Washington state. Not long after picking up a hitchhiker, the rider brandished a tire iron he'd found on the floor of Wayne's car. He was after Wayne's wallet. Wayne was not a guy to be trifled with and he casually, but very effectively, responded with a karate chop to his rider's throat. That neutralized the would-be assailant, who suddenly found himself getting his hands broken by the new possessor of the tire iron. Wayne then dropped him off at a police station. It had not been a good day for that hitchhiker. My day was going much better and Wayne dropped me off in Sisters, Oregon, my hands intact.

I was on a roll of momentum. In just a few minutes Nathan Poetzl, 19, of Colorado Springs, Colorado, picked me up. Nathan was a student at the Eugene Bible College. It was a fine coincidence that he was heading the 350 miles to Boise, Idaho. That was precisely where I was going. This is another case where I can claim fortune from the misfortune of others. Nathan was going to rescue his girlfriend who was stranded at the Boise Greyhound bus station. She was coming to Eugene for a visit from Springfield, Missouri. Unfortunately, she was in Boise when the bus drivers went on strike. But, fortunately for her, and me, Nathan had a car and was generous enough to play taxi driver on a 700 mile round trip.

Nathan's life in Colorado Springs had revolved around the pursuit of outdoor recreation. The 14,000 foot peaks of the Colorado Rockies were his playground for hiking, climbing, and skiing. He appeared strong, wiry, and healthy from years of high mountain activity. While in high school he was involved in wrestling. He was good enough to be considered for scholarships at a number of colleges. Disregarding those opportunities he selected a Bible-based Christian college for his continuing education. His father was a pastor and Nathan wished to follow in his footsteps and join the Christian ministry.

In addition to his academic training, he was training for the real world by working at the Eugene Mission. It was quite a coincidence that my last two rides had been closely associated with the Mission. He was concerned about the physical and spiritual condition of the many people he served there. Homelessness, hopelessness, alcoholism, violence, emotional and mental illnesses, physical handicaps, and disease were the enemies that Nathan and other volunteers at the Mission were fighting. Through his efforts, and with the help of God, Nathan knew he could help make a difference in people's lives. He was learning that to change the world for the better it required personal involvement and dedication to a cause. It wasn't just going to happen on its own.

There was something inherently optimistic about this young man. He was compelled to take things as they came and tried to diminish the effects of the bad things with a positive attitude. He felt blessed by his family, lovely girlfriend, education opportunities, and his intrinsic abilities. He was deeply devoted to his faith and enjoyed the view he held from his perch on top of the world.

I was enjoying the view from my perch in the passenger seat. U.S. 20 from Sisters to Ontario, Oregon, is as pleasant a drive as I've ever been on. Leaving mountains like the Three Sisters, Mt. Jefferson, Mt. Hood, and Broken Top behind, the smooth highway struck out into the high, semi-arid, eastern plains of Oregon. The settlements are tiny and far apart in this gigantic wilderness.

The sky was partly cloudy. The sun, shining through broken clouds, illuminated the surrounding sagebrush and rocks in soft browns, yellows, blacks, and reds. Once in a while we would drive through the violent frenzy of rain and snow squalls. Coming out the other side of the squall we would face more gentle earth tone colors across views of twenty to thirty miles distant. By the time we had scaled Stinkingwater and Drinkwater Passes it was getting dark. We followed the crooked course of Malheur Creek into Idaho in complete darkness.

We arrived in Boise around 10:00 pm. It had been a 400 mile day and I'd had enough. Nathan dropped me off at a south central exit ramp. I laid down just off the freeway entrance ramp amongst road construction and old cow pies. The construction was claiming pastureland along the southern edge of Boise but I was able to find a little patch of grass. Sometimes I'm not very choosy about where I sleep. I didn't have the energy to walk around an unfamiliar interchange looking for a better place. It was flat, grassy, dry, reasonably discreet, and conveniently close to the freeway.

I hadn't set up the tent, so the following morning I crawled out of my sleeping bag into chilly, wet conditions. I was kind of cranky that morning. The constant din of engines and tires on pavement, in such close proximity to my bed, had interfered with my sleep. When I hit the road my luck was poor, adding to my crankiness. I ended up walking three miles, to the last Boise interchange, trying to escape the Monday morning rush hour traffic. I didn't think Boise had the population numbers to actually support a freeway traffic jam. It was an unusual welcome to the not quite so wide open spaces of the Rocky Mountain west.

I finally decided to stop walking and waited at Boise's easternmost interchange. It was poorly designed for my hitchhiking needs. The merging lane of the entrance ramp connected with the freeway on a bridge. There was no shoulder available for drivers to safely pull over. Wanting to be as visible as possible to people entering the freeway and those already travelling on it, I had to position myself carefully. I had to attract the attention of drivers entering the freeway before they built up too much speed. If they didn't see me and decide before they began merging it would be impossible for them to stop because of the bridge. For those already travelling the freeway I needed to allow plenty of distance between me and the merging lane. They needed some shoulder to work with or it would have been impossible for them to pick me up. To satisfy all these technical requirements I stood on the freeway very close to the interchange overpass.

After a brief wait I caught the attention of a driver as he had just turned onto the entrance ramp. When he slowed down, I quickly gathered my gear and turned to begin the 75 yard trudge up the grassy slope to the top of the ramp where I assumed he'd be waiting. Wrong! He casually wheeled his four-wheel-drive GMC Jimmy straight down the grassy hill to the shoulder where I waited, dumbstruck. I loaded my stuff while the Jimmy sat idling with its front wheels on the freeway shoulder and its rear wheels down in the ditch. After I had buckled myself in, and introduced myself to Bill Scantlin, he spun the wheels and we leaped out of the ditch, onto the pavement.

BILL SCANTLIN
Mountain Home, Idaho

Bill's display of anarchistic tendencies made me feel pretty good. Up until that little maneuver I had thought I'd seen it all from my roadside perspective. It felt great to still be able to experience such surprise, despite the jading of thousands of miles. I've got to give Bill credit, he surprised the heck out of me.

Bill's family had a huge ranch near Mountain Home, Idaho. They ran 5000 head of cattle. His involvement in the operation was as a buyer. Travelling the northwestern United States year-round, he purchased stock they could use as a guard against any genetic inbreeding amongst the herd.

I learned a lot about cattle ranching during that ride; corporate cattle ranching. There were nineteen employees, 2500 acres of private land plus public domain Bureau of Land Management land they used for free, as long as they took care of it. I'm not exactly sure what taking care of the land actually meant. It seemed like a rather ambiguous concept to me. The entire ranch was geared to a sub-contract for the Simplot Corporation. Because the ranch operated under a contract it had a guaranteed market. In other words, Simplot would automatically purchase all the livestock the ranch produced. This was no example of the poor, little, downtrodden American family farm, mortgaged up to the axles of their tractors. It was a big, booming business. The boom in Mountain Home would surely continue until Americans lost their taste for steak.

Except for my sorry presence, the Mountain Home exit was empty that morning. There was no snow at this elevation but I was being buffeted by a strong, freezing wind. The source of the wind was indeterminate. Surrounding me on three sides was the high, dry, Snake River Plain. To the north were the vast forests and mountains of the central Idaho wilderness. Cradled in the snowy peaks, 100 miles northeast of where I stood, was the elite playground for the rich, Sun Valley.

Desperate to find relief from the piercing wind I tried using a light pole as a wind break. If I stood sideways and sucked in my breath, I could almost become skinny enough to take advantage of its protection. I had to entertain myself because there was no activity in sight. No cars, people, or wildlife were available as a distraction from the wind. Even so my attitude was good and I felt sure a ride was forthcoming. It wasn't. After a cold, lonely two hour wait I began having visions of the interminable wait back in Cactus Springs, Nevada.

Traffic going east on I-84 was sparse. When a guy finally came down the entrance ramp I gave him a good, hard look. As he accelerated past me the hopeless feeling became further entrenched. When he suddenly hit the brakes I hit the sky with excitement. Sheldon Bluestein hadn't really planned on picking me up, but after getting a careful look at me and my stuff he decided to take the risk. He was a recreational equipment junkie and had noticed my Kelty backpack and gore-tex mountain parka. He had convinced himself to pick me up by thinking, "Any guy with equipment like yours can't be all bad!" Being properly prepared for the road had paid off in the unexpected dividend of product recognition.

Sheldon worked as a cartographer for the state of Idaho. In addition to many other similar interests, it was a remarkable coincidence that both of our careers included mapping for the Department of Revenue of two western states.

He loved outdoor pursuits and had written two books on hiking in Idaho's desert country and in the mountains of northern Idaho. He was enthusiastic about preserving desert areas from overuse and general degradation. The books included advice on how to step lightly when traversing fragile desert and alpine environments. Sheldon had an impressive grasp of the geography of the western states.

Along the way, Sheldon bought me lunch at one of his favorite cafes in Burley. He also wanted to show me tiny Declo, Idaho, home of state legislator, Denton Darlington. There was a joke in there somewhere. I think it would have been better appreciated if I'd been more familiar with the political climate of Idaho.

We rode together for over 200 miles to Blackfoot, Idaho, where we drove straight into a wet snowstorm. With the temperature hovering at 32°F, Sheldon left me at a grimy, sloppy interchange.

As I waited at the entrance ramp, a man driving a van stopped. He didn't have room for me in his vehicle but stopped anyway. He was a vendor/distributor of beef jerky and assorted snacks. Just in case I was hungry, he had stopped to offer me a handful of his product. I gratefully accepted his gift. That anonymous man warmed up the cockles of my heart on that cold, snowy afternoon. Was there no end to the surprises this trip would reveal? It was undoubtedly showing me how stifled and inadequate my imagination actually was.

After my little snack, a pick-up truck pulled onto the shoulder about 70 yards down the road. The driver had come across from the left lane and had taken a few extra yards to slow down under the slippery road conditions. Sam Poole was hauling scrap metal into Idaho Falls, 25 miles ahead. He made as many trips as possible each day and was paid in accordance with the amount of material hauled. He was in a bit of a rush because the weather was threatening to keep him from making another run that day. I, too, was pressing my luck by continuing into the bad weather and oncoming darkness.

My luck held in Idaho Falls with a ride in Ken Smith's Cadillac. Ken was essentially retired but helped his wife sell melaleuca health products. The products contain a derivative of the Australian melaleuca plant, "the wonder from down under." Its medicinal properties could apparently cure everything from diaper rash to high blood pressure. The distribution scheme worked on an Amway-like pyramid basis. He was a very friendly guy, just doing his thing, but I wasn't quite convinced of melaleuca's miraculous healing potential. I'm such a cynic.

Ken lived in tiny Island Park, Idaho, just south of West Yellowstone, Montana on U.S. 20. Ken dropped me off near his home.

The weather was particularly unpleasant at Island Park's 6000 foot elevation. To the north were the 7000 foot passes and 11,000 foot peaks of the continental divide. To the east and southeast were the summits of the Grand Tetons and the high plateau of Yellowstone National Park. It was like standing in the middle of a snow factory. Snowflakes that seemed to be the size of autumn maple leaves were piling up all around. I was lucky there was no wind that afternoon. Any kind of wind would have molded the snow into impregnable drifts.

Primarily a summer tourist town, most of the businesses in Island Park were still closed for the winter season. The only place to stand and hitchhike was at the driveway entrance to the only open gas station in town. The snow was piled five feet high everywhere else, with no room between the snowbanks and the road. While I stood there, waiting for the rare vehicle to go by, I peered through the curtain of falling snow, seeking a place to set up my tent. I didn't expect a ride. In fact, I didn't even expect to see any more cars pass by on the highway. The cars that were going by were heavily laden with snow on their roofs and hoods. Dirty brown ice clogged their wheel covers and fenders. They crept along at 25 mph. Their window defrosters on full blast, windshield wipers working hard, head-lights on, drivers hunched over their steering wheels trying to distinguish between the white of the road surface and the white wall of snow that rose out of the ditch. The weather was so foul that no people in their right minds would be out in it, except maybe skiers. They craved the white crystal stuff, like a bad drug.

Four guys, in a rented Chevy Suburban, pulled into the gas station to get some beer. Even though I was practically invisible, I made sure they got a good look at me smiling and waving and appearing extremely enthu-siastic. They had plenty of room in the vehicle and invited me in. Charlie, Jeff and Dave worked for auto manufacturers in Detroit, while Scott did interior design in West Palm Beach, Florida. They were old college bud-dies and enjoyed meeting out west each year for a week of skiing.

Before the boys picked me up the weather really had me worried. I was overjoyed when they stopped and even more so when they revealed their destination. They had been down skiing at Grand Targhee for the day and were returning to their rented cabin in the Gallatin Canyon, just out-side of Big Sky, Montana. That fit perfectly into my agenda because Big Sky was my next scheduled stop!

It was too early to celebrate, however. We weren't home yet. There was still 80 miles of rough road to battle before we'd be tucked safely into our cribs.

U.S. 191, between West Yellowstone and Bozeman, Montana, was treacherous under the best of weather conditions. I should know after having spent three years travelling between the two frontier type towns. Upon completing my hitchhiking trip to Alaska, I immediately moved to the Big Sky area, just north of Yellowstone, to become a ski bum. The locale is perfect for skiing but bad for driving. Snowbound for at least five months out of the year, the beauty of the surrounding mountain tops belie the dangers of an icy roadway for as many months. Living along the Gallatin River, whose jagged course the highway follows, I had witnessed the terrible driving conditions that ultimately took many lives.

THE BOYS
Big Sky, Montana

The conditions on that night were so bad that state highway officials must have strongly considered a complete highway closure. Throughout the drive, my only solace was the size and four-wheel-drive capability of the vehicle. As long as Dave kept the rig on the road I knew we could climb the divide between the Madison and Gallatin rivers. I sat in the back, with my seat belt snug, flanked by Charlie and Jeff, and drank beer. I assumed the only thing safer was a motel room in West Yellowstone. I, however, was willing to take a gamble for the chance to wake up in Big Sky.

By the time it got dark we were driving between 35 and 40 mph, all alone on the road. The snow was accumulating at over an inch an hour. The rising sun would bring a serious powder morning. There wasn't a skier in the region who wasn't getting ready to make first tracks on the mountain!

The final thirty miles were intense. There were no businesses to stop at to take a break. Any of the scenic turnouts available during the summer were now buried under four to five feet of snow. We were making our own first tracks in the roadway. There was no other traffic going our direction and we saw just a couple of trucks coming from the opposite direction. All of us acted as back-seat drivers, peering through the ice encrusted windshield, trying to help Dave see the road. We were relieved to see the final mileposts as we approached the cabin. We had survived the perilous drive and still had beer left over!

When we arrived at the cabin the guys proved their expertise at vacationing, for each had his task to perform and set about doing it. From unloading the car and putting stuff away, to building a fire and preparing dinner, they did everything efficiently.

I telephoned an old friend, Dave Gentholts, who lived nearby. He could taxi me over to his house in about an hour. In the meantime, my hosts at the cabin had invited me to join them for a spaghetti dinner. The talk at the table centered on skiing. Knowing the area intimately I found myself wishing I'd had my skis along so I could have made a few runs with them the following day. I wondered how much attention I would have garnered hitchhiking in South Carolina with skis sticking out of the top of my pack!

Silence dominated the outdoors. The snow acted as a sound insulator, or more accurately, a sound vacuum. Any sound produced was sucked into and muffled by the blanket of white. Dave drove noiselessly up to the cabin in his tall four-wheel-drive Ford. Snow billowed ten feet into the air as he plied his course. High suspension clearance was an absolute necessity under those conditions.

It was the kind of night Montana was made for. A cozy log home made warm by a fragrant pine fire, a pot of tea, and friendship awaited the arrival of my travel stressed bones. Dave and his wife Jane opened their arms to welcome this nomad, as they had done many times before.

With the help of some outstanding rides I had come an unbelievable 900 miles in two days. I may have been in western Montana facing winter once again, but couldn't have felt more at home.

March 8 found me continuing north on U.S. 191, headed for Bozeman. Seeing me standing in Big Sky waiting for a ride was nothing new for the local residents. I'd done it many times before. An acquaintance, Jean Palmer, and her son Jordan, stopped and brought me to a friend's house in Bozeman. She readily admitted that if she hadn't already known me she would not have picked me up.

The next two weeks would be easy street for me. I knew my way around having hitched nearly every road in western Montana. Friends were scattered from Big Sky in the south to West Glacier in the north. I would be visiting someone every hundred miles or so, until I got to Canada. I planned on taking my sweet time going north because winter was still hanging around. I didn't think it too wise to tangle with a lingering Canadian winter, if it could possibly be avoided.

I left Bozeman on March 9 and headed for Helena, the capital city of Montana. I was beginning the 74th day of the trip. Shy Jim Cadwallader took me part way across town to the freeway entrance ramp on I-90. Another short ride in a car full of backwoods folks got me to Belgrade, the next exit.

One of the most satisfying things about hitchhiking in Montana is the freedom to walk along the freeway shoulder without the fear of harassment from law enforcement. There are no signs at each entrance ramp listing all the restrictions pertaining to highway right of way usage. In Montana, freedom blew in the wind.

The sign I carried said, "HELENA." It attracted Robert Wood's attention and he picked me up. A student at Rocky Mountain College in Billings, he was transporting a repossessed car from Billings to Helena. It was his spring break job. Driving around the state for a week delivering cars sounded to me like a good way to make money.

Robert was an aspiring actor. He was a theater arts major with an emphasis in classical stage acting. Among the roles he'd played so far was

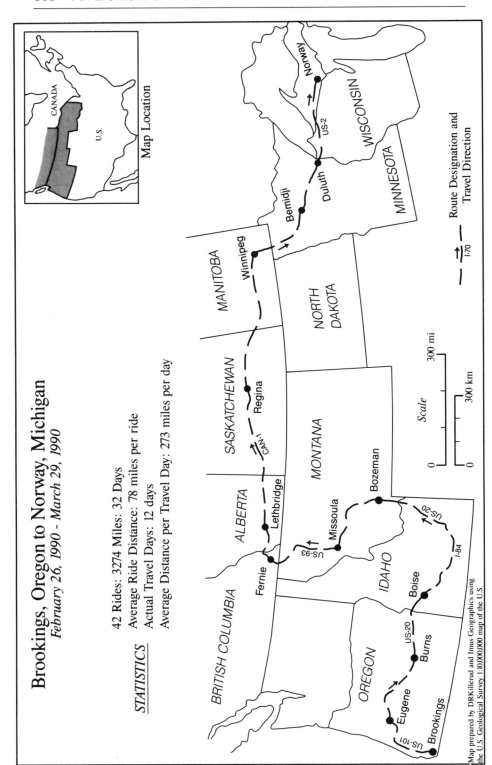

Brookings, Oregon to Norway, Michigan
February 26, 1990 - March 29, 1990

STATISTICS

42 Rides: 3274 Miles: 32 Days
Average Ride Distance: 78 miles per ride
Actual Travel Days: 12 days
Average Distance per Travel Day: 273 miles per day

Map prepared by DR Killerud and Imus Geographics using the U.S. Geological Survey 1:10,000,000 map of the U.S.

John Merrick, the Elephant Man. There were no special effects nor make-up in that particular production. The role required Robert to distort his facial features and motor capabilities to imitate the debilities of the character. It became an extremely stressful situation for him, both emotionally and physically. The character became a large part of his personal life. He was pleased to have successfully faced the challenge of Merrick's character, but was relieved when the show finally closed.

One of Robert's goals was to establish a community theater that would bring certain biblical parables to life. He claimed to have a liberal interpretation of the Bible. According to Robert, some of his interpretations and imagery were a little too bold for the administrators of the Rocky Mountain College stage.

Robert dropped me off in Helena at a friend's house. I continued to be amazed at the variety of personalities I had encountered thus far: cartographers, deep-sea divers, exotic dancers, authors, laborers, and now an actor. It was so exciting to anticipate the next character. You could never guess, so the game remained new with each ride.

Helena is a lovely town. It was founded on the strength of a gold rush in the mid-1800s. The downtown area remains crammed into an old mining feature named Last Chance Gulch. Surrounding the gulch, clinging to hills that rise 500 feet from the valley floor, are giant Victorian homes and mansions. Remarkably preserved by caring owners and an arid climate, the houses were built in the days when fortunes were made, and often lost, in speculative gold and copper mining.

As the sun went down and the city lights flickered in the cold night air, Helena looked magnificent from any viewpoint.

A few miles to the east were the waters of the mighty Missouri River. Back in 1804 the Lewis and Clark expedition had its first encounter with the Rocky Mountains at a point 25 miles northeast of Helena. Navigating the river in their canoes they were stunned by the towering cliffs on both banks. They named this impressive handiwork by the Missouri River, Gates of the Mountains.

On yet another cold, snowy Monday morning, I waited for over an hour in Helena before getting a ride with Jeff Westfall. Jeff was a student at the University of Montana, in Missoula, and was returning to take a final exam from one of my former professors. (I had left the ski resort business back in 1982 to pursue a graduate degree in geography at the U of M.) Missoula also happened to be the next city on my Montana tour.

In addition to being a student, Jeff was a member of the National Guard. During the summer he also fought fires for the Forest Service to help pay for school. A true outdoorsman, he talked about his love of hunting. Even though he hunted with a rifle at times, he claimed the greatest challenge in sport hunting was with a bow and arrow. He had spent years tramping around the mountains of western Montana. Jeff loved the life there and made it clear that he had no intention of making his home elsewhere upon his graduation from college.

Like Russ, back in Missouri, Jeff was another driver who felt compelled to give someone else a lift because of recent car trouble. His car had broken down earlier that year and he needed to hitchhike. Some extended waits for rides convinced him to pick up hitchhikers in the future. A lot of drivers never think about stopping until they're the one on the side of the road, begging a lift. Lessons like that are hard to unlearn.

It was day 78, 9400 miles into my journey and I was happy to be in Missoula. I celebrated by stopping at my favorite bakery, tea house, and a little Greek restaurant to get a gyros sandwich for lunch. That evening I went to a bluegrass concert and saw a bunch of old friends. It felt as though I had never even been away.

While visiting the Geography department at the University, I was told they needed a temporary cartography instructor for the next winter and spring quarters. I told the department head I was available and was offered the position. Just my luck. Now I didn't need to worry about starving to death next winter!

On March 14 my friends Bonnie and Jim set me on U.S. highway 93, headed north to Kalispell, Montana. I faced yet another gray and gloomy day on the road. At least it wasn't snowing.

University of Montana student Gregg Webster, of Ronan, took me along for the scenic drive north. I'd hitched and driven U.S. 93 dozens of times before. It is a beautiful road. After climbing out of the Clark Fork River valley it enters the Flathead Indian Reservation. Within the reservation sits the Moiese National Bison Range, in addition to two other national wildlife refuges. As you crest the hill past the bison range, the broad Flathead River valley stretches out in front of you for forty miles. The valley is bounded on the southeast by the Mission Mountains. During the winter and spring, that mountain wilderness is a stark, snowy landscape of jagged, 10,000 foot peaks. It is an unforgettable sight.

Gregg dropped me off in Pablo, a small town just south of magnificent Flathead Lake. There was a lot of traffic going past but the problem I faced was a lack of shoulder space for drivers to pull over and stop. It didn't seem to be much of a problem for my next driver.

As I hitched north, the entrance to the Salish-Kootenai Community College was immediately behind me. A car heading south turned into the college parking lot behind and to my left. It was a 1971 Datsun, or at least something of that ilk. If it had had a number painted on its doors I would have thought it was the loser of a demolition derby! It was unencumbered by things like an exhaust system, headlights or grill. It had dents from every conceivable angle and the windshield was threaded with cracks. I could hardly tell if the oil spewing out of the car was burning or just going from the crankcase to the air without any physical alteration from a liquid to a gas. Burning implies some sort of combustion but I don't think that was what was happening.

The driver stopped behind me and rolled down the window. Obnoxious little cars like that put me in a foul mood. It didn't look like he was going my direction so I didn't feel like talking. He was distracting me from the business of getting a ride.

He asked where I was headed and I replied Kalispell. He said he couldn't get me that far but was willing to backtrack the seven miles to Polson at the southern tip of the lake. The young student's name was Tim Fromm. He didn't have class scheduled for twenty more minutes and wanted to help me out. I was impressed and felt like a jerk for silently condemning both car and driver at first sight.

I wondered how many times I'd need to be reminded of the goodness of people and change my negative attitudes. Perhaps my thick skull would eventually get thin and I'd even learn a thing or two after having the lesson beaten into me five or six times. Without the benefit of a trip such as this, my eyes probably would have always been critical and hateful. It's so sad to become jaded. Perhaps in some cases blindness is a blessing. If we were blind, we couldn't judge books, or rides, by their covers.

I figured the spot in Polson was a good one. I was wrong. After an hour wait I started walking. Again, a driver going the opposite direction turned back to give me a lift. Kyle Mattson could get me across town, and considerably farther, as it turned out.

Kyle was missing at least ten days out of his life. Back in 1979, he was drunk for five days before being involved in a serious auto accident.

During the five days following the accident he was comatose. He wound up with some amnesia and lots of aches and pains. Compared to some of the crowd he used to hang out with, Kyle got off reasonably well. One guy fried his brains on acid (LSD) and another hung himself in jail. The inner cities of our country aren't the only places where substance abuse creates an atmosphere of hopelessness. Rural Montana has plenty of its own problems with unemployment, domestic violence, and serious substance abuse. Looking upward, toward the incredibly beautiful surrounding mountains against a blazing blue sky, it seemed like we were in paradise. Turning my gaze closer to the ground, I could see that all of the earthbound problems of humanity remained.

Ten years after the accident, Kyle was still trying to get back on his feet. He was definitely dealing with some loneliness and emotional stress. He hoped to snap out of his torpor by applying for admission to the community college. Going to class every day, thinking about projects and assignments would be just the thing to keep his mind busy.

My cross-town ride ended up being 55 miles; 110 miles out of Kyle's way. He had a lot to talk about and put the hour of driving to good use. We talked all the way into Kalispell. I hoped the sacrifice he had made for me in terms of time and fuel consumed was equaled by my inadvertent conversational therapy.

Occasionally, my trip exposed personal suffering. It certainly isn't limited to hardship cases on the road. None of us are immune to pain and suffering. It is just the unfriendly portion of our emotional make-up that keeps us human.

I visited in Kalispell for a day then left for West Glacier. A short ride from Gerrard Byrd got me to tiny Martin City.

Natural history and documentary movie producer Ron Shade brought me from Martin City to beautiful Glacier National Park. Ron's enviable profession required him to explore the park and record wildlife roaming in their untamed habitat. There are so many nice places in North America with great scenic value, but I think Glacier is one of the most satisfying.

Glacier Park is actually a misnomer. There are only a few active glaciers in the park, and they are only tiny remnants of the once vast rivers of ice that carved the lush valleys and jagged summits. The wildlife, high alpine lakes, waterfalls, and snow capped peaks are the true scenic draw, not the glaciers.

When I was a graduate student in Missoula I applied for a summer season, geographic research position in Glacier Park. I got the job and returned every June for the next four years. My good fortune and youthful exuberance enabled me to hike, climb, and thoroughly explore the million acres of wilderness parkland.

In West Glacier I found myself at home again. I considered it home because I returned there on a more consistent basis than anyplace else except for Willow River. I never live in one place for very long. My desire to experience new people, places and things keeps me moving. When I do stay in a locale for a few months it starts feeling like home. My criteria in defining the term home is quite different from most people's. Many people complain of being trapped in the town they grew up in. The adventures they face are with clients at work, paying bills, and raising their children. For some its more like a prison sentence than a life.

Each lifestyle requires sacrifices and an occasional longing for something different. While some crave the chance to get away I often find myself pitching about in the rough seas of life without the anchor of a place to call my own. Sitting in the living room of Carl and Lindy Key, looking out the window at the tiny residential area of West Glacier buried under four months of heavy mountain snows, I felt about as close to home as I ever have.

A few days later I continued north, headed for southeastern British Columbia. Whitefish, Montana, was about twenty-five miles from West Glacier. I had been dropped off by my friend Terry, who lived there. I was still worried about the weather. Although it was a clear, warm, 21st of March when I left Whitefish for the Canadian border, there was enough snow left on the ground to remind me that spring had not quite sprung. People were still skiing up at the Big Mountain ski resort that was in view from my wait spot.

The last time I'd waited for a ride in that same spot, going north on U.S. 93, was back in 1979, with my friend Chuck, on our way to Alaska. It had taken us a long time to get out. We became so bored waiting around, that as a distraction, we scrounged a 3' by 5' piece of cardboard and made the largest hitchhiking sign anybody had ever seen. It simply read, CANADA, in big letters. It was pretty entertaining for us and the passing traffic. I only needed a normal sized sign this time. It read, "EUREKA."

Gordon Sands brought me ten miles out of Whitefish into the middle of nowhere. The highway was a good two lane road and the mountains on either side were covered with thick forests. There were no houses in sight. I knew they were around but were secluded within the cover of woodlands and hills.

Gordon had been raised in the heavily forested area and enjoyed the peace and quiet the environment offered. He said it was so quiet at his place that he was able to hear the snowflakes fall to the ground. Employed as a logger, the end result of his daily labor was a clear-cut portion of a mountain slope. Clear-cuts are an unpopular scene, not only for most people, but for Gordon too. Those conflicting factors contributed to a kind of non-clinical schizophrenia in Gordon. Although he worked in the lumber industry and had a vested interest in the access to public timberlands, he also considered himself an environmentalist and believed there had been a lot of ill-conceived timber sales and harvests. Much of western Montana is under the public domain, managed by the U.S. Forest Service and Bureau of Land Management. Loggers and environmentalists are constantly butting heads over the proper use of these public lands. The polarization that exists in the small surrounding timber communities, regarding forest usage, is really sad. Gordon was stuck in the middle.

The place Gordon dropped me was two miles short of the nearest village. There was almost no traffic so I started walking. Forty-five minutes later I arrived in Olney, Montana. The next wide spot in the road, lucky enough to be blessed with a name, was twenty miles farther. I had no desire to walk there so opted to wait in Olney.

Seventy-year-old Ella West was heading home to Eureka, after visiting her sister in Whitefish. The first thing she said when I climbed into her car was that her son would kill her if he knew she was picking up a hitchhiker. I couldn't make any promises not to tell.

Ella was a warm, wonderful, enthusiastic, great-grandmother. She had lived her entire life in Eureka. She and her husband had operated an outfitting business and hunting camp in the Bob Marshall Wilderness Area for forty years. "The Bob" is one of the largest wilderness areas in the United States. Located just south of Glacier National Park, it runs along the continental divide for about fifty miles.

Over the course of her forty hunting and fishing seasons in the woods, she had whipped up a lot of pancakes, steaks, and eggs for clients over a stove in a canvas wall tent. Conditions had to be tough, even dangerous at times, working deep in the wilderness. Grizzly bears, freak, early season blizzards, and dependence on mules and horses for transportation required a great deal of self reliance. She had apparently enjoyed that rugged lifestyle, despite the hardships. Perhaps she enjoyed it because of them.

ELLA WEST
Eureka, Montana

Since retiring, Ella had found time to travel outside her Montana corner of the world. Among her travels she claimed Norway, England, Hawaii, Alaska, Mexico, and a recent trip to the Seychelles, just northeast of Madagascar. Her favorite trip of them all was a raft excursion down the Colorado River through the Grand Canyon. Even after all of the exciting things she had done, the Grand Canyon was more than just a tour. The fantastic colors of the desert, intimidating cliffs, thrilling sections of whitewater, and calm reflective moments in the warm sun made it the adventure of a lifetime. Next on her list of places to go were Australia and New Zealand.

It was a real privilege getting to know Ella. In Eureka, she bought me a cup of tea and a pastry before taking me the remaining seven miles to the border crossing at Roosville. It was a warm, sunny afternoon when we arrived at the border. Things were going great. Now, all I had to do was convince the Canadian Customs officials that I wasn't insane to attempt hitchhiking across their country in what, for them, was still winter.

Chapter Six

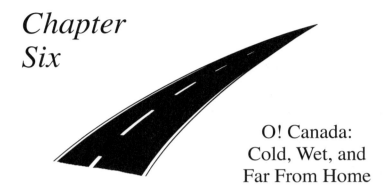

O! Canada: Cold, Wet, and Far From Home

Customs. It's amazing how the word conjures up images of baggage and personal searches, sneaky questions, document checks, long waits in line and hopes that you aren't forgetting to claim something that would ultimately get you thrown into jail. Even if you are the cleanest, most honest person in the world, no, make that the entire universe, a customs agent can make you feel as unwelcome as the plague.

I knew what to expect. A person on foot at the Canadian frontier, in the middle of nowhere, makes even the most relaxed customs agent sit up and take notice. They try to remain calm but just can't help anticipating what might come up on the computer screen as they key in your name. They never just wave you through like they do if you're Mr. and Mrs. Middle Class America in your brand new Ford. They just know something will be wrong and they can go home from work knowing they've saved their country from being violated by an outlander.

Following a diatribe like that, you'd expect an anecdote from travelling hell. For now, the official that took care of me was relatively casual. He still ran through all the usual checks and took a quick look at my gear, but found nothing. There was nothing to find but smashed clothing. He checked my available cash. They do that because they can deny entrance based upon how rich you are. I was carrying a couple hundred bucks in travellers checks because I knew of the cash requirement. That was it. Everything was cool that time and I strolled through the gate and into the huge expanse of Canada.

So, there I was in Roosville, British Columbia. There wasn't a village anywhere nearby. Roosville was just a port of entry. I was twenty-three miles south of the next highway junction in Elko. Once in Elko I would turn east, taking Crow's Nest Pass over the Canadian Rockies. There were very few cars passing through customs that Wednesday afternoon. Having hitched this same stretch of road with Chuck, I knew traffic would be sparse and rides would be slow to come. I started out walking and enjoyed the scenic beauty of the surrounding farmland and adjacent mountains.

I was surprised by the lack of snow that remained on the valley floor. The ditch along the road harbored the occasional dirty patches of snow amongst matted brown grass and weeds. Higher up along the hillsides and summits, the snow continued to battle for survival against the inevitable spring thaw. It was the 21st of March, the first day of spring, and the snow was fading fast. As I walked along, the air temperature increased considerably. It was a gorgeous day, far warmer than I had expected. I had dressed for much colder temperatures and was forced to remove my thermal underwear. There was so little traffic I changed clothes right there on the highway shoulder. Nobody drove by while I dropped layers of clothing.

Much of the traffic that did exist consisted of truckers and they had no time for the likes of me. I wound up walking about three miles before Chris Thompson stopped. He'd been visiting his girlfriend in Kalispell and was returning to his home in Fernie, British Columbia. I was happy to be off my feet. The synthetic fleece lined "duck" boots I wore weren't really suited to long distance walking and my feet had quickly blistered on the hot pavement.

Chris had only lived in southeastern British Columbia for two months. He owned a company in Fernie that manufactured, and rebuilt, electric motors. Prior to that he'd been an electrical contractor in the Cayman Islands which are located south of Cuba. In addition to the tropical temperatures, his favorite thing about the islands was their tax free status. I'm not sure how the government there financed any public services. It sounded too good to be true. There probably weren't any public services.

We hit Elko and took a right turn to go east on highway 3. By the time we reached Fernie, fifteen minutes later, the weather had taken a turn for the worse. We had started the climb into the mountains and were met by cold rain. As I stood waiting on the east edge of Fernie, that little, wet slap in the face was an important reminder of how fickle mountain climates can be. I was angry at myself for stashing my warm clothes too soon. Putting my thermal underwear back on under those poor conditions was a complicated and uncomfortable prospect.

As the late morning clouds gathered closer around my head, Rob Wadewest gave me shelter in his pick-up truck. He was coming off his graveyard shift at the coal mine. The area was rife with mines and Rob's job was driving a 170 ton rock truck. It sounded like a dangerous thing to do on the night shift. It must have been tough keeping his eyes open between 3:00 and 6:00 am.

I don't see how people can do it. I worked a night shift for a couple of months, and I couldn't have devised a worse torture if I'd had a computer program to help me. I got so little sleep that my life literally fell apart. It was like being on drugs, twenty-four hours a day. I eventually had to quit the job to get my internal clock fixed.

It was a short ride with Rob and he left me in Sparwood. Snow flurries swirled around me for forty-five minutes before John Talerico pulled over in his brand new Nissan 240Z. I couldn't remember if I'd ever gotten a ride in a new sports car before and was quite surprised when he stopped. I looked forward to a smooth, fast, 130 mile ride into his home town of Lethbridge, Alberta.

While I ooohed and aaahed at the surrounding mountain scenery, John played the tour guide. There was a lot of mining history in the area and John knew about most of it. The most fascinating tidbit was about a rock avalanche that had entombed an entire town. The Frank Slide so completely devastated the town that nobody ever bothered trying to dig anything out. The government re-cut the highway through the rubble and left the rest as it lay. It became a natural memorial to the lives of hundreds of families who never knew what hit them. It was an eerie feeling to pass through that small corner of Alberta knowing we were surrounded by the unmarked graves of hundreds of people.

The ride with John had been extremely pleasant. We had negotiated Crows Nest Pass without incident. The mountains may not have given us too much trouble but the weather conditions on the high plains near Lethbridge were seriously threatening. A large drop in the temperature allowed the snow to adhere to the pavement making for treacherous driving. We arrived safely in Lethbridge, and said our goodbyes in the midst of rapidly accumulating snow.

Luckily, Rory Lorencz stopped immediately and took me the nine miles to Coaldale.

Rory was a classic car collector on his way to look at a prospective purchase. I was envious because he owned a 1956 Chevy show car. I love old cars and once owned a beat up 1960 Chevrolet Impala. As close as it ever got to a show was on the red carpet of an auction block. When the gavel fell, I had lost $700.00 out of my original investment. With that sort of business acumen, it should be obvious why I'm hitchhiking.

In Coaldale, Walter and Josephine Grigor, a wonderfully sweet elderly couple, stopped and took me a few miles farther, to Barnwell, Alberta. I was hoping they'd invite me in for the night. I didn't ask, although I probably should have. It was dusk and the flurries of earlier that day had turned into a raging blizzard. Under those weather conditions I don't think they would have turned me down. They were charming folks and I was wishing for more of an opportunity to hear about their long lives on the high prairie.

Bill Thomsen brought me a few more miles to Taber, where he turned north. Now, I was in trouble. Those readers from the western plains will understand the fury I faced that night.

I was on the eastern edge of Taber, Alberta. It was completely dark and the snow was flying horizontally on a razor-sharp wind coming off the mountains to the west. Much to my dismay, the temperature was dropping fast. Most of my warm clothes were still in my pack from when I did my roadside striptease back in Roosville.

I stood on the side of a two lane road with no place for a driver to pull over. Under those blizzard conditions I knew I was invisible, even though I was near a street light. It would have been impossible to set up my tent because the wind was gusting at about 45 mph and there was no wooded protection in sight. But then, my visibility was limited to about forty yards.

I stood there for a while, the wind blasting ice crystals into my eyes, hoping someone would notice me. A pick-up truck drove by on the frontage road that ran parallel to highway 3 and pulled into a nearby farm. After about ten minutes the truck came out and I flagged down the driver, Emory. I was desperate. I told him I needed some kind of shelter from the wind for the night. I asked if I could use one of the outbuildings on his farm. He said he only worked at the farm as a hand, but assured me the owner would accommodate me.

With my hopes buoyed I ran over to the house to meet Jerry Holtman. He looked to be about forty-years-old. I caught him in the middle of dinner. He had been delivering calves all day and was using this brief respite to squeeze in a meal.

I told him of my journey and present predicament. Despite his frantic pace, he welcomed me and was happy to offer lodging for as long as I needed. There was a second house on the property that had just been vacated by some renters. Jerry brought me over there and showed me the accommodations. It had a kitchen, plumbing, and a perfectly functioning furnace. He apologized for the absence of furniture and asked if it would be okay. Out on the road, a few minutes earlier I had been hoping for the chance to sleep in a hayloft. Now I was trying to convince Jerry that I was being well taken care of with or without furniture. I told him I didn't need any furniture because all I was going to do was sleep.

I curled up in my sleeping bag, right in front of the heater. As it pumped out warm air I lay listening to the wind roar past the little house on the prairie. The snow clicked against the windows in a vicious staccato. It had been a fearful evening. Now completely safe, my heart beat rapidly as I considered my good fortune. It took a long time for my mind and body to settle down. Even after I did, I slept fitfully while the fury of the blizzard pounded the prairie, only a few feet away from my head.

The next morning I went out looking for Jerry to thank him for his hospitality. I found him out in the yard and he said that if I wanted to stay until the weather had warmed a little, I was more than welcome to do so. The temperature was terribly cold at around 10°F but at least the snow had stopped falling. My slow pace through Montana had made me restless and I wanted to speed across the huge farms and ranches of Saskatchewan and Manitoba. I thanked him for his generosity, but hit the road, hoping to reach warmer temperatures to the east.

Things sure looked different at the east edge of Taber in the bright sunshine. It had snowed four to five inches during the night although the wind had blown most of it away. The traffic that went by on the road had compacted some of the snow into ice. The wind carried what remained of loose snow across the icy road surface and polished it to a crystal-like sheen. I wore at least five layers of clothing against the cold wind. I was seriously reconsidering Jerry's offer of staying another day when George Kambeitz slid to a stop just behind me. I climbed in and was committed to continue east, back into winter.

George still lived on the same farm his grandfather had settled in 1907 south of Grassy Lake. He claimed the only way to be a successful farmer was to commit your life to it. It wasn't a career you could jump into and out of. It took years of understanding and care to build and/or maintain an efficient operation. His successful operation included surface irrigated spring wheat, flax, and sunflowers.

It was a short wait in Grassy Lake. Fred Clarke pulled over and offered me a ride to Medicine Hat, Alberta. Fred was an optimistic, high energy man who acted as though he was thrilled to be alive. He lived in Lethbridge and traveled southern Alberta as an electrical inspector of irrigation equipment.

When he was sixteen-years-old, Fred fell in love with a fourteen-year-old girl. It must have been true love because as I spoke to him they'd been married for thirty-seven years. He had put his kids through college and was proud of their successes. His family was, unquestionably, the most important thing in his life. They clearly contributed to his enthusiastic outlook on life.

FRED CLARKE
Medicine Hat, Alberta

Fred left me in the center of Medicine Hat with my own positive outlook. Although the sun was shining brightly, it was too cold to stand in one spot. I decided to start walking immediately assuming I'd have a ride in no time. My luck had been so good in Canada thus far I was feeling cocky. The east edge of town was a three mile walk and much to my dismay that was exactly how I got there. Beyond that, there was nothing but tiny towns spread far apart. I wasn't about to head off on foot into the seemingly boundless prairie. I quit walking and settled in for a windy wait. It was still too cold to stand in one spot, but I was left with no alternative.

The wind seems to be ever present out on the road. It is one of those extremes you have to deal with between each ride. It doesn't matter what part of the country you're standing in. On the highway side you are utterly exposed to its sometimes ferocious bite. It always makes you tired and often cold. You stand there and wonder why the prevailing wind is always in your face. It's meteorologically impossible and you try convincing yourself of its truth. If mother nature happens to be in a calm mood, the semi-trucks roaring by prove an ample replacement. The rush of the wind is inescapable, until you climb into your next ride.

Despite the wind, I was in a great spot, or so I thought. I waited at a stop light and had plenty of highway shoulder space to work with. There was mall traffic coming and going, and I also enjoyed the added luxury of sunshine. Nevertheless, the long walk had slightly dampened my spirit and the wait in the cold was getting to me.

Sadly, my spirit struggled to endure those conditions for another two hours before Gilles Therrien finally pulled over. He could take me to within a few miles of the Saskatchewan line. I was so glad to be moving again.

Gilles was going to the little town of Irvine where he owned a small house that he was fixing up. His plan was to move away from the city as soon as the house was ready. He, too, wanted to get out of Medicine Hat, but probably not as badly as I did that day. I asked Gilles to turn the heater on full blast so I could thaw out a bit before facing another long wait. My feet were frozen and my hands weren't doing too well, either. The day before, in the mountains of British Columbia, I had walked in tee shirt and shorts. My body wasn't prepared for the shock of 0°F air temperatures and wind chills well below zero. Irvine was a wide spot in the road. Unfortunately, the widest part was on the other side of the road from where I stood. It consisted of a tiny coffee shop with a single gas pump. I did feel fortunate that there was a commercial establishment so close by. Any wait longer than an hour would be enough to force me inside.

In Medicine Hat, highway 3 had ended at its junction with the Trans-Canada Highway. I was now travelling east on the TCH. This far out of town the highway had become a narrow two lane strip, with no shoulder. I was surprised at the large amount of traffic going by. Even so, I was reaching the limits of my patience and frost-bite-pain threshold, before Joe Kokoski finally stopped.

Joe was rocketing along in a nice, big pick-up truck. Unlike my ride into Phoenix, Joe let me inside the cab. I finally had a long ride, out of the cold. We were heading to Regina, Saskatchewan, ignoring speed limits across the 275 mile stretch of empty plains!

Joe reported on some bad things that were happening economically and culturally in Canada. He claimed Saskatchewan was a dying province. There wasn't much work available and as a result many people were giving it up and leaving. Presently employed, he worked with a contractor laying cable, wire, fiber optics, and gas pipelines. Even typically stable utility work like that was in short supply and he had to travel great distances from his home in Regina to find work. He was glad to be working despite the travel. He couldn't understand why Canada continued to accept immigrants while so many Canadian citizens remained unemployed.

Clearly, Canadians had to deal with about as many stupid problems as Americans: excessive foreign aid out of a bankrupt government budget; immigrant Sikh's demanding to wear turbans as employees of the Royal Canadian Mounted Police, instead of the traditional head dress worn by officers; Quebec province demanding political and cultural concessions from the federal government as it threatens to seek sovereign nation status; rebellious Indians finally organizing after decades of confusion; and serious economic woes in the maritime provinces. This is but a brief list of the socio-economic problems confronting our brothers and sisters to the north.

Joe came in contact with Americans quite often. He couldn't believe the average American citizen's ignorance of Canada's geography and current events. Canadians are far better informed about the United States because their public schools teach a lot of U.S. history and geography. The print and electronic media also provide Canadians with a large dose of U.S. news reports. Joe need not have felt slighted. The average American knew little about any country, even their own United States.

The ride with Joe had been great. When he dropped me off on the east edge of Regina, my travel distance for the day was approaching 400 miles. Fatigue had already started to set in even before we had reached Regina. Once there, I had no energy for a long wait. Fortunately, Shaun Farrell stopped immediately and brought me a short distance, to the eastern edge of the little town of Balgonie.

It was getting dark and I was about a mile out of town. The weather was absolutely terrible. The air was bitter cold and a steady 30 mph wind was blowing straight into my face. Even though I had been warmed by the last series of rides, I couldn't take it for more than half an hour. There would be no more hitchhiking that night. I could see the lights of some businesses but didn't want to walk back toward town, straight into a head-wind. My entire body ached and the fight in me was gone. As on the previous night, I was forced to seek shelter at the nearest farmstead. I would not have been capable of setting up my tent under those violent conditions.

I walked across the snowy, frozen stubble of a wheat field to the only dwelling in sight. I was desperately counting on these people for some kind of protection from the wind. If they denied me I would have to walk back into town to seek a motel room. If there was no motel room available, I would have to start knocking on doors. This had suddenly become serious business.

Farmers are always surprised when someone knocks on their front door. Nobody uses it except strangers. Friends always use the back door. I'm sure the folks at this farmstead weren't expecting company to be pounding on their front door that cold, cruel night.

With a maximum effort, I spoke as slowly and clearly as I possibly could through my stiff lips. Frustrated at not being able to do anything about it, I could hear my words slurring like a drunk as I struggled to tell them of my need for a place out of the wind. They didn't seem to be too thrilled about having me around, but acquiesced to my ice-laden request for shelter. A man named Don showed me a couple of options. I chose to set my tent up in their cavernous machine shed. It wasn't heated but was lighted and offered complete protection from the wind. That was all I required to survive and all I expected. I was practically gushing with grate-fulness.

The temperature dropped to -10°F that morning of March 23rd. I got little, if any, sleep. Although I was wearing nearly everything and using what was left of my clothing as an extra insulating layer from the ground, I froze. I spent the entire night knocking my feet together, to aid circulation, in a failed attempt at keeping them warm.

In the morning I packed as quickly as I could. I had to keep moving because the cold was seeping deeper into my core and I was worried about hypothermia. My hosts had apparently faced many intrusions from transients, so I didn't feel like troubling them further. I figured I'd have to walk the mile back into town and find a coffee shop where I could thaw out. I had to promise myself that I would stand at the highway for no longer than ten minutes before beginning the walk back into town. It was important that I make an absolute commitment and time limit because I was worried about slipping into a hypothermia induced lethargy.

Good things will eventually happen if one is patient and perseveres. That fact was proven to me again, that morning. The first vehicle that approached stopped. It was Chris Serratore and his teething puppy, Caino. His little pick-up truck was packed tightly with just about everything he owned. He had been living in western British Columbia for the past few years and was returning to London, Ontario, to attend school and be near his family. After much frenzied rearranging and numerous futile attempts to warm up our hands, we all squeezed into the cab of Chris' rig.

My cardboard sign had read "WINNIPEG" and I couldn't believe Chris was going that far, and much farther, in my direction. His route would drop south into the States and continue on to London across northern Wisconsin and the Upper Peninsula of Michigan. It was faster and far less expensive in fuel costs to travel in the United States. It also turned out to be very convenient for me. He would be driving right through Duluth, Minnesota!

CHRIS SERRATORE
Winnipeg, Manitoba

While living in British Columbia, Chris had worked as a tree planter. After a couple of years, planting about a jillion trees, he became disillusioned with the entire forest industry. He observed a tremendous lack of environmental concern by both government and industry. Even though his efforts promoted regrowth and reforestation, he wasn't interested in remaining associated with it. What he did as a planter didn't actually rec-reate a forest ecosystem; it simply re-established a crop to be harvested when it ripened. He didn't even consider the work professional forestry. It was strictly agricultural: tree farming.

When he began his education again, in London, he intended to study native Canadian issues. He felt much of the racial tension between white and native Canadians stemmed from a lack of understanding of historical and cultural differences on both sides. At 24, Chris seemed to have a good understanding of what his priorities were, plus idealistic goals to pursue. It was a pleasure to ride with this bright young man over those many miles.

Caino, the big puppy, was kind of tough to take, however. He was full of energy and excited about having extra company to chew on. Poor Chris' hands were all scratched and bruised from Caino's constant chew-ing. Teething must be a drag for puppies, too.

Two events on that long journey should be noted. The first was a speeding ticket in Winnipeg. Bummer! The wide open spaces of Manitoba and Saskatchewan had turned Chris into a speed demon and he didn't even notice that he was going fifteen clicks over the speed limit. The second big event was the border crossing into northwestern Minnesota on U.S. 59. All of my border crossings were memorable and this one was no exception.

An elderly lady was working alone at the tiny United States customs inspection station. She had found our completely truthful stories highly suspicious. She just knew we were going to enter the United States and get jobs. She asked me numerous times if I was sure I was a U.S. citizen and Chris if he was sure he wasn't going to try finding work in the states. Our answers weren't convincing enough. She needed a reason to deny us entry so began a search of our possessions for drugs.

Her search turned up some pennyroyal in a plastic bag. It was an herbal remedy Chris used on Caino to combat fleas. Because it wasn't packaged in some glossy container, she immediately figured it was dope and ran some tests. I'm sure she was disappointed when the test results showed nothing illicit.

By the time she had done all this investigating there were three vehi-cles waiting behind us. She felt the pressure of those waiting people and reluctantly let us through.

I recognize the need for border guards and the thankless task of pro-tecting the country from unhindered entry by political and economic refu-gees. Even so, I still think it's sad when the first impression travellers get of a country is of some little creep in a uniform interrogating them while rifling through their personal possessions. It's such a shame that free countries have to condone such shabby treatment of their guests and citizens alike. The further down the economic ladder you are, the worse the treatment. It's as if you have done something wrong by being unable to spend $50 to $60 per night on hotels during your visit. There is no welcome for you as a human being; only for your ability to spend money on the tourist trade. There is no trust at the border. Perhaps there never can be with terrorists, smugglers, cheats, sneaks, and liars to contend with.

Chris had picked me up at about 8:00 am on Friday, March 23, and we drove 750 miles in 15 hours. It easily ranked the longest ride of the trip. It couldn't have come at a more opportune time. One minute I was freezing my toes off in unfamiliar territory, and a minute later I was in a vehicle heading for Duluth. Perseverance paid off that time.

It was late on March 23rd when I pulled into Willow River. Chris had dropped me in Duluth at the intersection of U.S. 2 and I-35. I called my father and he came up and brought me back to the farm. I needed to stop in for a couple of days to take care of some business.

It would have been easy to blow off the rest of the trip at that point. The weather was cold and uncooperative; I was spending too much money; I was worn down physically; and the remainder of the trip would be through areas I'd never travelled before. The fear of the unknown had begun to rear it's ugly head since I had no acquaintances east of Detroit. I would be on my own for nearly 6000 miles!

I just couldn't talk myself out of continuing the journey. There were too many places to see and people to meet. On March 28, my parents brought me to U.S. 2 in Superior, Wisconsin, to continue my trip east. Superior is across the St. Louis River from Duluth. Despite the slight break in time, I wanted to maintain the continuity of my route as much as possible. I postponed my departure date when we arrived in Superior in the middle of a wet snowstorm. I didn't even bother to stick out my thumb. We tried again on the following day. Much better. It was still chilly and gloomy, but at least the roads had been cleared of snow by undoubtedly overworked snowplow operators.

Highway 2 at the east edge of Superior has four lanes and plenty of shoulder space. The snow had been plowed well off the roadway and provided a good safety margin between me and the traffic. That margin also kept me far enough away from the traffic so the spray coming off tires was not covering me in salty filth. This part of the country can receive quite a bit of snow, and the accumulation that remained in the woods, this late in March, was testimony to a very wet winter.

My parents didn't have to wait and watch for long. Roy Johnson stopped less than fifteen minutes after my folks dropped me off. Roy used to be a truck driver for US Steel. He had retired from that segment of the transportation industry, and now drove as a postal contractor delivering mail. The deer were thick in northern Wisconsin and he claimed to have seen 122 along U.S. 2 in one day. Our combined good fortune got us the twenty-five miles into Iron River without striking, or even seeing, a deer. There was plenty of traffic through little Iron River and I expected to be out of town quickly. Instead, it took over two hours before University of Minnesota-Duluth student Jason Ray stopped. He passed me by at first. After making up his mind he swung back around to get me.

Things were looking pretty odd as Jason pulled up next to me. The outside temperature was around 40°F and he was shirt-less behind the steering wheel. When I opened the car door I understood why he was dressed for the beach. His car's heater was stuck on hot. I, in turn, took a few layers of clothing off and made myself comfortable for the half hour ride into Ashland, Wisconsin. The two hours of standing around in 40°F temperatures had cooled me off and I welcomed the tropical air inside of Jason's car.

JASON RAY
Ashland, Wisconsin

Mike Barker got me to Ironwood, Michigan, and Joe Lucania took me a few more miles to Wakefield. Joe was a published writer. He called the science fiction stories he wrote, "info-tainment." Entertaining, but loaded with social and technical information used to broaden our educational horizons. It was a short, but fun ride in his new, sleek Ford Probe.

Things were going slow in Wakefield when Karen Barkley and Shawn Tesch stopped to bring me to Marenisco, the next town. I was feeling fortunate to have gotten a ride with Karen and Shawn. There was very little traffic heading east and the next large town was 100 miles away. The little towns in between were neatly spaced at twenty-five miles apart. They were too far apart to consider doing any walking.

It wasn't really getting late but the gray skies and cool air made it seem like dusk in the middle of the afternoon. Karen and Shawn dropped me off at a good spot on the highway, east of Marenisco. Although it looked good, it was a lonely place. There were no businesses or homes in sight. The highway was narrow with no shoulder to speak of. The snow and trees of the surrounding forest looked as though they were anxious to reclaim the pavement for their seedling progeny, leaning into the right-of-way as if to intimidate anyone foolish enough to disregard their resolute mandate. Looking down the roadway in the direction of the little town of Watersmeet, it appeared as though the wilderness had won. The arrow straight highway seemed to disappear, swallowed up by the encroaching black wall of tree trunks and descending gray sky.

The first car to come down the long hill toward me stopped and chased my worries away. People driving in remote areas are incredible. They beat the odds every time. In the city it can take 5000 cars before someone will stop. If it ever took 5000 cars at a solitary intersection like Marenisco it would take half a lifetime to get a ride.

Dave Schaefer of Amasa, Michigan, brought me the seventy-two miles to Crystal Falls. As a sort of salesman, he spent a lot of time on the road. He worked for a small business lobby group. He travelled from town to town trying to enlist small businesses into his group. He said Michigan politics, economics, and tax rates discouraged small business ventures. His group felt these entrepreneurs needed a stronger voice to make the business climate more open. It was the lobby group's job to make that voice heard.

Being on the road promoting his group and coming home late after long days was taking its toll on Dave. He wasn't sure the stress was worth the money. He longed for the days when he was a boat pilot on the water taxi run to Isle Royale National Park. Isle Royale is a large wilderness island in Lake Superior, and Dave enjoyed serving the people who sought out the remoteness of the park. The taxi was a seasonal concession and he hoped to work there during the coming summer.

As we pulled into Crystal Falls, the sun came out from behind a cloud just long enough to set. As it set, I found myself riding with Bob Whiting into Iron Mountain, Michigan. Bob spent as much time on the road as Dave did. He had put on about 14,000 miles over the last three months. Bob was an auto insurance claims adjuster. In that part of the country a lot of insurance claims were due to collisions with deer. Night-time encounters with deer are a deadly prospect. Bambi and all of his friends can create havoc when they tangle with a couple of tons of steel travelling at 55 mph, plus.

It was completely dark when we arrived in Iron Mountain. Bob was kind enough to give me his phone number, in case I couldn't get a ride out of town that night and needed a place to stay. I wanted to try getting another ride as I was hoping to make it to my sister's place near Detroit the next day. It seemed like a long way away at that point.

Despite the darkness, it didn't take long before D.J. stopped and brought me six more miles to the little town of Norway, Michigan. I decided that there wasn't much use trying to continue in the dark. It had been a productive day and I was tired. Stopping here would give me the opportunity to spend some extra time getting to know this man who had picked me up.

Lonely. We use one form of the word to describe areas devoid of human occupation or activity. The hitchhiker thinks of wide open spaces, roads with little or no traffic, and long distances between towns, as lonely. On a more personal level loneliness refers to the absence of company. It is a very complex concept. One can be completely alone despite being surrounded by throngs of humanity. The company must be sympathetic and interested or the person seeking company and attention will fail to alleviate their loneliness.

D.J. was a young man who seemed to have a profound loneliness. He picked me up to help me out, and to have somebody to talk to. He said he'd never passed by a hitchhiker. It was his lucky day whenever he had an opportunity to meet someone new. Unlike my missed opportunity with Terry McClennan back in Rodney, Ohio, I wasn't going to be bashful.

When we got to Norway I straight out asked him if I could camp out at his place.

He was agreeable but said that he had to call home first. He had recently suffered a nervous breakdown and was living with his mother and stepfather until he could get on his feet again. He talked to his mother and she said it would be fine to bring me home. What concerned D.J. was his wicked stepfather's reaction to a guest. The old man worked a graveyard shift and we had to be quiet, so as not to disturb his sleep before he went to work. D.J. was clearly intimidated by him.

We arrived at their rural home and I set up my tent in their back yard. We went in to meet his mother and get something to drink. While sitting at the kitchen table enjoying a cold beverage, I wrote a bit and visited with D.J. Even though we were as quiet as church mice, his dad was roused. He came out grumbling and made stern demands of D.J. to do this or that. Stupid stuff, like rolling the windows up on the car. He wasn't at all interested in his yard guest. It was as though I wasn't even there except as an enemy to be ignored; a potential free spirit in his house of tyranny. When he was through putting a little fear into D.J. he disappeared down a dark hallway to continue his much needed beauty sleep.

D.J.'s mother lived under a cloud of blue tobacco smoke. She sat in the dark watching late night soaps sucking on one cigarette after another. D.J. and I sat at the kitchen table, under the only light on in the house, talking in hushed tones and drinking cherry flavored kool-aid. It was like a scene out of the bizarre underground movie, Eraserhead. Everything was in black and white. There was little dialogue between the characters. Much of the communication came in the form of grunts and scowls. The only things missing were the sounds of high winds blowing through wide gaps in window and door frames, and the clanking of an adjacent factory.

Our opportunity to visit was limited, to say the least. I wanted to be out in my tent when D.J.'s stepfather started getting ready for work at 11:30 pm. For D.J., a complete recovery from his nervous breakdown seemed far off. There were many factors against him: his stepfather, no self-confidence, and a lack of job skills. I was touched by his personal anguish. Not even feeling comfortable at home, must have been incredibly stressful. A house filled with that sort of tension could easily break a person's will to pursue happiness. One could forget all the possibilities and joys life had to offer, and be forced to concentrate strictly on survival. The most important lesson I learned that night was the value of emotional strength and independence of mind.

The morning of Friday, March 30th, was clear and cold at 21°F. I was packing up my gear at 5:00 am, and we were out on the road early to get D.J. to work on time. D.J.'s place of employment was just off of U.S. 2, east of town. I did not feel light-hearted that morning. I left him to skulk through his life, depressed and lonely, sweeping the floor at some mill for $4.50 an hour. He was a good man and I hoped he could reassemble the shattered fragments of his psyche and spend more of his time smiling and laughing instead of wincing and grimacing in pain.

A guy named Larry made a dangerous stop in the middle of highway 2. A couple of cars swerved to miss him and honked angrily. Lousy drivers are like car magnets. You can be on a road completely devoid of traffic, then somebody pulls a stupid stunt like that, and suddenly there are cars swerving everywhere. Despite Larry's lack of driving skills we survived the trip into Powers with no further mishap.

Although it was still early in the morning, the weather was sunny and warming up nicely. My mood was starting to improve but it seemed like there weren't many friendly faces among the drivers passing by. Trying not to let the unfriendly masks bother me, I waited for two boring hours in Powers before a trucker finally stopped. He had passed me, going the opposite direction, a long time ago and was surprised to see me still waiting there. In the time since he had passed me by the first time he had travelled over fifty miles round trip to Iron Mountain and unloaded his cargo. Running empty back to Escanaba, Michigan, he sympathized with my plight and was willing to carry me along for the last twenty-two miles.

I had waited only a few minutes on the eastern edge of Escanaba when Todd Olsen pulled over. Todd was my age but lived the opposite lifestyle. He'd been married for eleven years and was raising four kids. He wanted to have a dozen but his wife wasn't that ambitious and put a halt to the baby making at four. He figured he had a good marriage and his best advice to bachelors was to marry the woman who had become your best friend.

In addition to dabbling in a little pre-marriage counseling, Todd laid bricks for a living. He worked on the night shift. The construction season was short that far north, and construction companies scheduled three crews that worked around the clock to finish projects. Jobs were scarce in the upper peninsula, so he was willing to travel far from home during the week and commute back on weekends. It was Friday afternoon and he was homeward bound.

Todd was an interesting and extremely friendly guy. He was mellow and took a very casual approach when inquiring about my spirituality. We had a pleasant discussion concerning the existence of God, afterlife, morals in today's world and other matters of spiritual importance. As a member of the Seventh Day Adventist faith he believed in spiritual redemption through the belief in Christ. Although I was raised in the Lutheran Church, I was unconvinced by biblical teachings regarding the existence of a supreme being. Todd didn't get all bent out of shape about my lack of faith. He accepted my beliefs as my own but encouraged me to keep looking for answers to the larger questions of life and death and rebirth. His tolerance, coupled with encouragement, seemed to me to be the best way to promote a change toward enlightenment. Those characteristics are something we all can appreciate as we search for answers.

Todd wanted to share a beautiful, local, natural phenomenon with me called Big Spring. He drove out of his way to get there. The area was still snow covered so we parked where the plowed road ended and walked a little way into the woods. We soon came upon a crystal clear pond. It had a diameter of about seventy-five feet. There was a suspended cable attached to a raft which was in turn, moored to a dock. The cable reached across the length of the pond. We climbed aboard the raft and released the moorings. Todd, using the suspended cable and a wooden lever, pulled us out to the center of the pond. From there we could look down through the water and see sand billowing along the bottom where the spring water entered the pool. The colors of the sand and water ranged from muted yellows and browns to brilliant blues and greens. The wind was non-existent in this little pocket of the woods. There was no noise other than tiny riffles along the water surface lapping the pontoons of the raft. I enjoyed those few special moments of peace, away from the rush of automobiles and pavement covered earth. Perfect for smoothing out a stressful day, it was the kind of place D.J. might have been able to put to good use.

When we piled back into the car, Todd was determined to buy me lunch. We stuffed our faces at a local pizza place. With all of our distractions it had taken about two hours to go fifty straight line miles. I wanted to hit the Detroit area that night so declined his kind invitation to stay with him and his family.

After eating lunch, I waited for a ride directly in front of the Michigan Highway Patrol station in Manistique. Places like that were always reassuring to people driving by. They reasonably assumed that if you were an insane criminal on the loose, the last place you'd hang out was on the sidewalk in front of a police station.

Joe Golden stopped soon after I'd started hitching. Joe was anxious to get home to Marine City, Michigan, just northeast of Detroit. Like Todd, he had worked a week in Iron Mountain and was on his commute home. The difference was that Joe was travelling 300 miles toward my destination. I finally had a long ride after nickel and diming my way across Wisconsin and Upper Michigan. Although my luck had been quite good since leaving Superior, I was still relieved at this big boost. It would be a good opportunity for an extended conversation and viewing the trees, lakes, and small towns while we were on the move. Driving most of the way at 80 mph we were definitely on the move!

We enjoyed ninety miles of fine woodland scenery and views of Lake Michigan before reaching the Mackinac Bridge. The bridge was an incredible structure which spanned the strait between Lake Michigan and Lake Huron. It was frightening being hundreds of feet above the water with a very marginal guard rail protecting the edge. The driving surface was of a metal grating design. The wind blowing across the strait could also come up from below, through the grate.

One could almost sense the wind, bridge, and lake acting as conspirators. The bridge would let the wind pass up through it from below, to raise the vehicle off the surface. The cross-wind would then sweep it off the deck, relieving the bridge of its burden. The lake would hungrily devour any unlucky vehicle, removing any trace of foul play by the other players.

Crossing the bridge we left the upper peninsula of Michigan and were driving south on I-75. The miles slipped by rapidly.

At 39, Joe had lived in Michigan all his life but had never been to the upper peninsula before his most recent job. The country was nice enough to look at, but he hated travelling so far from home. He had been working at a paper mill as a millwright. Quitting only hours before because of a back injury on the job, he figured it would take surgery to fix him up this time. Major injuries happened so often, they had become just an inconvenience. He had even broken his back in 1981. Erecting heavy machinery under close tolerances was clearly dangerous to one's health, and from the sound of it, he was always an accident waiting to happen.

Joe considered himself a highly skilled professional. Some of the jobs he'd had were in paper mills, nuclear power plants, automobile factories, coal fired power plants, steel mills, food processing plants, and more. It was quite a collection of experience.

Unfortunately, Joe was a chain smoker. He was sensitive enough to my non-smoking preference to keep his window cracked while he indulged. He had once gone to a hypnotist to help him kick the habit. Three days after experiencing the hypnotic suggestion he went to a bar and started smoking again. He hadn't slowed down since. So much for the effectiveness of that treatment.

As we zoomed across the state and into Saginaw, I was reminded of Paul Simon's immortal reference about hitchhiking out of Saginaw on the search for an elusive America. I think it's impossible for a hitchhiker passing through Saginaw, or Winslow, Arizona, not to hear certain songs ramble through their minds.

Joe was heading east at Flint where we finally left I-75. I rode with him fifteen miles farther on I-69, to the little town of Lapeer. As we approached Lapeer, I was discouraged to see signs warning motorists not to pick up hitchhikers. A maximum security prison had just been completed and put into service within sight of the road. Oops! I found myself in the wrong place at the wrong time.

Joe dropped me off at the junction of I-69 and Michigan 24. The prison facility was on the other side of the freeway. It was dusk, and Lapeer was still twenty-five miles away from my sister's home in the northern suburb of Rochester Hills. I figured I was completely screwed. There wasn't a telephone in sight. In fact, there wasn't anything in sight except the prison. The traffic going by seemed determined not to slow down.

As I slowly walked south on highway 24, I looked for a place to pitch my tent for the rapidly falling night. While walking and hitching I was also looking for the best place to stand and wait for a ride. When I found a good spot I began to mentally prepare myself for a cold night in one of the adjacent, snowy farm fields. Detroit wasn't exactly known for its peaceful urban life. Approaching the city I had expected a considerable amount of wariness from the citizens, even if I hadn't been standing adjacent to a penitentiary.

Soon after I stopped and stuck out my thumb I was amazed to watch Andy Szadyr, of Lake Orion, Michigan, pull over. I was so excited at the prospect of a ride out of there, I started to exclaim my thanks as soon as I opened the door. Andy immediately shushed me and pointed to the back seat where his infant daughter was sound asleep in her car seat. Her older sister, of three or four years, was next to her enjoying an ice cream cone. I was astonished at the entire scenario. Under those circumstances I wouldn't have expected a ride even after a long wait. But Andy wasn't cognizant of my location, nor the time of day. He only noticed my need for a ride. Not only did he give me a ride as far as he was going, he took me a few miles out of his way to my sister's doorstep. Too good to be true? Nope, it was true.

On Wednesday, April 4th, after visiting family in Rochester Hills, my sister Diana drove me north to the border crossing at Sarnia, Ontario. It was one of those big plaza things with about ten car lanes. Not too many people were entering Canada on foot that morning and I wound up waiting in line with the cars. I had the self-conscious feeling you'd get if you were standing in line behind a bunch of cars, waiting to use the drive through service at a bank. If you can't picture yourself being a little self-conscious, try actually doing it.

When I'd made it to the head of the line, the inspector in the booth quickly filled out some paperwork to get me out of his life, and then sent me to some building where they would continue my processing. The young woman who dealt with me next did not want me in her country. I had ample cash, a major credit card, camera equipment, my journals, a job waiting for me in Montana in two months, a passport, and a plethora of good reasons why she should let me into Canada. Thank goodness I didn't mention I played a radical sport like Ultimate frisbee. She would have surely sent me back home.

She didn't have any good reason to turn me away except that maybe she didn't like my looks. I volunteered as much information and tried to be as helpful and persuasive as possible. I knew she was considering sending me back for no reason at all. They can do that. Barely convinced, she did some more paperwork and released me onto the next stage of this process. All the while she kept warning me not to work in Canada. I told her that I avoided work everywhere I went and all the menial employment that remained in Canada was safe from my exploitation. She was so business-like it was impossible to tell if she was a likeable person. She had learned her lessons at the academy well. Too bad.

In the next office they sort of looked me and my pack over and decided it wasn't worth the bother of browsing through my dirty laundry. I was finally welcomed into Canada. They actually said, "Welcome to Canada."

I would be in southern Ontario for less than ten hours. From Sarnia I would cross Ontario and enter the United States again at Niagara Falls, New York. From there I would travel on into New England. I was in completely unfamiliar territory. This portion of the trip would have no familiar faces and many places were still gripped by winter-like conditions. I was nervous.

Things started out from Sarnia on a positive note when Chris Rooney stopped before I'd even set my pack down. Chris sold beef and poultry contracts to restaurants throughout southern Ontario. He was very busy, selling a quality product he sincerely believed in. I was riding with the quintessential salesman. We raced across the plain for almost an hour, into Strathroy where Chris would call upon another client.

At the Strathroy exit there was nothing around to stop the wind. Long before, sometime during the Pleistocene Era, the glaciers had scraped away any relief that may have existed, making the landscape as flat as a pancake. The farmers did the rest by chopping all the trees down. It was a long, cold wait under high, hazy, slate gray skies before Glen Giroux took me to one of the London exits. I was glad for the chance to warm up, even if it was for only half an hour.

The London entrance ramp was an inconvenient, looping affair and it took a few moments for me to figure out where I should stand. I must have found the best place because Martin P. Elderhorst stopped immediately and offered me a ride to Woodstock, Ontario.

Martin held the distinction of having the most fascinating job of all the drivers I'd met on this journey. He worked with bells. His family had been in the business since the early 1900s. Martin, and his brother who lived in Pennsylvania, continued the family tradition. Martin did a lot of repair work on cast iron bells and carillons. Carillons are musical devices with a number of different sized bells that produce a chime of a different pitch when struck. It's like an organ that plays bells instead of pipes. He installed a lot of clocks and bells in shopping malls, the cathedrals of the 1990s. In addition to cast-iron bells, he did some work with electronically produced bells and chimes.

Martin's business required considerable travel and he enjoyed picking people up as a diversion from the dashed white lines. It was a most enjoyable diversion for me as well.

Reed Porter of Lambeth got me to Brandtford, Ontario, and Ed Laverick got me to a place called Duff's Corner on highway 53, just south of Hamilton. I had decided to take smaller roads to Niagara Falls because the freeway traffic was getting heavier and the cities were getting bigger. I didn't like that mix.

It was an hour wait at Duff's Corner before a rough looking character named Harry pulled his pick-up truck over. He was heavily into motorcycles and used to ride with the British Columbia chapter of the Hell's Angels. He quickly admitted to being crazy a while back. He assured me he was better now. Noticing the big knife sheathed on his hip, I found myself relieved at his improved condition. I'm not a psychologist, but insanity and weapons didn't sound like a healthy combination. It was almost as dangerous as the combination of politicians and armaments.

"HARRY"
Niagara Falls, Ontario

Harry talked a lot about the biking brotherhood that exists among motorcycle club (gang?) members. There were rights of passage, general brawling, and alliances that you'd die (or kill?) for. They were a coterie with an undying respect and loyalty for North American manufactured motorcycles. Harry would have loved Bruce Kiper's antique motorcycle shop in Land O' Lakes, Florida. Especially the pit bull that attacked Japanese bikes. Harry had all the proper regalia: tattoos, silver skull rings, scars, long hair, big, black leather boots, and of course, beer. I was riding with the genuine article. He was as friendly and helpful as nearly any ride

I'd had, despite his rough cut appearance. He even bought me a sandwich for lunch.

While rolling into Niagara Falls, Ontario, the deluge began. Harry could take me no closer than a few miles from the waterfall itself and the bridge that led back into the United States. I was drenched the minute I stepped out of his truck. The fastest route to the bridge would have been along the tollway through town but pedestrians were strictly forbidden. I was forced to wind my way on foot through residential streets that approximately paralleled the tollway. The rain never let up for a second.

After sloshing through deep puddles for a couple of miles, David Reynolds, proprietor of the Rainbow View Bed and Breakfast, stopped to offer me a lift. I loaded my stuff into his tiny, sub-compact car and we were off to his place for a nice cup of tea. He offered me an inexpensive room at his lovely inn for the night. I was anxious to return to the States and wanted to try getting east out of Niagara Falls that night. I foolishly declined his generous offer and turned myself out into the grim weather once again.

From the Rainbow View, it was an easy walk to the bridge where I caught sight of the falls. It looked considerably different from most post card shots one normally sees of it. At that time of year, a large portion of it was still frozen. Frozen or not it was still an impressive sight.

The entire area was choked with tourist traps. Where it would normally be teeming with tourists for most of the year, I happened to be the only person in sight. I'm serious! There was nobody around. The weather had driven everyone who had a place to be, to that place. It was like the nuclear winter had begun. It did not portend the perfect evening of a sightseeing vacation. All the curio shops were locked up tight. So, I stood where millions of lovers had gazed out across this romantic, natural wonder, with my own imaginary sweetheart (maybe that exotic dancer from Florida!) and watched the Niagara River rush over a frozen cliff while the rain pummelled me from a completely overcast sky. It was more like a Hitchcock movie than a romance novel. What's the difference if I didn't come in out of the rain? Romance didn't exist in the nuclear winter, anyway.

Tired, I clomped up a flight of stairs to gain access to the bridge. I readied myself to cross the bridge and face another border interrogation. Before I could cross the bridge though I had to cough up a dime for the pedestrian toll. It was a far better alternative to swimming the river or jumping from ice floe to ice floe to gain the New York state line. I was angry because I didn't have a dime handy and had to dig through a bunch of wet gear to find one. Sorely tempted to jump over the unattended turn-stile, I decided against it. Throwing off my pack and opening my parka, I loosened my rain pants and unbuttoned a pant pocket before retrieving my wallet. I opened it up and fished out my only dime, an American dime. I was on the Canadian side and hoped the gate accepted U.S. coin. I put myself back together, shoved the dime in and walked through the turnstile with my head held high like the Sultan of Brunei. As I said, despite my decidedly soggy mood, it was better than swimming.

Entering the United States at Niagara Falls, New York, I faced my simplest border interrogation. It wasn't so easy, however, for another trav-eller I noticed. While I waltzed through, I saw a foreign woman trapped in "between country limbo." It looked like a nightmare. While visiting in Canada her U.S. visa had run out. Now she was trying to re-enter the U.S. to catch a plane for home. They wouldn't let her back in because of her expired visa. Canada didn't want to let her back in, so she stood and cried and waited for something to happen. Yikes! Some of my Canadian friends refer to customs officials as border Nazis. You decide.

I may have been lost, exhausted, and standing in the pouring rain, but I was about as free as you could be, in America. I was apparently free to walk, as well. Rides were not happening that night. Darkness was rap-idly moving in, aided by the thick, saturated clouds that emptied their loads on Niagara Falls. There was a little park nearby with a small pavilion that I used for a temporary shelter. I rested and ate a meager dinner. There was no table to sit at so I sat on a dry patch of concrete about as big as my butt.

I realized I couldn't spend the night under this marginal shelter in the middle of a business district, so when I finished a couple of sandwiches and a piece of fruit, I started walking along a road I thought would eventu-ally get me to the east edge of town. It turned into a detour and I was forced to walk through residential areas. Hitchhiking was impossible.

While walking endless blocks and feeling pretty low about life, I came upon a large city park. There were playing fields, a lake, gardens, and some nice old trees. Everything was drenched but I would be sleeping there no matter what. I was out of mental and physical strength. I sneaked around searching for a relatively dry spot to sleep. I'm sure I looked pretty rough under those conditions. I felt like a real fugitive. Fortunately, being invisible was commonplace for me and I was able to remain inconspicu-ous. I found a small pavilion that was used during the winter months as a storage spot for the park's picnic tables. There was one table that had been rotated a little out of place which left a gap just large enough for me to lie down in.

I was suddenly gleeful at the prospect of spending that awful night in this little alcove. Wind protection, privacy, incidental lights, drying racks for all of my wet gear, and a dry concrete pad upon which to lay my body, was much more than I ever could have hoped for. I didn't even worry about where I was going in the morning. I was living for, and savoring, the moment.

The stuff in my pack, like sleeping bag, tent, and extra clothes stayed dry because I had a nylon pack cover that shed water pretty effectively. Using the surrounding picnic tables as clothes drying racks I hung up all the clothing I had worn that day. With all the moisture in the air and cold temperatures I realized the cloth stuff wouldn't dry much, but the slight breeze would dry out my polypropylene long underwear, gore-tex parka, and nylon rain pants. It was a solid start toward a dry next day.

The morning of Thursday, April 5th, found me continuing my walk across the city. I finally settled on a road I thought could get me to Lockport, New York. I had a general direction in mind but had no idea which route might get me northeast with the least amount of complications.

Finally, after walking the entire length of Niagara Falls, somebody pulled over. Dan Jeffores was going to Pennsylvania to visit an Army buddy. On his recommendation I chose U.S. 20 to cross the state toward Albany. It required a slight southern detour but I felt I needed to get some momentum started.

Dan was suffering the aches and pains of a couple of bad traffic accidents. In 1980, after far too many cocktails, he wrecked his car and found himself waking from a coma four weeks later. In 1986, while riding a motorcycle, he hit a deer. The first accident was due to irresponsibility and the second was due to bad luck. Either way, I didn't feel too confident riding with him after hearing those stories, but he was driving at a prudent 45 mph so I actually had little to worry about.

As we drove away from the Great Lakes we climbed in elevation. The temperature began to drop and we were soon driving through a snowstorm.

Dan brought me to U.S. 20, just south of Batavia. At that junction there was virtually no traffic going east. I wasn't at all surprised by the lack of traffic. Driving conditions and visibility were poor due to the heavy snow falling. After about a thirty minute wait, I decided to go back towards

Batavia and try my luck on the entrance ramp of the New York State Thruway. I hated to do it but there seemed to be nothing going my way on 20.

Allen Galbraith stopped and took me back to Batavia. He was a local farmer who also ran a short-haul trucking business. That day he was out searching for tractor parts. The equipment shop in Batavia didn't have the part he needed, but their sister store in Canandaigua, fifty miles east on U.S. 20, did. His inconvenience turned out to be my good fortune. He needed the part that day so we were quickly on our way. I had lucked out by avoiding the thruway and was still taking a big chunk of mileage out of U.S. 20 east!

Allen termed this area of west central New York state the "snow belt." It consistently received excessive amounts of winter precipitation. Because of the area's reputation for rough winter conditions, residents there, and in similar communities around the country, bragged about how it kept the riff-raff out. The landscape was primarily rural with an occasional medium sized town, strategically located. The farmland is rich, and the water, plentiful. Allen used to have a dairy operation but sold out in the late 1980s when the government was trying to discourage dairy over-production. Then he went to growing sweet corn, dry beans, and other cash crops.

There was a bit of history associated with the area. All of the little towns we passed through were established in the late 1700s. Those towns had not only survived the past 200 years, they seemed to be thriving despite a national recession.

I found myself passing through this part of the country with its graceful rolling hills, partially forested landscape, large narrow lakes extending the length of valleys, and wondering what it was like 400 years ago, before the advent of European technology. Covered by vast forests that would quickly dampen any noise, one could hardly imagine the kind of silence that blanketed the land. No automobiles, farm implements, airplanes, trains, chain saws, lawn mowers, or even gas powered leaf blowers existed to disturb the quiet. The only sounds four centuries ago were the songs of birds, water chattering in a stream-bed, and the wind rustling the needles and leaves of trees.

The ride with Allen was very pleasant. He was a tremendously friendly, hard-working, family man. I was glad he had to drive a few extra miles to get his tractor part.

U.S. 20 was an excellent choice of route. I was able to travel through interesting, scenic little towns, while avoiding the freeway bleakness and larger cities to the north.

While I stood in Canandaigua, New York, the weather couldn't decide what it wanted to do. It went from winter to summer, and back to winter in fifteen minute intervals. I had dressed for cold, wind, and snow. I had to be prepared for the worst conditions and was glad I had done so. Luckily, Tim Clarke came along and got me into Geneva. The weather had improved one hundred percent in those few, short miles. When Tim left me, I was so warm I removed a couple of clothing layers.

Under nice weather conditions I continued east by a series of short rides, with short waits in between. I enjoyed the mix of people. A couple, my age, took me out of their way to Seneca Falls. From there, three surveyors in a crappy old Jeep Cherokee, with a gaping hole rusted through the floor, got me to Skaneateles. Then a young man brought me down the road to his house. He was kind enough to let me use the bathroom. My water supply was gone and that stop enabled me to refill my bottle. Dehydration can sneak up on a hitchhiker. I constantly forced myself to drink water.

The young man's house was in a rural area. There was no intersection nearby so I just started walking. The day remained beautiful. From the hills and curves on the road I viewed magnificent scenery. It was early April and the forests and farm fields were starting to green up nicely, but the view wasn't awe-inspiring like the mountains and deserts of the west. Out there, eyes popped out of their heads at fantastic, forbidding landforms. The vistas of central New York produced a more peaceful, comfortable, soothing, and welcoming sensation. It was a place for the eyes to rest. A place to quench the sensuous desires of sight. I had been a long time in the dreary colors of winter rains and frozen brown fields. My eyes drank in the sights, smells, and relative quiet of the hills. I immediately knew that I wanted to come back to this part of the country someday.

Brick-layer, Bob Seymour, took me on a short ride through the apple orchards of the Tully Valley into Lafayette, just south of Syracuse, New York. After an hour wait, Don Casler drove by, only to return moments later. He had practically no room in his pick-up truck for me. Certain I wouldn't fit, he was still willing to try squeezing me in anyway. Although my skills as a contortionist were limited, I was definitely game for a try. The waits had been getting progressively longer between each ride and I wanted to keep moving through Lafayette. It was very tight in Don's truck. I may have been uncomfortable, cramped in a fetal position in the front

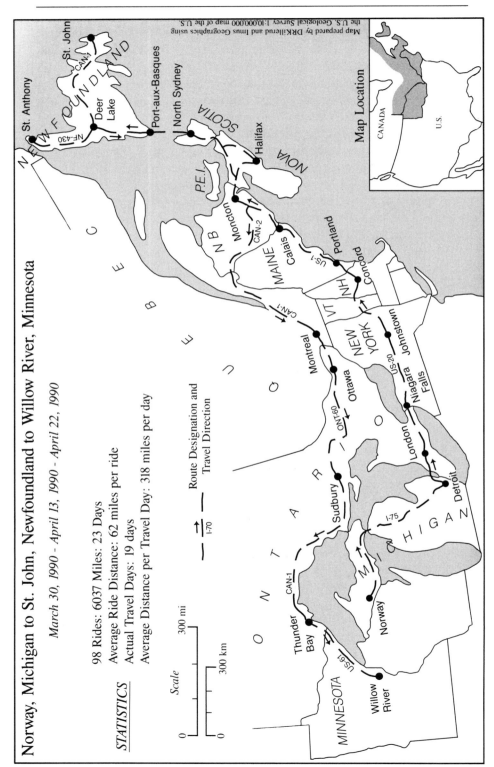

Norway, Michigan to St. John, Newfoundland to Willow River, Minnesota

March 30, 1990 - April 13, 1990 - April 22, 1990

STATISTICS

98 Rides: 6037 Miles: 23 Days
Average Ride Distance: 62 miles per ride
Actual Travel Days: 19 days
Average Distance per Travel Day: 318 miles per day

Scale
0   300 mi
0   300 km

↑↓ Route Designation and
I-70   Travel Direction

Map prepared by DRKillerud and Imus Geographics using
the U.S. Geological Survey 1:10,000,000 map of the U.S.

Map Location

CANADA
U.S.

seat for the seventeen miles to Cazenovia, but I was also thrilled to be moving.

In Cazenovia, I finally got a good long ride. It was also my final ride of the day. Timothy Lundstrom was my age but lived the life of a business professional as opposed to mine as a vagabond. He worked for a small company that did construction and land development. He enjoyed the intense activity and responsibility that came with his position. He made good money and had recently purchased a huge, old, Victorian house in Johnstown, New York, where he now lived. It was a virtual mansion by my standards. It had thirteen rooms and a carriage house in the back yard. Timothy was hauling a sailboat home and planned on storing it inside the cavernous carriage house.

When we arrived at his house, we found ourselves walking on pins and needles. His wife was not interested in having some guy off the street as company that night, nor any night for that matter. Even after being introduced and talking for a while, she would not consent to my night's lodging under her roof, despite an invitation extended earlier by Timothy. Timothy wasn't one to put up too big of a fuss over the matter with his newly acquired wife. It didn't look like a situation that could be reversed, anyway. I couldn't really blame him for not arguing our case further, since he had to live with her, while I didn't.

I was disappointed to have received such a cold reception, but not surprised. It is a rather unusual situation to be faced with. One moment you're sitting at home reading Redbook magazine, the next you're face to face with a goon in a backpack who wants to sleep on the floor of guest room number eleven. Not a pretty picture to have to deal with. How could your husband do this to you?!

So, I got thrown out of the house. Timothy made his apologies to me and offered a suggestion for a place to sleep. He drove me to the entrance of a cemetery. He said it was the nicest place around and was adjacent to New York Highway 29 east, the road I would be on in the morning.

I would have enjoyed spending the night in a mansion and perhaps touring Johnstown in the morning. Instead, I slept in the cemetery. The only touring I did was in an attempt to avoid tripping over stone monuments to dead people. I climbed up a hill, looking for a dry, level spot. It was cold and foggy that night. I took it as a direct attempt by Mother Nature to challenge my courage by creating a scenario that was as spooky as possible. The only things missing were the hoots of owls, the scratching of rats, and the baying of hounds. I found a nice grassy spot to sleep next to a little chapel, flanked by woodlands. I slept great and apparently didn't disturb too many of the spiritual residents.

I was up before dawn. I wanted to make sure I was gone before any maintenance personnel arrived early to dig some graves. There was also the possibility of having some decedent's last wish to be interred at dawn. I could just see a huge motorcade parked right in front of my tent as I crawled out in my underwear. My imagination tended to run a little on the bizarre side when slumbering in a graveyard.

Standing on highway 29 at 5:30 am, I didn't even expect to see any cars, much less get a lift. The first car to approach was driven by Todd Byrns, again proving how foolish my lack of faith was. Todd had the day off and was going fishing. He got me about ten miles up the road and another driver quickly brought me a few more.

While waiting at the junction of highways 29 and 147, Ron Williams pulled up. He was the foreman of a carpentry crew, and was on his way to a job site. He lived in the tiny village of Sprakers, just off the New York State Thruway. Despite its proximity to the thruway, he said his back-woods home was nice and quiet. Apparently, generations of his family loved out of the way places. He said his grandpa had lived in a shack in the woods until the day he died. Living in the shack with gramps had been twenty-seven cats and two dogs. It must have been a busy, odoriferous place. When the old man finally died it must have been a herculean effort to find new homes for all the pets.

Ron took me the forty miles to Glens Falls on the Hudson River. I had decided to go north to Whitehall, New York, then follow U.S. 4 across Vermont and on into Concord, New Hampshire. I had elected a more northerly route to avoid the big cities of Connecticut and Massachusetts. Of course, if I had gotten a ride with someone going all the way to Boston, I probably would have taken it. The route didn't really matter much, as long as it kept going in the general direction of the New Brunswick coast.

Rides were slow in coming and I did a lot of walking getting from one town to another. It wasn't any big deal. I just kept plugging along.

I rode with a guy and his pit bull a couple of miles into Hudson Falls. Then, three crazed roofers in an old, rattle trap pick-up truck, squeezed me in for eight more miles. They were a happy-go-lucky, foul-mouthed, snuff-spitting, beer-drinking, joke-telling bunch of dudes. Oddly enough, they were all missing most of their teeth and the ones that remained had an unusual greenish tint. I wondered why tooth loss plagued crazed roofers more than it did the rest of us.

My last ride with a lone female was all the way back at the Montana-British Columbia border with Ella West. It took nearly the length of the continent before finally experiencing the next one. I was treated to a twenty-five mile ride with Monica McGaughey of Lake Placid. She seemed like a strong and confident woman, pulling over to pick me up without hesitation. We rode together from Fort Ann, New York, to Castleton, Vermont.

U.S. 4 was a limited access highway. I waited at the top of the entrance ramp after reading a nasty sign. It had a list of things you couldn't do on the freeway, including hitchhiking and stopping for hitchhikers. Not familiar with attitudes of the populace and its police force I thought I'd better try getting a lift from nowhere near the freeway shoulder. I had waited in the shadow of tall pine trees for about forty-five minutes when Norman Bogart stopped. He brought me to the east edge of Rutland. This put me within striking distance of the Killington Ski Resort, which happened to be located right on U.S. 4.

NORMAN BOGART
Rutland, Vermont

My next ride, with Barry Lane, took me to the resort turn off. He was on his way to work as a chef at one of the restaurants there on the mountain. In addition to cooking, Barry taught writing skills at a correctional facility. He was also the author of a book entitled, Discovering the Writer Within. The book contained a series of exercises that were designed to help extract creative writing skills from people who didn't think of themselves as capable writers. He was driving an old, blue Chevy Nova that was pretty typical of the sort of vehicle I rode in throughout the trip: dented, rusted, and sagging. It reminded me of Axel Foley's car in the movie, Beverly Hills Cop. Barry was as proud of it as he could be.

I rode all the way from Killington, Vermont, to Concord, New Hampshire, with Jeanne Batch. I couldn't believe it. She was my second ride with a woman in one day!

Jeanne was a psychiatric nurse at a hospital in Massachusetts. She liked her job and enjoyed being around "crazy people." Used to an environment that catered to slightly wacky people, she didn't think anything of picking up a hitchhiker who looked like an emotionally stable guy. It was her day off work and she was checking out the ski slopes. She was hoping to ski with some friends in the coming week and wanted to see for herself how much snow cover remained this late in the season. Unimpressed by the snow cover, she told me that the New England States had three seasons; Winter, Mud, and the 4th of July. From what we had seen of the surrounding mountains, Winter was rapidly retreating into Mud on that April 6th.

If the ski conditions weren't satisfactory she could always go sailing. Jeanne crewed on yachts and loved to race. Raised as an Army brat, she had traveled the world over with her father. It sounded as though she had experienced much of what the world offered and continued to pursue exhilarating activities.

She left this self-professed crazy man at a good spot outside of Concord, New Hampshire. Not having a firm destination in mind I continued ambling along, still trying to avoid big cities. I chose U.S. 202 as the road to take into Portland, Maine. There I realized I would have to face some city traffic and complicated roads.

I got a quick ride out of Concord from a guy who took me only about two miles. I waited there for forty-five minutes before I started walking. After walking about a mile, twenty-year-old Adam Linnebur pulled over.

Adam was a fascinating young man. He claimed to be a budding writer and poet, and was an intense observer of all life. He hoped to write about the struggles his family faced while he was growing up: things like divorce, alcoholism, uprooting a large family, and serious financial challenges. He was heading for Dover, New Hampshire, to visit his best friends from college.

For his writing inspiration he chose gritty environments. The hard, dirty streets of large urban areas, mixed with the physical challenges provided by wilderness experiences, were his favorite stimulants. He looked forward to the experiences, both soft and harsh, that would round out his being and help him to fully understand the human condition. I was impressed with this thoughtful, fervent young man. We were both disappointed when our paths diverged after a short ride.

Jere Kalef brought me to the outside edge of Rochester, New Hampshire, and David Klepper took me into East Rochester.

I was in an interesting mode, a hitchhiking robot mode. I was going through all the motions and having really fantastic luck. I was very impressed at how brief my waits were and how the drivers would go out of their way to put me on a good intersection at the edges of towns. It's just that the rides were so many and so short, averaging twenty miles per ride, that I was numb for most of the conversations. I couldn't even tell you what the scenery was like across Vermont and New Hampshire. I fear I missed seeing a great deal of the natural beauty of the area which existed outside of the white lined road boundary.

It was my third day out of Detroit and I'd had thirty different rides across six-hundred miles when Mike Coyne picked me up in East Rochester. He invited me over to his house for a couple of beers and some grilled burgers with his family. I told him I was definitely interested in that action. Mike said I looked a little tired and insisted I stay with them that night. After the two previous nights, strolling through the rain in Niagara Falls and sleeping in a cemetery in Johnstown, it was funny he didn't say I looked like the living dead.

When Mike called his wife Debbie to tell her to expect a guest when she got home from work, I expected a reaction like the one I'd gotten the night of the cemetery sleep. (It seemed like it had been weeks since then, but it had only been the previous night.) The visit started out with some apprehension on Debbie's part. After spending a little time getting to know me she made me feel right at home. A bunch of the Coynes' friends came by and their house trailer was full of activity. Their two kids, Leah and Jimmy, harassed me like they would any uncle. I enjoyed my visit and we all had a fun time. It was a much needed social situation for my spirits and a comfortable rest for my body.

It probably sounds as though I needed more rest than any normal human being would on any given day. When I began the trip I didn't think it would be so tiring. After all, I mostly sat around in cars all day. Nevertheless, the constant movement in cars and on foot, extremes of weather and emotions, a poorly conceived diet, a different bed every night, conversing with a tremendous mix of people and personalities, and my attempts to get some feel for the geography of the terrain I travelled, all added up to stresses and fatigue that had me searching for a bed by 5:00 every evening.

On the morning of April 7th, I said good-bye to the rest of the Coyne family and rode with Mike from East Lebanon to Sanford, Maine, where he was employed. They had wanted me to stay for a day or two, but I was anxious to reach the maritime provinces of Canada. The Coynes had opened up their hearts to me, which made for a rather sad good-bye.

Don Landry was driving the first car to approach me in Sanford in the cold, white, morning light. He was a member of the Maine Air National Guard and was on his way to South Portland for duty. He lead a diverse life. He worked for Pratt and Whitney Aircraft as a production line specialist. He and his wife also had a seven acre hobby farm with livestock and a huge garden. Their house was originally built in 1836 and required considerable maintenance. He kept plenty busy with those many activities.

With Don stopping in South Portland, that meant I had to try hitchhiking across town. It was a bleak prospect on such a quiet Saturday morning. While studying a city map hanging in the window of a gas station, I managed to talk a guy into giving me a ride to some anonymous freeway junction. He wasn't leery about offering a ride and got me started in the right direction. Another guy took me across most of the remainder of town. Portland seemed like a pleasant place and I hoped to spend more time there at a later date. I began walking toward the northern outskirts. Leaving another city behind, I intended to trace scenic U.S. 1, along the rugged Atlantic coastline, until entering Canada.

It was going to be another day with many short rides. Michael DeRice saw me walking and took me to Yarmouth. Young Don Perkins got me to Freeport, Maine, and the intersection of I-95. The interstate paralleled U.S. 1 for a short stretch and I decided to use I-95 to try avoiding one and two mile rides. I used a sign that read, "BATH."

Bath, Maine, was on the east fork of a major split in the freeway. This was one of those few times when I didn't want a ride to an exit short of my destination sign. I didn't want to deal with the busy freeway traffic any more than this one time. If I made a good connection from Freeport to Bath, I'd be back on U.S. 1 and taking it slow and easy through lots of little towns.

I stood on the entrance ramp, squeezed between the white line and the guardrail, and there wasn't much room for anyone to safely pull over. Luckily, it was a sleepy Saturday morning and the intersection wasn't crowded with rapidly accelerating vehicles.

I felt sort of silly standing there with my Bath sign, so I flashed it with a sheepish grin. It seemed as though I was making a statement about my personal hygiene, rather than making an attempt at enticing a driver to stop.

Beautiful women, piloting turbo-charged Saab sports cars, don't normally stop for hitchhikers. At least that genotype had never recognized my existence before. Apparently, Kelly Doyle just couldn't say no. She entered the ramp and saw me with my silly sign and contagious smile. A big smile broke out across her face, she rolled her eyes at my ridiculous situation, and hit the brakes.

KELLY DOYLE
Wiscasset, Maine

On our way to Wiscasset, we stopped and had some breakfast at a little roadside cafe. I found out Kelly was five months pregnant. Giving me a ride under those circumstances showed a truly trusting nature. She and her mate lived in Richmond, Maine, in a big old house they had recently purchased. She expressed an interest in doing some long distance travelling, but her increasing domestic responsibilities put those desires farther down her priority list every day.

It was interesting to note that during the past two days, I'd had rides from three women. That had definitely shattered the previously established average of one female ride per 2000 miles. It was a welcome trend.

Long waits can get terribly boring. The only form of relief for the hitchhiker is walking. Even that's not much of a relief because it doesn't take long to get tired. In the western United States the towns are so far apart you don't want to strike out into the middle of nowhere on foot, alone. In the eastern States distances are much shorter between settlements, so it is far more tempting to start walking toward the next town. Rides were slow in coming on U.S. 1, so I would normally start walking immediately after I got dropped off because the next town was only a few miles ahead. That way I could try generating some of my own momentum and also have a chance to view a changing scene.

I had walked a couple of miles out of Wiscasset, Maine, when Steve Albahari stopped. He was living in North Bennington, Vermont, but was in the area for a job interview. Over the past ten years he had worked at a number of different jobs to survive. On the side he did landscape photography and hoped to make his living as a professional photographer someday. He had compiled a series of his best images into a promotional brochure. They were magnificent. It wasn't just nice scenery, it was fine art photography. I was wishing a bit of his photographic skills would rub off on me.

From Warren to Camden, Maine, I rode with a mentally ill man named Dan. He was clinically depressed and had a nervous disorder. Driving around, for lack of anything better to do, he was an insomniac and hadn't slept for a couple of days. His nerves were fried and his driving wasn't exactly tight. In his struggle to end his pain he had been counseled extensively by a Christian minister. Dan professed his faith in Jesus. He was hoping God would help him find a way out of his torment.

Either God was working in mysterious ways that day, or was on vacation. Sleep deprivation is apparently one of the most effective tortures for breaking the will of man. The human condition can be brutal and the human being named Dan was ready to snap. In Camden, I bid him a gentle good-bye and wished him well. I almost hoped he'd fall asleep at the wheel. If he softly rolled into a ditch and bumped his head just enough to knock him out, he could sleep in peace for a few hours. I found it a strange thing to wish for.

I was so busy getting into and out of cars and talking to drivers, that I didn't get much of a chance to examine the roadside scenery as I rolled along. No sightseeing for the frantic, I guess.

My ride out of Camden with Bruce Margarido was jammed with philosophical conversation. He even took me miles out of his way, just to extend our discussions.

Bruce had been self-employed for many years and felt it was the only way to be truly free. Still self-employed, he was starting a new business at age forty-one. He was in the process of establishing a travelling handyman/maintenance business. His intent was to approach his customer's needs with a new age, holistic service. The maintenance services he provided reflected a client's lifestyle and personal needs. He would help customers through their mentally frustrating battles against the mechanized world as it broke down, giving the customer the hope that they wouldn't be beaten in life by the likes of enamel appliances and plumbing.

Bruce mentioned the value of the "unknown" in our life's journey. He said that the unknown held the potential of our life's energy. If we could recognize that fact we could also better appreciate each moment of life by taking advantage of all it had to offer. He claimed we squander much of our personal potential by fretting over what tomorrow might bring, instead of using the unknown of the future as a source of free thought and action.

While building his business and enjoying the open freedom of the future, Bruce also planned to continue his education in the fields of chemical-use counseling and psychology for men. He said men faced tremendous struggles in the changing roles of gender. They needed advice, counseling, and a feeling of community when it seemed as though half the world's population was aligned against you just for being a man. His highest goal was to establish a men's retreat in the rural setting surrounding his home in Jackson, Maine.

The ride with Bruce and his dog Lupine was in stark contrast to my previous ride with Dan. My emotions were on a roller coaster ride again and I was starting to lose energy. I took some time out for lunch in a nice little roadside park in Bucksport, where Bruce had eventually dropped me off.

I was still struggling northeast along the Maine coastline with short rides. It took a couple more rides to get the twenty miles into Ellsworth. Evening was fast approaching as I walked out of Ellsworth.

Sixty-four year old Ernie was heading up to his partially constructed bayfront home in Harrington, Maine, thirty-five miles away. A machinist for most of his life, he had retired four years earlier. Not to be slowed down in retirement, he had taken up snow-skiing. He now spent his winters on the slopes instead of behind a steel lathe. He invited me to stay at his place in Harrington and I accepted. He wasn't married so there were no phone call clearance procedures for the invitation to be approved.

The homesite was in a secluded wooded area overlooking an arm of Pleasant Bay. Arriving just before dark, there wasn't too much to see. The skies were so cloudy there wasn't the opportunity for a pretty sunset. The ground was covered with four inches of crusty snow. The forest consisted of mixed deciduous and evergreen trees. Tucked away in the thick trees, the building site was so secluded that the bay was barely even visible. The house wasn't yet habitable so we spent the night in his tiny bunkhouse. It was quite cold that night, with temperatures dropping into the high teens. Ernie had successfully cranked up the old kerosene heater and we slept comfortably.

The next morning Ernie offered to take me the eighty miles to the border crossing at Calais, Maine, across the St. Croix estuary from St. Stephen, New Brunswick. It was a very generous offer and it saved me from another potentially long morning of short rides and long, cold waits.

At Canadian customs in St. Stephen I was directed to an officer who was most civil. He did his job by asking me all the necessary questions without any overt, condescending scrutiny. We had an enjoyable conversation and he sincerely welcomed me back into his part of Canada. It seemed like a great beginning for my final push to the easternmost point of my trip. The end was almost in sight and I was getting anxious for it to be over. Sunday, April 8th, was my 105th day out of Willow River and Ernie had been my 240th ride across 12,653 miles.

I had no idea what to expect from the maritime provinces in terms of geography or the populace. Because it was a slow Sunday morning, I wasn't surprised that I had to walk out of St. Stephen. I finally did get a lift, from Vincent Lindsay, a few miles to the St. Andrews turn off.

Sandy and Lee Miller were coming out of St. Andrews and were turning in my direction. They pulled over and Lee rolled down her window to ask where I was going and if I'd had lunch. I replied that Saint John, New Brunswick, was my immediate destination and that no, I hadn't had lunch. Although they weren't going as far as Saint John, she promptly invited me along for the ride to the next town, in addition to lunch at one of their favorite cafes. I threw my stuff in and we rode off to the little town of St. George. Along the way, Lee was knitting some sort of garment for retail sale at a local woolen shop. Knitting, as a passenger in a car, was a very efficient use of her time. If I'd have been so smart, after knitting for nearly 13,000 miles I probably could have knit sweaters for the entire Canadian Army.

LEE AND SANDY MILLER
St. Andrews, New Brunswick

Sandy and Lee had lived in St. Andrews for a long time. Sandy was the head gardener at the resort which made up the bulk of that small town. After church on Sunday they always went out for lunch. I happened to be in the right place at the right time.

They recommended the fish and chips at the little restaurant we visited. It was a fine choice. After treating me to lunch, they took me a few extra miles down the road, looking for the best place to drop me off. They were truly a delightful couple. I was wishing they didn't live so far away from me so I could visit them more often.

My next ride was the complete opposite. Sixty-nine year old Otis was a very strange man. You'd probably be pretty weird too, if you'd worked at a fish factory for forty-three years. Retired from forking fish, he went for a drive every day, just for something to do. He always picked up hitchhikers for someone to talk to. And talk he did! Mostly about his sex-

ual escapades. Bald, overweight, pimply, and toothless, I couldn't possibly
have had less interest in his sex life but I couldn't get the guy to shut up. A
bi-sexual, it sounded as if Otis had had sex with anything that was still
breathing, but I wouldn't have put necrophilia past him either. He claimed
he was wild before he got married and was still wild at age sixty-nine. I
thought that was an understatement.

I convinced him to take me across the bridge, to the north side of
Saint John Harbor, by shelling out the 75 cent toll. I thought it was a bargain. I was relieved he had taken me all the way into Saint John, even
though I'd had to endure an earful of gibberish.

When Mike Roy picked me up in Saint John that Sunday morning he
was still trying to sober up. He had been partying until late into the night.
Mike had spent the remainder of the cold night in the back seat of his car
trying to sleep the alcohol out of his system. He had tried to sleep indoors
but the friends he intended to stay with wouldn't answer the door. Apparently they were too drunk to make it to the door to let him in when he
knocked. Mike left me in his hometown of Hampton and went off to get
some sleep.

Mr. Desireé LeBlanc and Jocelyn Peach were going to Moncton,
New Brunswick. I'd finally hooked up with a ride that was going a reasonable distance. Over the next sixty miles I struggled to communicate with
them. The radio volume was high and their tiny Ford Fiesta didn't have
much sound insulation, making the road noise terrible. Somehow, over the
din, I found out that Desireé was a photographer and also worked in a glass
factory. Jocelyn was a mental health worker and psychiatry student. Both
were recovering alcoholics and proud of their continuing sobriety. The tremendous negative effect alcohol consumption has on people's lives is
absolutely unbelievable!

Moncton was a good-sized town and I chose to go around it on the
perimeter highway instead of through it. Where Desire and Jocelyn had
dropped me off left me six or seven miles from the road south, to Nova
Scotia. It had been a long, productive day and I wouldn't have minded
ending it where I was. I walked for a little while to loosen up and stay
warm. I kept hitchhiking but kept a sharp eye out for a good campsite. It
had been raining there all week and as I looked around for a potential
campsite, I found nothing but wet, spongy ground.

I was at the very outskirts of town. As I walked along I saw a few
homes carved out of the woods and a couple of businesses next to the highway. I could see nothing of downtown or residential Moncton. After three

or four quick excursions off the road to investigate the soggy ground conditions, I went back to the road each time hoping to get a good ride in the remaining minutes of daylight. I was hoping someone would either take me home or at least to someplace where the ground wasn't completely saturated with water.

The sun's light was just disappearing when Tim Oickle stopped his pick-up truck next to me. Hallelujah! He was going the 165 miles to Halifax, Nova Scotia, on business. He worked for a tree trimming service. His company worked all over the maritimes and this trip to Halifax for the coming week's work was commonplace.

I mentioned that on my return trip through New Brunswick I would be travelling along its east coast into Quebec. Tim was from northeastern New Brunswick and warned me of some potential problems I could encounter passing through that area. There had been a couple of ruthless murders in the village of Newcastle. The perpetrators had not been captured and everybody was frightened and paranoid. If I were going that way I could expect a very cold reception and some long waits. The residents of sleepy little Newcastle were getting a big dose of fear shoved down their throats. I thanked him for the forewarning and reconsidered my original plan. Any amount of violence in any place on earth can have far-reaching effects. In this particular instance my freedom to go where I pleased was suddenly at risk. It seems like an insignificant effect, but, when multiplied by millions of violent events worldwide, the effects suddenly grow to unwieldy proportions.

In an attempt to maintain a consistent easterly bearing, I hadn't intended to go as far south as Halifax, but Tim invited me to stay at his motel room in town. I couldn't pass up the opportunity for such an easy night. It would also give me a chance to see what the southeastern coastline was like. So, we drove across a dark Nova Scotia and into the big city.

Going straight to the motel, we arrived shortly after 11:00 pm. I took the first shift in the shower. I quickly stripped off my damp, sweat encrusted clothes and jumped in. The hot shower caressed my clammy skin. Satisfied that the temperature of my extremities had finally matched my core temperature, I relinquished the bathroom to Tim. Luxuriating in the comfort of the room I watched the late show on television. I was feeling giddy from a mix of fatigue and good fortune. I didn't want the day to be over. By the time I arose the next morning, Tim had already left for work. He had gone without disturbing my selfishly hoarded sleep. In a note I wished him success, thanked him for his kindness, and bid him farewell.

I looked out the motel window and tried to guess which direction to go. We had arrived late in the night and I was having a hard time getting my bearings straight. Halifax is a town that is split, and seemingly surrounded, by water. I started walking along a busy road that appeared to be headed for downtown. I had low expectations for getting a quick ride that close to town. I paced myself for an extended walk across the city.

Paul Aubrecht dissolved those expectations, stopping directly in traffic to load me up. There was no shoulder on the narrow, two-lane road and a curb made it impossible to pull off the roadway. He wasn't worried about slowing traffic up for a few seconds, nor did the people behind us seem to mind. I certainly appreciated their attitude. It was like being in a two-bit, Montana cow town. I felt right at home.

Paul was originally from Antigonish, Nova Scotia, located northeast of Halifax. Upon completion of an architecture degree, he found employment in the bustling city of Toronto, Ontario. He disliked the fast pace of Toronto and after a couple of years decided to return to Halifax. I could understand why he loved this city. It was truly a seaside gem. Nice neighborhoods dotting the surrounding hills, ample green park lands, and a spotless downtown made it seem quite liveable. After a brief tour, Paul directed me to a few more interesting sites downtown. He also told me how to reach the ferry terminal where I would cross the harbor to Halifax's sister city, Dartmouth, Nova Scotia.

The sightseeing highlight of my brief tour was the Citadel. Located on a lush, grass-covered hilltop, adjacent to downtown, it was a magnificent granite fortress built during British and French conflicts to protect the city. It was actually a small city unto itself. Its ominous black cannons still sat in the battlements with a 360 degree view to guard against any land, or sea-borne enemies. It was an impressive, everlasting monument to the amount of natural and human resources wasted on armed conflict.

The ferry ride to Dartmouth was short and scenic. Fantastic bridges criss-crossed Halifax Harbour; boats ranging in size from little two person sailboats to gigantic barges plied the waters; and the full skyline of downtown came into view as the ferry came to a stop on the other side. In Dartmouth, I strolled across town trying to locate the Marine Drive Highway. I would follow that coastal byway for the next 140 miles. I expected no rides out of downtown Dartmouth and didn't receive any, though I did stick my thumb out occasionally, just in case.

I finally reached a hilltop that looked like the edge of town. I set my pack down and watched a lot of traffic go by. I was on the Marine Drive and felt remarkably patient. It was a fine clear day and I enjoyed my hilltop view.

After a couple of hours, Raymond Salter finally got me started. A resident of nearby Porters Lake, that was where he brought me. Raymond had been retired for five years. He wasn't all that fond of it and didn't recommend retiring early. It was too boring. He had enjoyed his twenty-five years working at a naval dockyard, followed by ten years sailing on oil tankers. Maybe he would have appreciated his retirement more if he had been spending it in the cramped quarters of a ship sailing the high seas.

The short rides continued with Gerald and Lorraine Homans. During my two hour wait in Dartmouth, they had passed me as they did errands in town. Now that they were finished, they picked me up on their way home.

The Homans left me in the village of Jeddore. I waited for a while at a nice spot overlooking a rocky Atlantic Ocean beach. My patience began to wane. Even though it was a relatively warm, sunny day, my itchy feet started carrying me and my pack down the road after about a twenty minute wait.

I hadn't walked more than a mile before Dr. J.E. Harris Miller stopped. He was a very calm, handsome, sophisticated, and articulate man. He was recently retired as the Deputy Minister of Public Health for the province of Nova Scotia. His long and distinguished career included private medical practice, directing a Veterans Hospital, public health administration, and serving as an artillery commander during World War II. His leadership capabilities had been tested early on, as he found himself in command of 150 men at the tender age of nineteen.

Dr. J.E. Harris Miller
Moser River, Nova Scotia

Among his war stories he recalled the unusual German threat to the security of the North American continent. While stationed at Cape Spear, on the eastern tip of the island of Newfoundland, German submarines were torpedoing both merchant and military targets in large numbers. Every vessel was a potential target because North American industry was supplying much of the armament and food stuffs to Great Britain, in defense of the encroaching Reich. German U-boat commanders were even so bold as to attack ships in Conception Bay, just west of the city of St. John's, Newfoundland.

Dr. Miller enjoyed picking up hitchhikers because he loved to hear their stories, and to share a few of his own. When we arrived at his summer home, a small, tidy cabin on the ocean shore, he invited me to join him for tea and toast. I savored his elegant hospitality and good natured demeanor. This gentlest of gentlemen had the ability to make me feel very special, and right at home, so far from home.

After tea, Dr. Miller brought me up the road a few more miles to Moser River, Nova Scotia. I thanked him for his kindness and we said goodbye. I was feeling very positive about my rides thus far in Canada and had been making excellent time.

I was more in the mood for walking than standing around waiting for a ride. Traffic coming through Moser River could be gauged somewhere between light and non-existent. The next tiny village was Necum Teuch, then Ecum Secum. Those names and other exotic names like Mushaboom, Musquodoboit, East Quoddy, and Gegogan littered the map along the Nova Scotia coastline. They were all as quaint as they sounded.

After walking a couple of miles, two young men in their late teens, Paul Soontiens and Tom Barkhouse, brought me to Marie Joseph, Nova Scotia. Paul was planning an adventurous 6000 mile canoe trip across the entire length of Canada. Those plans made my trip seem pretty tame. Tom was a journalism student at King's College in Halifax.

They took me slightly out of their way to show me a bit of local natural history. We went to a place called Fancy's Beach where ocean tides and wave action had built a natural dam. The dam consisted of billions of small, smooth stones which stood between the salt water ocean, and a fresh water lake. There was less than fifty yards between the two bodies of water. It was an interesting feature. I felt lucky to have met such nice young men to chauffeur me along this remote stretch of road.

Upon our arrival in Marie Joseph my good luck with rides had ended for the day. I walked northeast out of town for about four miles and it was so quiet only a couple of vehicles passed me. When I reached the tiny settlement of Liscomb Mills, I ran into Johnny and Connie Langille. They weren't driving their car, a black '86 Monte Carlo, they were washing it.

Practically parked in the stream bed, they were using creek water, bailed with a bucket to wash and rinse their car. Unlike the other Monte Carlo drivers I'd encountered, the Langilles treated theirs with tender loving care. I talked with them until they had put the finishing touches on their job and decided to test the waters, so to speak. I asked them if I could set up camp in their yard for the night. They were agreeable to it and directed me to their house a block away. I was relieved to have made sleeping arrangements for the night and was ready to take a load off my feet.

After I set up my tent in their small yard, next to the garage, the Langilles invited me in for tea. Johnny was a real talker and we chatted for hours. After the talk ran out I returned to my tent. I went to sleep exhausted and satisfied, even though it had been a relatively short-mileage day. The countryside had been ruggedly beautiful and the people I'd met were among the friendliest I'd encountered anywhere.

I awoke to a steady rain battering the tent fly early the next morning. I packed everything up soaking wet. Johnny worked up the road, in Sherbrooke. He had planned on taking me that far when he went to work that morning, but his construction crew didn't work under those lousy weather conditions. I would have to find my own way to Sherbrooke.

The Langilles referred to the dreadfully cold, rainy weather as "dirty." I, of course, had to go out into this dirty weather and slog down the road. Johnny and Connie wouldn't send me off on my slog, however, without a good breakfast and some more visiting.

I had walked out of Liscomb Mills to no place in particular when two brothers, Palmer and Lloyd Crost, stopped. They were driving a nice car and I was surprised when they rescued me from the rain, completely soaked. They didn't pay wet clothing any mind. I guess they'd seen plenty of rain in the nearly 150 years of Nova Scotia weather which they had experienced between them.

Palmer, at 77, and Lloyd, near 75, still had a living, Methuselah-like father who was 101 years old. I didn't ask for their secret to longevity, but assumed a casual home life and hard work was a big factor in their good health. Palmer dropped his brother Lloyd off in Liscomb and decided to run me up to Sherbrooke. He contrived some errand as an excuse to bring me there. It was mighty generous of him since it was not a pleasant day to be out driving around. Besides, I don't think he had much extra money to burn in gas.

LLOYD AND PALMER CROST
Liscomb, Nova Scotia

Even though I rode into Sherbrooke, I did a considerable amount of walking the remainder of that morning and early afternoon. By noon the rain had let up and slowed to a light drizzle. I got one short ride out of Sherbrooke, but spent the majority of five hours walking ten miles to the little town of Aspen. The long walk came as no surprise to me. I was travelling through a remote portion of Canada. I couldn't expect quick rides with so few vehicles in the area. In five hours of walking there were less than twenty cars an hour passing me.

I walked up to the mom and pop store in Aspen, where I intended to take a break. My feet were trashed. My boots were great for the duck loving weather I'd experienced that morning, but less than adequate support for the many miles I'd walked with a heavy pack. I needed some incentive to keep walking and chose an ice cream bar to satisfy my sweet tooth. I'd had enough pleasure denial for the day. It was time to lighten up.

While munching on my treat, I struck up a friendly conversation with Anita and Art MacEachren, mom and pop themselves. This was quite a switch from the attitude of the little twerp tending the store back in Montezuma, Iowa! They said they'd come here to escape the stresses of former jobs. Art had been in some type of supervisory position with the government. Even though it wasn't a position that was overtly political, there were a lot of decisions made based more on political expediency than in the best interests of the provincial population. He tired of that posturing and his own "paycheck junkie syndrome," and bought Aspen's little store. Both of them felt more relaxed, healthier, and generally happier.

Fortunately for me, Art had business to attend to in the town of Antigonish. He offered me a ride that I couldn't refuse. Antigonish was situated on a large, well travelled highway. It was the highway that would eventually bring me across the remainder of Nova Scotia in a straight shot.

Bernie MacDonald had a pick-up truck full of supplies but squeezed me in for a quick ride to Lower South River, Nova Scotia. It was only a couple of miles from where Art had left me, but he assured me it was a better place to hitch than where I was. It may very well have been, but I still wound up walking out because of a long wait. Nobody seemed interested in me.

Alvin Bowman was ending his workday as a nursing orderly. He picked me up on his way home to Monastery. He took me a few miles out of his way to the causeway across the Strait of Canso, which separates the Nova Scotia mainland from Cape Breton Island. He said it was no problem to help me out with a few extra miles.

The causeway had a narrow two lane road surface and I didn't feel safe walking its two or three mile length. I didn't have to worry about the trek because Dougal Stark stopped moments after Alvin left and took me to the other side.

When Dougal dropped me off, I ducked into the woods for a few necessary moments. I hurried back up to the road, hoping not to have missed a potential ride. Before I had even put my pack on my back and stuck out my thumb, Dennis Hotten was pulling over. Whew, that was a close one! If I'd been in the woods a minute longer I would have missed a three hour ride to North Sydney. It was the long ride I'd been hoping for. My timing in getting the ride was excellent but the timing of my traverse of Cape Breton Island left me somewhat disappointed. The weather remained dirty and gloomy, leaving the allegedly magnificent scenery looking no different than the inside of a wet shower curtain.

Raised in North Bay, Ontario, Dennis had since moved to Halifax and worked there for a maintenance contractor. Their only client was McDonald's restaurants. It was enough work to keep him busy and travelling all over the Atlantic Provinces. His present assignment was bringing him to Sydney.

It was snowing in North Sydney, Nova Scotia, when Dennis dropped me off at the ferry terminal. From that point, I would begin the longest water passage I'd ever made, crossing the 100 miles between Cape Breton Island and Channel Port-aux-Basques, Newfoundland.

I quickly determined the departure schedule and purchased my ticket. I was impressed with the price of the ticket. A foot passenger paid a mere $14.75 Canadian to travel the 100 miles on a large, comfortably appointed ship. It was around 8:30 pm and the boat left at 11:45 that evening. Perfect. I could wander about town, have a good meal, and return to the terminal in plenty of time to board.

I had a tasty, inexpensive, Chinese meal for dinner, with plenty of hot tea to chase the damp chill out of my bones. I was still soggy from the rain and sweat. I finished my meal with a fortune cookie that carried an important message, "Stop searching forever, happiness is just next to you." I did feel like my search was nearing its end, and if the good karma reflected in that simple sentence were true, happiness could be found in the drivers sitting next to me who would carry me home.

I dawdled, trying to kill time. I walked around town slowly, looking into store windows and strolling residential streets. With a continuing drop in temperature the weather remained lousy as the departure time approached. Arriving at the terminal waiting room with half an hour to spare, there was still a bit of snow blowing around as the vehicle traffic loaded up. The stern of the "Caribou" loomed out of the ink black darkness, illuminated by floodlights. The bow of the ship was virtually invisible from where I stood ashore.

I proceeded onto the ferry with more than a little trepidation. Past experiences with water had revealed to me its ruthless power and deadliness. While canoeing in the Boundary Waters Canoe Area of northern Minnesota, a friend and I faced death in the form of a waterfall current that was sweeping us to the brink. Another time I fell through the frail ice of a wilderness creek. I was wearing skis and a backpack at the time. I had obviously survived both incidents and took from them a tremendous respect for this formidable enemy which, at the scale of the ocean, could swallow the entire population of the world with barely a ripple. Recent maritime ferry disasters in Scandinavia did nothing to reassure me that a large boat was necessarily immune to mishap.

When I got on board and settled into the large common area designated for television viewing, I found out it was "hockey night in Canada." But then, every night in Canada is hockey night! Allegedly, there are a couple of days in the middle of July when Canadians forget about their violent national pastime, think gentle thoughts, and go on a picnic. No sticks, helmets, referees, penalty boxes, or ice anywhere to be found. Unfortunately, the picnic event often includes swimming. Their dip into icy cold water is a shocking reminder that they live in a land perennially locked by ice and snow. They rush out of the water as angry as a right wing tripped on a three on one break. This blunt reminder collectively sends all of Canada into a funk. Epidemic levels of fist fights, hooking, and slashing occur nationwide. Reacting to a paternal instinct the government legislates a requirement that everyone must don helmets and face guards for their own protection. The citizenry is resigned to sit on splintered benches, lacing and unlacing their skates. With vacant eyes they just sit and wait. They are unsure how to handle the remaining days of summer without their beloved hockey. It's a sorrowful state of affairs in this otherwise great country.

All is well, though, when lakes and rivers begin freezing on August 1st. Then one can witness scenes reminiscent of Hans Brinker and the Silver Skates. Rosy cheeks, gleaming eyes, and love affairs abound. Canada, once again, regains its stature as an industrial world power. Being from Minnesota, I'm well acquainted with a hockey-based culture. A little known fact, Minnesota is actually a part of Canada that was misplaced by surveyors.

We all took our seats and settled in to watch the big game as the nautical miles passed by. The television reception went bad after the first couple of minutes. God help us all! People were getting a little nervous about missing their hockey fix for the day. You could see the fear rising in their eyes as they looked around for somebody to blame. It was touch and go for the entire first period. The game finally came back on strong and clear during the second period. We could relax once more and watch the players (gladiators?) duke it out. Life in Canada was good once again.

Sometime during the first period break, I took note of the fact that the ferry was smashing into things. There was this muted crashing sound and the entire ship would shudder. Each crash was followed by a scraping sound that continued along the entire length of both sides of the vessel. I wondered what in the name of Poseidon was going on.

I donned my coat and rain pants and went out on deck to investigate. I pushed open a door that led to an outside deck. I had dressed appropriately. It was just awful out there and I hoped the door hadn't locked itself behind me. I was met by a strong cold wind that swirled the sleet around like a dervish. The metal deck was slick with a thin layer of ice. I shuffled over to the railing, taking note of the location of nearby lifeboats. I thought it strange that the ship wasn't pitching at all despite the wind. There was no threat of falling overboard because I stood on an upper deck with ten feet of lower deck width between me and the sea. Nonetheless, I had a firm grip on the railing in front of me. I was the only person outside. I must have really liked bad weather; I found myself enduring a lot of it.

The dim glow of the ship's running lights revealed large, flat, cakes of ice, completely surrounding us. Shaped like even sided polygons, the frozen slabs of sea water ground together as they rode the ocean swells. They were interlocked in a puzzle configuration, for as far as I could see. As the ship sliced through this puzzle, the pieces would be only temporarily displaced, separating long enough for us to pass, then closing behind us once again, leaving a bland white pattern that obscured any evidence of our passage.

As the wind slapped at my clothes, the sky rudely spit sleet in my face. Visions of the captain of the Titanic, announcing women and children first, clogged my panic stricken brain. We didn't have a chance. The crew, ignoring the captain's orders, would lower their own lifeboats first and leave us reading the lifeboat crane operations manual. It was written in Greek and nobody would know how to read it. We were doomed!

Reeling under the weight of these images, gripping the railing even tighter, I suddenly realized what would save me from a certain mental breakdown. I ran back inside, resolved to watch the last slapshot of the hockey game fly before we entered our chilly, black grave. I knew that's what a real Canadian would do!

When the game was over and we weren't yet mired in the muck at the bottom of the Cabot Strait, I wandered up to the forward-most passenger access of the boat to check for stress fractures or holes left by sneaky icebergs. Although I had no structural engineering training, I wanted to provide as much assistance to the captain as possible, just in case he was worried. All seemed in order. I noticed no gaping holes, gushing water.

While forward on my inspection tour I met a couple of characters in their mid-forties from southwest Nova Scotia. With good Scottish names like Lennis Corkum and Llewellyn Moore, where else could they possibly be from? It turned out that they were cabinet makers. They were on this God-forsaken boat to deliver some exhibit housings for a museum, 350 miles away at the northern tip of the island of Newfoundland.

If you're like I was, you don't have any idea about the proper pronunciation of the name, Newfoundland. Let me help. Say each syllable slowly and clearly to begin with. Knee-oo-fn-lan. After a little practice, say the entire word as fast as possible, with the accent and a full second time lapse on the final syllable. It won't seem so scary after the recommended practice. You'll be the envy of everyone at your next party!

Well, even though I could correctly pronounce Newfoundland, I was still a traveller without means. I asked Lennis and Llewellyn if I could join them on their journey to the town of St. Anthony and their cabinet making gig at L'Anse aux Meadows, National Historical Park. They agreed to haul me along. This required a bit of effort on their part. They had to re-pack their van to accommodate me and my gear. They had to wait until we made landfall because there was no access to the vehicle decks while out to sea. They didn't seem to mind the slight complication of their trip and welcomed the unusual company.

Excited about how well things were going, I returned to the television lounge and tried to catch some sleep. I stretched out on the floor with everybody else who didn't have a cabin and snoozed for a couple of hours.

When we arrived in Port-aux-Basques, Newfoundland, after the seven hour boat ride, I was happy to be on land again and quite relieved to have made arrangements with Lennis and Llewellyn. We witnessed a bleak scene as we disembarked. The terminal was consumed in a whiteout. Thick snowflakes flew horizontally through the air and everything that stood exposed to the wind had a drift built up behind it. The town of Port-aux-Basques was nowhere to be seen through the curtain of dull white.

The snowstorm was localized and disappeared shortly after leaving Port-aux-Basques. As we drove northeast on this remote version of the Trans-Canada Highway, I witnessed some of the most rugged terrain I'd ever seen. Huge rocky expanses with sparse tree cover, streams, frozen ponds and lakes, and towns spaced 50 to 100 miles apart. Much of it was covered with fresh snow.

We lunched at Deer Lake, a town that existed simply because it was at a crossroad. From there we turned north on the Viking Trail and hugged the coastline the entire distance to St. Anthony. Although the Viking Trail was paved and snow-free, it was quite rough. Frost heaving had buckled the road in hundreds of places. The effect of some of the larger ones picked us all up off of our seats and the cargo off the floor of the van. Smaller frost boils promoted the growth of potholes. Every set of tires that struck the pothole edge would send small chunks of tar flying, enlarging the diameter and increasing its depth. Off to the west, often only a stones throw away, we could see that the Gulf of St. Lawrence was frozen solid. Snow, cold winds, frost heaving, and salt water still frozen on April 11th got me to thinking about hockey again.

Lennis and Llewellyn were so friendly and homespun, our conversation was like that between old friends. We had a great time watching Newfoundland pass by our windows.

The named places we passed by were just tiny hamlets. Few of them even had fuel stations or grocery stores. Snow wasn't falling for the majority of the drive but the ground was still covered with a couple of feet of snow. Every ten or twenty miles we would come to a patch of woods that came right up to the road. A half dozen cars and pick-up trucks would be parked along the side of the road at these spots creating miniature traffic jams. Men and women were busy cutting and splitting wood, and stacking it in their trucks. They used snowmobiles with little sledges to retrieve the wood from the forest and bring it to the roadside. Because everyone had to have wood to keep their homes warm, everybody was out there working. The gatherings appeared to be quite a community social event.

It took ten hours for us to drive the 350 miles from Port-aux-Basques to St. Anthony. That northern outpost was covered with more snow than we'd seen on the island thus far. The guys had reservations at a motel and went to check in. I went along to see what it would cost for me to get a room. I wasn't interested in spending the night out in temperatures colder than 20 degrees F. They were staying at the cheaper of two motels in town and even that was $60 Canadian per night. I decided that it may have been snowy and cold, but not bad enough to shell out that kind of money for a night's lodging.

I walked up a street for a couple of blocks, where it dead-ended, along with the town. Walking up and over a knoll, I set up my tent in a little depression that obscured it from view. All the trees around were about four feet tall, stunted by the short growing season and poor, rocky soil. Rolling terrain and a lack of trees made the area perfect for a snowmobile playground. The snow all around my campsite was criss-crossed with snowmobile tracks. I had to set up my tent in a spot off the main thoroughfares. I didn't want some fourteen-year-old snowmoblie driver racing through the middle of my bed in the dark. People are always getting killed by those things and I didn't intend to be a victim that night.

My dinner consisted of a sandwich, an apple, some nuts and chocolate. Durable, high energy food. I was always so hungry from the calories burned from physical exertion, everything tasted awesome when I did eat.

The sunset was pretty, dropping off behind a treeless, three-hundred foot high ridge. I went to bed reasonably warm and dry and slept well. St.

Anthony was as far north as I was going to go. It was just good luck that I avoided spending the night in a raging blizzard.

Everything I packed up in the morning was stiff and cracking from the cold. I couldn't leave my hands unprotected for more than a few moments at a time. When I had finished that distasteful task I walked back to Lennis and Llewellyn's motel. I was planning to hang out with them all day as they worked. When they finished I would ride with them back south. I was unquestionably pursuing a surefire ride at that point. I did not want to be left standing in St. Anthony for a couple of days, or longer, waiting for a ride under really dicey weather conditions.

LENNIS CORKUM AND LLEWELLYN MOORE
Port-aux-Basques, Newfoundland

After breakfast we headed off to the museum at L'Anse aux Meadows which was less than ten miles out of town. We arrived there under near whiteout conditions. The snow along the road to the museum had drifted to ten feet deep. Lennis backed the van up to the entrance door through a trench carved out of the snow. As they went about unloading and assembling the exhibit cases, I spent the day relaxing and studying the museum's artifacts. It was nice to loaf around and enjoy the warmth of the building. The pleasure of living had been reduced to its simplest components; warmth, rest, and just enough food to keep my stomach from growling in protest.

L'Anse aux Meadows National Historical Park, a cold, naked, wind-whipped little plain, was reputed to be the first European settlement in North America. The short-time residents were of Nordic descent. The winters were harsh with virtually no growing season, and they struggled to survive here for only a few years before conditions forced them to return to Scandinavia. Even this close to spring, it was plain to see how difficult survival must have been for those earliest of pilgrims.

It took all day for Lennis and Llewellyn to finish their project. We headed south at 7:00 pm, as darkness and a violent storm moved in to replace the daylight. The temperature took a big plunge and the wind kept trying to blow us off the road. We drove along with almost no other traffic to accompany us on that terrifying, black night. The snow was blowing horizontally across our path and we had to slow down to a crawl to enable Llewellyn to see the roadway. When the van seemed to be running on only about five out of its eight cylinders, we looked at each other with anxious eyes. The carburetor was apparently freezing up. If the vehicle were to fail completely, there would be little chance for our survival. Driving a final stretch at about 15 mph, we were able to limp into a fuel station and set about bettering our situation.

During our stop we dumped in some fuel line de-icer along with plenty of gas. The van was getting about half of its normally atrocious gas mileage, due to the effects of the cold and wind. It was easily -50°F under the effects of a vicious wind chill. Facing the possibility of frostbitten face and fingers, Llewellyn was torturing himself under the hood, making sure everything in the vicinity of the carburetor was free from ice and moisture. While this flurry of automotive tending continued I went inside and asked to use the restroom. The attendant gave a little chuckle and shook her head. When I wondered aloud what was so funny she said that all the plumbing facilities were frozen solid. It wasn't a good sign. It wasn't even a funny joke. I had to go pretty badly, but wasn't willing to risk freezing my penis off squatting in a snowbank behind the building. I decided I could wait until I experienced some friendlier weather conditions before dropping my drawers.

We were able to continue down the road, mishap free, and eventually rolled into the junction town of Deer Lake again. With its large, modern fuel station and restaurant facilities, the town appeared as nothing less than an oasis. It was a welcome sight to our highway hypnotized eyes.

The snow had nearly stopped and it wasn't quite as cold. I decided to leave Lennis and Llewellyn to their own devices. They were continuing south, driving all night to catch the ferry which would leave from Port-aux-Basques in the morning. I was worried about letting a sure thing go, but wanted to complete the trip as planned. A little bad weather wasn't going to get in my way. If I didn't do it, now that I was so close, I'd probably never see the remainder of the island. I was determined to continue east from Deer Lake, to St. John's, Newfoundland.

From Deer Lake, St. John's was still 350 miles away. Lennis and Llewellyn had dropped me off at 2:00 am. It was Friday, the 13th of April. St. John's would just have to wait; there would be no more hitchhiking that night. I would try my luck on that superstition wracked date when daylight arrived. I found shelter from the wind under a semi-truck trailer, parked against a plowed snowbank. It was a nice, cozy, quiet place. Not exactly the Hilton but I still slept like a king.

Even a nasty night like that didn't really phase me. I had become one with the road. I knew where to look for the little nests I required for a night's rest. Even if I didn't find the perfect bedsite, the next best thing was usually plenty good enough. I felt comfortable damn near anywhere. It was a strange, but powerful feeling. I could go anywhere I wanted.

When the sun came up on my peculiar little camp the temperature of 20°F reflected springtime influences. I hit the road but had a long, boring, two hour wait to get out of Deer Lake. As I'd expected, traffic on the Trans-Canada Highway was sparse. Pete Shepard broke the two hour stalemate and brought me about fifty miles to the junction of highway 410. Pete was from Goose Bay, Labrador, and worked seasonally at the NATO defense base there. Labrador is the continental portion of Newfoundland. Despite its remoteness, Pete claimed Goose Bay was growing. New houses, businesses, and roads appeared every year.

Pete was on the island for a surprise birthday visit with his two-year-old daughter, Samantha. She lived here with her mother, and Pete only had the chance to visit them every six months. It was difficult and expensive to travel away from Goose Bay, so he'd never been far from Labrador. He was excited to be out and about.

Although it was a sunny morning, I was dressed in thermal underwear, wool cap, two pairs of mittens, down vest, mountain parka, rain pants, and snow boots, in an attempt to stay warm. Pete wore jeans, tee shirt and sunglasses. Despite the snow surrounding us, it was like a trip to the beach for him. The harbor of Goose Bay, some 400 miles north, was still confined under the grip of four to five feet of ice. It was a town that used snowmobiles more often than automobiles. Despite that fact, Pete seemed to be familiar enough with the throttle of automobiles. We zipped down the road at speeds approaching 100 miles per hour. That's what I called making time.

Junior Young, a lifelong Newfoundlander from Twillingate, was going home after dropping his wife and son off in Corner Brook. Corner Brook was a large town and the location of a hospital. Junior's wife had a kidney problem and would be staying there for a while to receive treatment.

Twillingate was on a tiny island in Notre Dame Bay. Junior worked seasonally at a fish plant and was altogether unemployed during the winter. He often watched icebergs drift by his front porch as they floated down from the ice pack on the Labrador current. It was a pastime that rarely, if ever, happened to those who lived on the coasts of the lower forty-eight states.

Junior left me at a place called Notre Dame junction eighty miles east of where Pete had dropped me off. A couple of fifteen mile rides with Ford Perry and Roy Burt got me to Gander. Gander was a reasonably-sized town and even had a busy international airport, but I had my sights set on St. John's, the provincial capital. Other than my initial two hour wait that morning I had been making excellent progress. I was determined to spend the night in St. John's.

By 1:00 pm, twenty-five year-old Ted Baker became my deliverer, taking me the remaining two-hundred miles. He was travelling from his place in Corner Brook to St. John's to surprise his family with an Easter visit. As we approached the coast, Ted learned of my desire to stand on Cape Spear. It was the eastern-most point of the North American continent. He was happy to act as a tour guide, bringing me there to accomplish that goal and helping with the obligatory photos.

Ted parked the car and we walked up to the lighthouse. The wind was cold but at least there was no snow to contend with. The area was a designated park and there were a couple of other people roaming around braving the cold. The view from this rocky outcrop was breathtaking. Portions of St. John's were visible. The coastline was mostly a series of steep hills that dipped straight into the ocean. There weren't any trees to obscure my line of sight inland. Looking out at the Atlantic Ocean, the water barrier that kept me from continuing east, I was ecstatic about completing this important leg of the trip. I had been breaking new ground with each mile for the last three-thousand.

The people of eastern Canada were proving to be as trusting and kind as the people of any geographic area. That was fortunate for me because the towns were far apart, cars were few, and the weather marginal at best.

Of course, after arriving at Cape Spear and looking around, I wanted to be instantly transported back to Willow River. Things didn't quite work out that way....

Chapter Seven

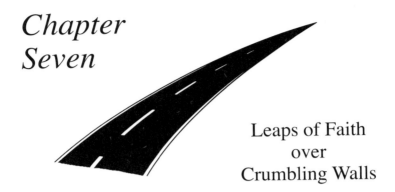

Leaps of Faith
over
Crumbling Walls

There's a lot to be said for innocence. I wonder how much of an effect it has on our day to day existence. Sometimes, when the activity around us becomes so overwhelming and out of control, our unknowing innocence can lead us directly into the line of fire. In that case our lives get squashed. Other times, our blissful naivete seems to provide us with a virtually impenetrable shield. Nothing can do us harm.

Often, fun and exciting activities look relatively safe, but are actually fraught with danger. Especially as youths, we found it difficult to recognize real danger. Surely everyone can recall circumstances in their young lives, where only a matter of inches decided between an end result of catastrophe or giggles. Cars miraculously avoided us when we darted out into the street from between parked cars; we skated across thin ice without falling through; we conked our heads when we fell off our bicycles but didn't get a concussion; we walked under ladders, fell down stairs, ate all kinds of gross stuff off the floor, and survived. As kids we were capable of walking through fire unscathed because we didn't even realize there had been a fire until we looked backward. After looking backward at danger enough times, experience taught us to begin turning our sights forward. Our hindsight eventually lead us to anticipate events in the immediate future, thereby enabling us to avoid the most obvious threats. As this process of increasing awareness progressed we lost our blind innocence a little bit at a time. Along with it went the invisible shield that ignorance had endowed us with. Some of us survived it all to become adults.

Even as adults, there is so much we don't understand and can't control. We have to maintain an unconscious mix of adult savvy and childish innocence to keep us going. Unfortunately, both qualities will eventually fail and we'll suddenly be dead.

If it's not innocence, perhaps it is just dumb luck. Is that what I'm talking about? Maybe we're just shoved out into the world with an invisible number stamped on our foreheads. The number indicates the quantity of good luck we carry. Each good luck experience we take advantage of throughout our lives is automatically deducted from our accounts. Eventually, our accounts reach the minimum balance and close. We're history because there's no accommodation for overdrafts. You could also liken it to fouling out of a basketball game. After the fifth foul you hit the bench. You used up your allotted number and that's that.

I must have had some brand of middle-aged innocence, as well as a high number of good luck opportunities in my account to have made it as far as Newfoundland. Even after my visit to St.John's, I was still in the game. Innocence? Luck? Poor calls by blind referees in my favor? Ted Baker and I had a chance to find out how much of that stuff we had left between our two, silly souls.

St. John's, Newfoundland is a beautiful city of around 100,000 people. Its downtown district is on St. John's Harbor. The rest of the town has grown up on the steep hills above the harbor and the rolling hills up and away from the water.

Ted's poor old Toyota station wagon was a genuine rust bucket. It clanked, rattled, and wobbled down the hills and curves of eastern Newfoundland. Pieces of the car body were practically dissolving before our eyes under the relentless chemical reactions that took place in an environment of salt, water, and steel. I knew we were leaving a trail of red dust wherever we rolled.

As Ted drove the hills from Cape Spear back into town, he complained about the Toyota's brakes. It's no wonder. They sounded frightful. The pads must have been worn down to rivets and provided very little braking friction against the rotors. What we heard was the screeching sound of metal on metal. As long as it stopped the car, I could live with the noise. It was a sound I was familiar with because I used to have brakes with no pads, during my "lean years" after college.

As a passenger I had no idea how badly the brakes were actually performing. Ted was worried enough that he stopped, as it were, practically brakeless, and checked underneath. We both went out to look around, but didn't notice anything unusual during our quick inspection, so we continued on into town, still talking about the sights and doing the tourist thing. Even with metal pads on metal rotors, I knew we still had the capability to stop, as long as the master cylinder was still intact.

Once in town, Ted turned onto a steep uphill grade. The road was en route to a camping spot he knew of that was outside of downtown, yet convenient. We proceeded uphill a few blocks before stopping for a traffic signal. The hill was even steeper by then and we rolled to a stop at the intersection. Ted went to use his brakes, to keep us from rolling backwards, and his right foot went to the floor with no resistance. I tasted bile. The brakes had utterly, and completely, failed.

The Toyota had a standard transmission and was in neutral. Ted's left foot still had the clutch depressed as gravity began living up to the tenets of physics. While he was stomping on the brake pedal, trying to generate some kind of pressure in the brake line, we both went for the emergency brake. With two desperately strong, panic stricken grips, we damn near ripped the handle out of its certainly rusted mount before the brake began to grab hold, ever so slightly. It slowed our backward progress long enough for Ted to sensibly shift into first gear and drop the clutch, thereby using the engine to keep us in place.

Things happened really fast in that situation. There was none of that slow motion perception that you hear about before certain accidents happen. As Ted revved the engine and let the clutch slip to hold us in place, we glanced at each other and cracked nervous smiles. Inches and giggles. There was fear in our eyes as we looked back down our former pathway. We took a few seconds to contemplate the frightening possibilities of our barely averted plunge through downtown and into the harbor, then decided we needed to get off of that damn hill. Hills always become "damn hills" when you don't have any brakes.

After our single application of the emergency brake, it had reached the end of its rope. Its adjustment was so far off that it was no longer of any use in slowing us down. Having lived there all his life, in addition to nearly dying there, Ted knew the safest route across St. John's to the park where I could sleep. We drove slowly. I didn't want him to hurry, but I wanted to be out of that car and into bed. I wanted my mommy, my blankie, and a bottle of something stronger than warm milk! You know, that mix of childhood innocence and adult savvy that keeps us going. I'd had enough of that stressful situation.

We arrived safely at the park and found a place to leave the car for the night. I went to camp and Ted went to phone for a ride home. He was too shaken up to drive that thing another foot. I slept that night in a small wooded area along the shore of a pond, having used up yet another of my good luck credits. Life was good! I must have been spending those credits like crazy to pay for it though. I was paying for inches and giggles....

The following morning I met up with Ted to help figure out what had gone wrong with the brakes. He rode up alone on his motorcycle although I was expecting him to bring along some help. Since he hadn't, it was up to us to figure it all out. While taking up a position underneath the car as he pumped the brake pedal, I noticed a line leaking brake fluid. A heavy part of the suspension frame had been so weakened by rust that it had snapped. The brake line was mounted directly onto it and had snapped accordingly. As Ted worked the pedal, the brake fluid came streaming out. The problem wasn't a pinhole leak like you would normally find. It was a gaping hole caused by a complete fracture of the line. With absolutely no chance for pressure to build up in the system it was no wonder there weren't any brakes.

Ted Baker
St. John's, Newfoundland

I had a compelling interest in the repair of Ted's Toyota. I was planning on riding back to Corner Brook with him the following day, but I preferred riding in a vehicle that could stop at a moment's notice. Go ahead, call me demanding.

Slowly and cautiously, never even shifting out of first gear, Ted drove the car to a nearby garage. The mechanic said they could fix it by later that day if they could find the needed parts. I kept my fingers crossed.

I took advantage of the sunny weather and roamed about St. John's all day. I didn't waste any precious moments worrying about whether or not the car would be ready. I'd be able to find my own way out of town easily enough.

As I walked about town that day, the thing that struck me most about St. John's was the colors. The grass wasn't quite green yet because it was still awakening from its winter dormancy. The air temperature was still cool, in the low 50s, and I noticed dirty patches of snow here and there lurking in the shadows. Despite the dull colors of grass and dingy little patches of snow, everything else in town seemed brilliant. The sky and ocean were a fantastic blue. Along the waterfront, colorful ships lined the docks. Blue, red, yellow, white, and black fishing boats were bedecked with fluorescent green nets, red and white floats, and yellow ropes. Huge container ships, with their shining hulls standing high in the blue water, were the sites of the most activity. Forklifts twirled around in a bizarre dance, leading their partners of cargo across the dance floor. When one trip across the floor was over, the fickle machines would abruptly dump their partner, go back across the room to find another, and the next dance would begin and end with a similar result. Silver cranes lifted large, rainbow-hued metal containers from the dock and carefully conveyed them into deep holds or neatly stacked them on the top deck of the ship.

The citizens kept their town neat and clean. Houses were nicely painted and yards well kept. People were out working on their gardens, and tulips of many colors graced the early spring.

The next day was April 15, Easter Sunday. It had been another chilly, damp night in my camp next to a little lake. Trying to take advantage of the bright sunshine of the morning, I lay in bed until the tent was dry and the air temperature had warmed up to 50°F. By the time I finally hauled myself out of bed it was 9:30 am.

Ted was supposed to come by at 10:00 am and we'd set off across the huge island for Corner Brook, over four-hundred miles away. I packed up and waited until 10:45 before deciding to split. Ted didn't necessarily owe me a ride and he may have changed his mind about leaving so early. Easter was a big day for family fellowship. The only reason he had to leave some time that day was because he had to be at work the following morning.

Getting out of St. John's was a snap thanks to Ted's foresight. There was no need to dodge around town to find the right road out. I was camped only a hundred yards from the Trans-Canada Highway so I began my walk west looking for the perfect hitchhiking spot.

Julie Huntington, of Torbay, just north of St. John's, picked me up while I was still walking my first mile. She was on her way to do some scuba diving. She was a diving instructor and was seeking a nice place to bring her students for their lessons. The classes must have been for advanced students because she would be teaching them in the hostile world of the north Atlantic. Originally from Milwaukee, Wisconsin, she worked as a fisheries technologist with the University of Newfoundland. The primary goal of her profession was to figure out better ways to harvest the seas of its fish.

My ride with Julie was less than half-an-hour long and I found myself walking once again. I fully expected Ted to be driving up any minute, and he did so before I'd walked another half mile.

Ted Baker was a wonderful young man and I was fortunate to be sharing his company once again. He had been born and raised in Newfoundland, and reflected the personal openness that was legend for the population of this isolated rock in the Atlantic. He was temporarily employed at the college in Corner Brook as registrar. Upon termination of his appointment in December, he would travel to Indonesia as a volunteer with a cross-cultural program called Crossroads.

Although his tenure with Crossroads would only be four months long, participants were expected to bring home and share their knowledge of the host country's problems and challenges. As bright and articulate as Ted was, I felt confident the Canadians he came into contact with, following his mission, would gain a good understanding of what the people in Indonesia had to face to survive.

While in St. John's, Ted and I had gone to some drinking and dining establishments for food and drink, and I had met several of his friends. They were as pleasant as he was. Ted was an athlete as well as a goodwill ambassador. He competed at the national level in whitewater canoeing and kayaking.

He told me the reason he stood me up earlier that day was due to a delay at home. He had every intention of coming by my camp and taking me to Corner Brook and said he was surprised to have found me gone.

We spent that Easter Sunday driving 400 hard miles. Even though we arrived at the Corner Brook junction near dark, I wanted to squeeze a few more miles into the day. I'm not sure what my big hurry was. The next town was thirty miles away and traffic had disappeared with the sunlight. I said good-bye to one of my longest rides, with the happy knowledge that we had dodged a rusty bullet together.

I had no success getting out of there that evening. The junction where I stood was a couple of miles out of Corner Brook. I didn't really need to go to town for anything but water, so I decided to forgo a town trip and walked up the road a bit, looking for a place in the woods to camp.

A stiff wind blew out of the island's central highlands, carrying the temperature to well below freezing. The snow was at least four feet deep in the surrounding woods. I had a difficult time even getting off the road, due to the high snowplow berm along the ditches. I eventually found a well protected spot and set up my tent. I fell through the snow up to my crotch about ten times while getting to, and setting up camp. The wind in the treetops whistled a lullaby over that unusual land and my exhausted body quickly succumbed to sleep.

On Monday morning, April 16th, I dragged myself out of my cozy cocoon, packed up my wet gear, and was on the road by 9:00 am. Rick Patey always picked people up and was happy to take me the twenty-five miles to the Stephenville junction. Unfortunately, this junction was still ten miles away from the closest town, and nearly twenty miles from the next junction on the Trans-Canada Highway.

I waited there for what seemed like the entire morning before I gave up and started walking. It was a stupid thing to do because there was no place to walk to. Like the deserts of Texas and Nevada, the distances around there were huge. I wouldn't be catching somebody turning onto the road up ahead, because there weren't any roads for people to turn from. Besides that, I was walking straight into the teeth of the northern version of a typhoon.

It rained thick sheets of water. I was completely soaked in a matter of moments. My Gore-tex coat and nylon pants were no match for this deluge. The wind was in my face and I had to lean hard into it to remain on my feet.

There was a surprising amount of traffic that breezed past me, despite the conditions. During a half hour of walking, I must have seen ten or fifteen cars and trucks go by. That was a car at least every two or three minutes. Practically gridlock for those parts.

I was experiencing a lot of conflicting emotions out there. I was really angry at the inhospitable traffic. I also screamed at the top of my lungs at the weather, demanding it to take it a little easier on me. In opposition to that turmoil, I walked along, amazed at the interesting predicament I found myself in. I felt fortunate to be out there alone, experiencing the thrill of facing an unmerciful tempest. Once again, my respect for what mother nature was capable of dishing out was enhanced.

I had walked a couple of miles before Dave Bursey took pity on me and awakened me from my watery philosophizing. He brought me into the steel-gray gloom that enveloped Port-aux-Basques. Dave would be working in town but I would be riding the first ferry out. We had arrived ten minutes too late to catch the morning ferry, which left me with an eight hour wait until the next departure. I crammed my gear into a locker, then went back out into the rain to rummage around town looking for something to do. My budget didn't include funds for sitting around in bars and drinking, so I found little to do. I exchanged money at the bank, bought a thick, trashy, paperback novel about vampires, did some grocery shopping, and walked up and down the small hills and along the narrow streets for hours.

When the ferry left Port-aux-Basques that evening, the conditions were similar to the ride over. We were hitting the same ice floes and facing the same wind and sleet. The only thing missing was the hockey game.

To pass the time before going to sleep, I roamed the ferry. In one of the corridors there was a little photographic display reviewing the history of the Canadian Atlantic ferry system. There were photos of various ships, with notations regarding original construction, chain of ownership, previous service, and last but not least, their fates. Under the present weather conditions, the final sentences were not comforting reading. Much of the ferry fleet had ultimately become lost at sea. Those simple black and white words on the little note cards did nothing to express the terror that must have been felt by the doomed passengers and crew. A lively imagination like mine, along with ice floes crashing into the bow, helped to bring those terrifying images to life. Why couldn't they have had a nice display where they talked about eastern Canadian food recipes, instead?

Once again, I had survived Cabot Strait and arrived in North Sydney, Nova Scotia, just after dawn on Tuesday, April 17th. It was a beautiful spring morning. I didn't know where the clouds of the night before had gone, but was glad they had dispersed.

I hurried off the ferry to catch the first cars and trucks that would soon be streaming off the boat to all points of Canada. Unfortunately, nobody driving off the ferry that morning would pick me up so I had to walk out of and away from the terminal to find some more traffic. A young man heading for work stopped, but only took me a couple of miles.

A brief walk from there brought me to a short, narrow bridge. Halfway across, Dave McDonald waved me along to the end of the bridge where he could safely pull over and load me up. I was grateful for his patience while he waited for me to catch up with him. I had been dreading long walks and short rides and was excited that my walking would soon come to an end. My excitement was a little premature.

DAVE MCDONALD
Cape Breton Island, Nova Scotia

Dave was on his way to the town of Margaree, on Cape Breton Island. He owned and operated a tourist lodging business called the Norma Way Inn. It was located along the Cabot Trail Highway, reputed to be the most scenic road in North America. It followed the rugged island coastline, which consisted of high bluffs rising vertically out of the sea. I wouldn't ride on the Cabot Trail during that trip, but the descriptions of a beauty not to be missed left me with a good excuse to return.

Dave was an extremely pleasant man. The culture he was raised in, on the island, was one of trust and neighborliness. His own roots with family and friends ran deep. Everyone knew everybody else and all shared in the joys and problems of life and its struggles. I could hear the affection in his voice and see it in his eyes as he spoke of this beloved land. I didn't foresee Dave leaving the small community life of the area, for the larger financial rewards possibly awaiting him in some cold-hearted city.

I was disappointed at the short duration of my ride with Dave. I wanted to hear more of his life on the island. He left me in the tiny village of Nyanza, where he turned off, heading for Margaree and the coast.

While waiting for a ride out of Nyanza, an elderly woman approached the junction from a side road. She then turned down the road in the direction I was headed. She stopped alongside me and waved me over to her window. She wanted to tell me that she was just running an errand a few blocks down the road. She wanted to assure me she wasn't just going to pass me by and leave me standing because she didn't like my looks or something. When she returned from her errand, she tooted her horn and waved. She was an especially kind person and I appreciated her consideration of my feelings. It cut a bit of the loneliness out of an otherwise long, solitary wait.

After an hour wait in Nyanza I started walking. I walked over four miles before coming to another intersection. I tried my luck there for yet another hour with no success. Completely frustrated once again, I started walking. There were so few cars I began to think about how long it might take me to walk the 2000 miles from there to Willow River.

Another mile brought me to the crest of a hill with a wide turnout. I decided to make a new sign using the Lathrop Wells strategy. While kneeling down, working on the sign, an approaching semi-truck driver noticed me and slammed on his brakes. Led by the two front tires toward the shoulder, the other sixteen grabbed at the pavement. The big rig screeched to a dusty halt right behind me, and the door of the cab opened to a seat next to Alden Gordon of Upper Kent, New Brunswick. I would be retracing two sections of road to the town of Sussex just south of Moncton, and as luck would have it, Alden was on his way across Nova Scotia to Moncton. I had a long ride, at last! I knew I'd have a ride for at least the next 275 miles.

Trust didn't come easily for a long haul trucker like Alden. He'd heard all the troubling stories from other drivers and run into a few bad characters himself. The bad characters weren't necessarily hitchhikers but had some sort of criminal element involving the road. He wouldn't have picked me up without some proof that I was legitimate. My legitimacy was determined after he remembered seeing me all the way back in Corner Brook. He was driving one of the vehicles that had passed me by in the middle of the torrential downpour. He reasoned that if I had made it this far since then, I must have safely experienced a number of rides. He could see I wasn't in jail, nor was I driving a stolen car. It was accurate reasoning as far as I was concerned.

Alden drove a truck for a big retail discount chain, delivering products throughout the maritimes. Every Monday morning he could be seen loading his rig onto the ferry, with deliveries to Corner Brook, Gander, and St. John's, Newfoundland. They were the only towns with a population large enough to support department stores. He had come across on the same ferry as I had the night before. The reason he wasn't far ahead of me was because he had made a couple of deliveries along the way. That's how our timing brought us together on the crest of that particular hill.

We rode together to New Glasgow, Nova Scotia. He had to make another delivery there. He dropped me off saying he'd pick me up again if I hadn't gotten a ride by the time he returned. Then there would be no more stopping and we'd have a straight shot the remaining miles to Moncton. I thanked him and looked forward to continuing our conversation.

Where Alden had dropped me off, on the east edge of New Glasgow, there was a lot of highway construction taking place. It was a bad place to wait so I set off walking through that mess, all the way to the west side of town. An hour later, I stood at an excellent freeway interchange with the city of Truro twenty-five miles away.

Blair Morrow, of Halifax, took me to his southern turn off at Truro. He worked as a consulting building inspector. A soft-spoken man, his friendly demeanor was that of a man without an enemy in the world.

Despite some long waits in this corner of Canada, the people who stopped were very kind. I was glad for that because I was a little on edge, anxious to get home and rather impatient. I was pushing the mileage every day. With my patience short, long waits had become agonizing. Once again I had been reduced to a hitchhiking machine. By their very nature, these kind people settled me down and helped me to enjoy their unique and beautiful part of Canada. Nobody can appreciate the countryside, or friendly people, if they are in a big rush.

In Truro, Alden came by again and picked me up. It was still over a hundred miles into Moncton and I was getting tired. The passenger seat of a cab-over style semi-truck is uncomfortable and the bumps in the freeway were taking their toll on my stamina. As we approached the city, the rain started coming down hard. Before dropping me off, Alden stopped at a card-controlled fueling stop. This one happened to have a shower, and he let me use the facilities for a quick clean up while he gassed up. I hadn't bathed since the motel room in Halifax, over a week earlier. I really needed a shower after all the tough walking and rainy conditions I had endured. Unfortunately, my clothes were a mess too. Everything was dirty and damp. The beneficial effects of the shower were short-lived.

Alden left me at a great spot, on the very western edge of Moncton. There was a motel, restaurant, fuel station, and a little store right there. The rain never let up for a minute. My only sane option was to try scrounging a room at the motel. I chose the insane option of relying on my gear to protect me and provide me with a good night's sleep. Being stubborn, I wanted to tough it out, just for fun.

As fresh and clean as I could be from my recent shower, and bundled up in my rain gear, I headed out into the wet, black void to find a place to camp. The surrounding landscape was practically under water. I stumbled down the road toward a single bright light on the right side of the road. It was the yard light of a small church. I was exhausted and needed to get horizontal. Choosing a spot on the lee side of the structure, I set up my tent as fast as I could. There was a shadow that I could squeeze into so that my camp wouldn't be noticed.

The wind was blowing so hard that the building provided little protection from it. A few minutes after crawling into my sleeping bag, I had to crawl back out of it. I needed to move some of my gear around the inside of the tent to hold the corners in place. The wind certainly wasn't going to blow the tent away with me inside, but the breeze was determined to blow it to shreds. As the cold, wet, nylon tent walls slapped me in the head, I wished I were someplace else. The night was no longer the sort of entertainment I wanted to participate in.

I couldn't possibly sleep under those conditions and needed to try something else. I climbed out of my sleeping bag again, then all of the way out of the tent, in the hope of finding a better location with more wind protection. As I zipped up the door on the rain fly and walked into the rain, the tent started rolling away. Except for what I wore, I had all my gear inside. Even that wasn't enough weight to keep it in one place. I was able to corral it, then anchor it, and continue my search.

Now, the side with the least wind was in the church parking lot, directly under the light. I opted for a quick move, even though the spot I chose was completely visible to anyone driving along the road. I normally preferred a more discreet bed.

My tent was of a free-standing design and required no disassembly to move. To do so I just had to grab two of the supporting poles and drag the whole mess around the corner, then along the side to the middle of the building under the light. When I crawled back inside the tent, I saw that everything had gathered into a big pile along the back wall. It was a slimy, clammy, cold catastrophe.

After remaking my bed, I entered my sleeping bag with my wet Gore-tex parka, wool hat, and mittens on. It wasn't below freezing, yet, but I knew it would be before long. I wanted to be prepared for the worst, and then forget about it. I wasn't going to worry about what tomorrow would bring. It would come whether I wasted time thinking about it or not. My move was a good one and I slept alright. Exhaustion had worked its magic on me, once again.

I awoke to find a heavy frost on everything. I tried, unsuccessfully, to brush it off the tent. My freezing hands packed the wet tent away. The wind wasn't blowing at hurricane velocities that morning, but it remained a dangerous chilling factor. I hit the road at a fast walk, hoping to warm up a bit. My goal was the driveway back at the gas station complex where Alden had dropped me off the previous night.

I was hoping for a short wait because of the cold. My hopes were rewarded almost immediately by trucker Pete Johnson. Not only was the truck interior warm but so was Pete's smile. He seemed to be knowledgeable on nearly every topic of discussion, be it politics, history, geography, or economics. His thirty-six years belied a very mature understanding of life and happiness. He was as comfortable in his truck with a stranger as a grandfather might be with his grandkids in a fishing boat.

PETE JOHNSON
Sussex, New Brunswick

I rode with Pete for about an hour into Sussex, New Brunswick. It was enough to get me warmed up and dried out a little. From there, he headed southwest to Saint John, while I continued west toward Fredericton, the capital of New Brunswick. I had a depressing wait in Sussex.

There seemed to be plenty of traffic, but no one was giving me a second look. The rotten wind was cutting through my clothing like I wasn't even dressed. With no emergency shelter visible from my spot on the road I began to worry. It was so bitterly cold!

When I was on the road in the United States I had acquaintances to use as destinations. They weren't really very far apart in terms of time or distance. I could be at a friends house after a couple of days out, or five days at the most. In the eastern United States and Canada, that luxury was not available to me. That fact took a lot of the enjoyment out of being on the road. I was still meeting the coolest people around but had little chance to reflect on their kindness and generosity. I was too busy trying to get the next ride out of the cold spots where I waited. Home, the one destination I had left, was still thousands of miles away.

When John Morrison finally stopped for me in Sussex, my mouth was barely functioning well enough to greet and thank him. I felt like the Tin Man in The Wizard of Oz asking for oil through rusted lips and jaw.

John was on the road as a hydraulic component sales-and-service man. Long hours away from his wife and teen-aged kids made him regret wasted time driving from one town to the next. Spending his life travelling wasn't his idea of a good time. To make it more tolerable, he helped other travellers when he could and enjoyed their company. He said he never passed up hitchhikers. Whether or not he trusted a particular individual along the road didn't come into the decision making process. He just automatically chose to help anyone who needed a lift.

JOHN MORRISON
Wicklow, New Brunswick

In our continuing conversation on trust, John related two stories that showed a breakdown of trust on both an institutional and human level.

The first story involved John and his twenty years of military service. John had joined the Royal Canadian Air Force right out of high school. He was trained in helicopter maintenance and served for fifteen years, at which point he was transferred, cross-service, into the Navy. There, he was assigned menial, miserable jobs and hated every minute of it. He suffered through another five years, only to obtain the minimum pension available to Canadian service personnel.

The reason any of this was especially notable was because John claimed the existence of an armed services retirement scam. He said the Canadian government purposefully transferred people into different branches of service, to essentially disenfranchise them. The point was to make them so miserable that they would quit the service before being eligible for full retirement benefits. The institution of the Canadian Armed Services had not acted in good faith and caused harm to many of its citizens. No one expects institutions to perform perfectly; however, it isn't too much to ask that they act in good faith toward those with whom commitments had been made. It was disappointing hearing this story from such a gentle and generous man.

When talk turned to the trust associated with human interaction, John noted a decline in neighborliness and personal responsibility. They are concepts that are less and less visible and are even becoming difficult to recognize. When someone we don't know treats us kindly we automatically assume its some kind of a scam being set up or a sales gimmick. Our trust in strangers has been worn down by the corruptness of people and business associates we are frequently in contact with. If people won't take responsibility for their own actions or mistakes, they assume nobody else will either. Who might get stuck with the blame often has little to do with who was actually responsible.

Its impossible to trust people in that sort of environment. We need to recognize that we're all guilty of certain things. It doesn't necessarily mean that everybody is basically bad. We just need to be conscious of our shortcomings and try to do better. Our own imperfections are a reflection of the flaws of others. With the understanding that everybody has similar flaws, we could work on them together, and maybe even fix some of them. Wouldn't it be great if we could be a good neighbor to the family next door, as well as our neighbors in countries across the globe. Everything we do is cumulative. Both the good, and the bad things we do have an effect in places we've never even heard of. I'm sure an accumulation of good activity would be of great benefit to the global population, and it would add up fast if we all worked at it.

After a delicious hot lunch at one of John's favorite cafes, he left me at the tiny town of Wicklow, just north of Florenceville, in west-central New Brunswick. John had inspired me with his good nature and thoughtful conversation. I was grateful for the long, 170 mile ride; it had given me plenty of time to learn from this man of peace. I hoped the same sort of good will he spread to every rider he picked up would be carried outward by those riders and become contagious on an epidemic level

.

Maine was almost close enough for me to throw a rock into it. John had taken me through Fredericton, then west and north along the Trans-Canada Highway. The next big town was Edmundston, sixty miles away. Even though I had made pretty good time getting into Wicklow, the traffic was unbelievably light for a mid-week afternoon. There didn't seem like much of a chance to get many more miles in before dark. The ride with John had turned me from a frozen hitchhiking machine back into a human being. My patience had returned and I even enjoyed the scenery. The hilly countryside was beginning to show some color. The fact that I was no longer faced with freezing rain might have also been an important factor in my improving state of mind.

It was an extended, windy wait on the top of a long down grade in Wicklow. Even though the sun was shining, it was still quite chilly and the wind was in my face. I got tired of fighting the buffeting breeze, turned my back to it, and started walking. I hiked two slow miles before Michel Allard blew by me and hit the brakes.

Michel lived in Edmundston, New Brunswick. Working as a salesman for Ralston Purina livestock feeds, he was relatively new at the job. It required a lot of travel, but with a small territory, he didn't have to be away from home overnight very often. In his mid-thirties, with a family, it was important for Michel to be home as much as possible. I was fortunate enough to meet his four-year-old son when we arrived in Edmundston. Michel picked him up from a day care center before taking me to the edge of town. It was really sweet to watch them interact. Michel was bi-lingual, French and English, but spoke French to his son. It was beautiful listening to native French speakers in melodic conversation.

I bid Michel au revoir with my mid-western accent at a fine intersection at the northern edge of Edmundston. The highway sign above me read, QUEBEC. I was only a few miles away from that large, mysterious, and influential province.

The political, legal, and constitutional challenges facing Canada are enormous. Most of the challenges originate from the autonomy demanded by French-speaking Quebecois. Quebec remained stubbornly devoted to its French oriented culture, in response to the pressure directed by the other provinces to conform to a British Commonwealth culture. The existence of two official languages caused a national identity crisis of sorts. The crisis has led to a wide enough rift that the province of Quebec has threatened a split from Canada. If a secessionist movement is successful it will deal a potentially fatal blow to Canada's already faltering economy. Quebec is rich in timber, mineral, and water resources. It controls the water transportation routes of the St. Lawrence River into the Atlantic. Montreal is a business center in which many Canadian and multinational corporations are headquartered.

It sounded as though both parties involved were desperately trying to solve the issues that threatened to dissolve modern Canada. Despite the harsh words and misunderstandings that had occurred in the political spotlight, most Canadians I talked with quietly hoped their country would remain whole. The citizens had a sincere interest in working out the cultural differences between conflicting cultures. Tribal leaders of native Canadians were also pursuing constitutional recognition of their rights and culture. It was one more political element that would either break Canada's back or make her stronger than ever by welcoming diverse peoples into the decision making mainstream.

As I contemplated Canada's problems, the first car that came by pulled right over. The fancy new Camaro had been special-ordered from the factory by Rejean Trudeau. The day before, Rejean had been released from six years of service in the Navy. After being stationed in Halifax and seeing three European tours of duty, he was thrilled to be heading home for what he hoped would be a more normal life. Normal life, for him, included staying in one place with his girlfriend and family, while working for IBM.

Rejean, a bright, quiet, twenty-five-year-old man, viewed the world unlike many of the other drivers I'd met. He really enjoyed a materialistic lifestyle. After spending so much time stationed in the maritime provinces, he looked forward to a more urbane existence in Montreal, or some other large city. He enjoyed the New York City/Montreal connection of styles, culture, and urban attitudes. Perhaps I found this conversation so fascinating because I do my level best to avoid an urban lifestyle. As I mentioned earlier, I seldom rode with people with aspirations such as Rejean. Everybody else seemed to want to escape the confines of tall buildings and traffic jams. I was glad to have had a glimpse into his idea of a perfect world.

The ride with Rejean was doubly productive. In addition to a great visit, I rode with him practically the entire distance to Montreal. Eighty miles out of Edmundston we caught the freeway at Riviere du Loup. 200 fast, freeway miles later, Rejean pulled over in Drummondville. He was turning south, toward Sherbrooke, at the Drummondville freeway exit. It was about 11:00 pm when he dropped me at the exit ramp. I was too tired to try for the city at so late an hour. The bright lights of the big city would have to wait one more day before this buckaroo saw them.

The area where I was, between Quebec City and Montreal, consisted of quaint rural villages surrounded by rich farmland. As I walked away from the lights of the freeway interchange, I sought a concealed campsite in a pasture. The spot I found was in some trees, but still within sight of the highway. I was too fatigued to walk any farther and decided it was as good a place as any to spend the night. The weather was pleasant, so I didn't bother setting up my tent. There was no snow left and the ground was remarkably dry for a day in early spring.

From my little center of the universe, in a farmer's field, I woke up to a crystal clear morning. I loafed around in my sleeping bag until the sun warmed me up enough to motivate my morning packing routine. Maybe it was the weather, or my generally western progress, but I was feeling close to home. I took my time assembling my stuff, for what seemed like the millionth time. It was actually the morning of day 116. I was hoping to catch my 276th ride without walking down the highway.

My luck was awesome. A young man stopped only moments after I reached the freeway entrance ramp. He spoke no English so I had no idea what he said as I piled in. What I had missed, with the lack of a French speaking translator, was that he was only going a short distance. That wouldn't have been so bad, but he left me at a split in the highway. There was only an exit ramp and the freeway continuing into Montreal. There was no entrance ramp to stand on, so I had to walk along the freeway shoulder. That was normally my preferred method of freeway hitchhiking, but I hated doing it so close to a metropolis. As I walked toward the next entrance ramp, watching hundreds of cars race by, I tried hitching with a sign that proclaimed "MONTREAL."

Danny Poirer lived in Montreal and had lots of room in his pick-up truck. I was glad that I had not only caught his eye, but that he was in the lane closest to me. If he had been in the outside lane it would have been nearly impossible for him to get over to the shoulder. The traffic was so heavy and fast, I had been feeling invisible again.

Danny worked as a truck dispatcher in the city and was on his way to punch the clock. His father worked for the Greyhound Bus company, so Danny had been around the transportation business all his life. Although a Canadian, he had lived in the U.S. for a number of years. I am always impressed with bi-lingual abilities and Danny spoke excellent English, as a second language. This wonderful, friendly young man was getting married in a few months. His fiancee had apparently made an excellent choice.

As we approached central Montreal we found ourselves at a standstill in four lanes of traffic. It was quite a switch from the nearly empty byways of the maritime provinces!

Danny got me as far into town as his job site was. He was a bit late for work so couldn't afford the time to take me any farther across town. At least I was slightly west of the center of town which was better than being slightly east of center. The freeway was crowded with fast moving cars and semi-trucks. The urban entrance ramps had a design that made it impossible for a hitchhiker to stand or a vehicle to stop. I struggled along, trying both the frontage road and freeway shoulder. As I walked along, I came to the complicated junction of the freeway, and the access road for the international airport. Yuk!

After walking for a couple of hours in intense traffic along scary roads, I found a patch of green grass, adjacent to a busy intersection. Dumping the burden of my pack onto the ground, I lay my weary muscles on this minuscule meadow. I shut down my hassled nerves and ate a bit of lunch. The two stretches of walking I'd already done that morning had a slight dejecting influence. I tried to relax under the scrutiny of hundreds of people. I had all the privacy of an oddly costumed performer at center stage. In cities I felt out of control. It seemed like there were invisible influences pushing me around. As opposed to aiding my transport, the complicated roads and heavy traffic were an enemy that existed to slow, or even halt, my progress. This was in huge contrast to the benign country roads surrounding big cities or out in the middle of nowhere. Fortunately the weather in Montreal was pleasant, leaving me with one less negative aspect to contend with. During my little rest I had a chance to work on a solution to my predicament.

The highway and parallel frontage roads left almost no opportunity to hitchhike out of the city because of the traffic danger. Montreal was large enough that walking out was not a good option either. It was a city built on an island. If I had to walk out I would eventually reach a bridge that was not designed for pedestrian traffic. My feet were continually sore and any more than three hours of walking made life miserable. It seemed like public transit was the only way to go. When I picked my pack up off of my little patch of green to continue west, I vowed to seek out the nearest telephone and give transit information a call.

Fifteen more minutes of walking brought me to a public phone. The bus connections turned out to be relatively simple. I could hop on any bus in the area and ride to some big mall that served as a transit hub. From there I could transfer to a bus that would bring me to Ste. Anne de Bellvue. Ste. Anne de Bellvue was essentially the western-most suburb of Montreal. It sat at the end of the island and the beginning of a long bridge that attached the island to the mainland.

I always felt pretty self-conscious on public transit, hauling so much gear and not really knowing my way around. I need not have felt that way in Montreal. I met a woman on the first bus who made sure I was in the right place at the right time to make my mall connection. Among the friendly people I met on the bus was Fred Fizet. He was getting off at the same place I was at Ste. Anne de Bellvue. I needed some water and asked if I could get some at his house. He was happy to oblige and we went up to his apartment. There I met his lovely wife, Jackie. They were gracious enough to fix me a sandwich and beverage before sending me out to the highway. They were kindred spirits in that they had travelled extensively in Europe. They knew how nice it was to be taken in for even a short time for rest and refreshment.

After my brief rest, Fred drove me to the last exit on the freeway before the bridge. The bridge was long and narrow, too dangerous to walk across with the high volume of traffic it carried so close to rush hour. Another difficult effect to contend with at that hour was the sunset. As it set behind my back, it was directly in the eyes of the drivers coming toward me. I searched the area for possible campsites, under the assumption that there was no chance of getting a ride out that night. It had taken the entire day to get approximately fifty miles to where I stood. Even so, I was still under the urban influence of Montreal. Freedom seemed to lie at the end of a mile long bridge.

Deliverance came in the form of twenty-nine-year-old Jean Gagon. He had pulled over to pick me up without passing by to get a look. I was so excited I had turned into a blathering idiot, and was trembling as I loaded up. When I found out that he was going all the way to Ottawa, Ontario, one-hundred miles away, I almost cried. The day had taken a lot out of me and my emotions were trashed. The stress of the day was finally over and I was now in the hands of a most capable traveller.

Jean Gagon was a French Canadian from St.-Jean-Port-Joli, located halfway between Quebec City and Riviere-du-Loup, on the St. Lawrence River. When Jean was twenty-years-old he left his hometown to experience what the world had to offer. His goal was to travel and work his way around all of North America. Throughout his journey he considered himself an ambassador of goodwill. In the process he would learn the English language. He hitchhiked around the United States, Canada, and Mexico, for eight months. During that time, over 1000 people expressed an element of trust and helped him along his way. He was truly a vagabond on his trip. He carried very little extra clothing or gear and slept outside, without a tent, seeking shelter wherever it could be found. He learned English, and also Spanish as an added bonus.

JEAN GAGON
Ottawa, Ontario

After that first taste of adventure, he continued his travels with even more extensive wanderings. Among his unofficial ambassadorial accomplishments was a 28,000 kilometer bicycle tour of the world. He also bicycled from Bombay, India to Katmandu, Nepal. On that trip, he fell sick often but never found his personal safety threatened by the people. In fact, the only time he was robbed was in Mexico, and then only his watch had been taken. It was a remarkable record of safety across a huge number of miles.

Jean was not into speed. He said that if he ever bicycled again it would be on the big, heavy clunkers that the countries' residents rode. It's not only far slower that way, allowing one to experience even more of the countryside and culture, but easier to get parts after mechanical breakdowns along the road. An even slower pace would be to walk. He was planning a walk from Helsinki, Finland, to Peking, China. After speaking with this man, I couldn't doubt his sincerity and determination. He would undoubtedly achieve his goals.

When he wasn't actually traveling for pleasure, he worked as a mechanic for a plastics manufacturer. His work was what brought us together. He was going to Ottawa to prepare a bid on a work contract. He invited me to stay at his hotel, downtown. After luxuriating in a thorough shower, I offered to take him out to dinner. We ate heartily, but we both were too tired to explore any more of the downtown area. At 10:00 pm it was far past my bed time.

The following morning, Jean took me to the western edge of Ottawa and bid me farewell. It had been a real pleasure meeting this fascinating man. Proof, once again, of how enriched our lives can become by seeking out the many strangers who have interesting lives, behind their unfamiliar faces. I found the pull of those opportunities nearly ruling me. It was so much fun meeting those people. They're not famous in a public sense, but their accomplishments are extremely valuable to the global community by making the world a more diverse and exciting place in which to live.

On April 20th, just outside of Ottawa, it didn't feel much like spring. I stood on the Trans-Canada Highway, buffeted by a cold wind, while rain threatened to drench me.

It was a short wait before John Pollard, of Ottawa, took me a few miles to the junction of highway 7. After my depressing Montreal walk, I was back in control of things. I felt like I owned the road and nobody could slow me down. With my mental attitude in complete control, I had no interest in rushing along, however. Things couldn't have been better.

Beautiful Jackie Churcher was on the sad errand of attending a funeral for a close friend's father. She was travelling from Ottawa to a small town west of Algonquin Provincial Park. I had planned on following the Trans-Canada into North Bay, Ontario, but chose to ride with Jackie through Algonquin Park on highway 60. I would eventually pass through North Bay but would enjoy the scenic trip through Algonquin first. I wasn't about to bail out of this nice change of pace. No longer a machine,

I was willing to take a minor detour to continue a conversation and view some parkland.

Jackie, 24, lived the life of a sophisticated, urban professional. A recent graduate of Queens University of Kingsbury, Ontario, she worked as a research analyst for an economics management consulting firm. Despite her urban lifestyle she had spent two summers working in Banff, Alberta, in the Canadian Rockies. She also enjoyed camping and canoeing.

JACKIE CHURCHER
Emsdale, Ontario

She never picked up hitchhikers, but had decided to make an exception on this trip. She wanted to see what it was like to give somebody a ride. I was glad fate left me standing along the road when she tried her little experiment. We had a nice conversation and I enjoyed our 180-mile-long ride together which had brought me to tiny Emsdale, just south of North Bay.

A lot of drivers find themselves reluctant to drop hitchhikers off. It's kind of a shock for drivers to suddenly dump their new friend out along some unfamiliar stretch of road. Jackie's negative reaction to "just leaving me standing out in the middle of nowhere," was similar to many of the other drivers I'd met. It was very endearing. She wondered if there was anything else she could do or if I'd be warm and dry enough standing in a light drizzle. I assured her that she had been more than generous and reminded her that it would be ridiculous for her to take me five, or five-hundred miles farther. It had to end someplace, why not in a convenient place like Emsdale?

Frank "Phudd" Gerrard gave me a quick lift to Burk's Falls, and I rode the remaining fifty miles to North Bay with Reuben Sollman.

Reuben's mood matched the weather: gray and gloomy, with a cold wind. After twenty-nine years of marriage, he was struggling to recover from a recent divorce. He treated me fine but didn't have many good things to say about his ex-wife. He just couldn't get his bearings back after experiencing a bitter breakup. He knew he'd live through it but didn't look forward to the long, painful, heartmending period.

In North Bay, I left him with best wishes, hurried out to the road, and started walking. It was on the verge of snowing and I needed to keep moving to stay warm. All of the lakes around there were still frozen solid. I wanted winter out of my life.

I was back on the Trans-Canada Highway and headed toward Sudbury. Before I had walked two blocks, a woman named Christine pulled over and said she could take me to a town about forty miles west of Sudbury. Great! Yet another lovely young woman to ride with that day.

Christine was an intellectual and spiritual powerhouse. At 29, she already had a long list of personal accomplishments. She had travelled extensively in Europe, and especially enjoyed France. She held a master's degree in International Government and Law from a French University. As a French Canadian, she was very proud of her Quebec heritage. Through her education and experience she was fluent in both English and French.

While on a trip to Europe she had experienced the challenge of walking the ancient pilgrimage route of St. James of Compostella. While on that road she witnessed and felt the personal struggles of the faithful as they trudged toward their goal. Christine was compelled to believe in the beauty of God's creation and had experienced a newfound hope for the condition of humanity.

In her willingness to help make the world a better place, she was working with the Jesuit Order of the Roman Catholic Church. Her present project involved a management study of a Church sponsored spiritual retreat. It was originally established for the benefit of native Canadian Indians living in central Ontario. Her faith in Christianity was unwavering, believing that an increasingly influential church would lead to a more accommodating, peaceloving world.

Before arriving in Espanola, Ontario, we stopped for a beer and something to eat. I came to admire her spirit and healthy energy. I was feeling a lack of energy, nearing the end of my own sort of pilgrimage. She offered a section of floor in her office to sleep on that night and I happily accepted. I got to visit with Christine a bit longer and had a warm, dry spot to sleep.

Although unmarried and childless, she was fascinated by the biological and spiritual mystery of childbirth and the total development and raising of the young. All of the scientific data in the world couldn't explain the existence of the so-called personality that made each individual unique. She felt that the nurturing of each of those individuals was an important responsibility and hoped for a chance to experience that responsibility with her own child. The spiritual gift of life on earth came only once and such a gift should not be squandered.

I hoped the thrill of childrearing would remain with her even after long nights with a crying baby, diapers, and the struggles of adolescence.

The following morning Christine brought me on a tour of the retreat facility. After a big breakfast, she brought me to the road and wished me continued good luck. I felt very close to home and was excited to be on my way. Less than 1000 miles remained, then I could finally unpack my pack and leave it so.

It was Saturday morning, April 21st, and rides were slow out of Espanola. I waited for over an hour before I started walking. I must have gone about five miles before someone stopped. Moved by the Holy Spirit, it was Richard Gross who stopped to give me a ride.

RICHARD GROSS
Webbwood, Ontario

Richard was a local man who had lived in the area all of his life. He admitted to looking me over about ten minutes before. He had passed by going the opposite direction to run errands in Espanola, and thought to himself, "Richard, steer clear of that fellow there. He looks like trouble!"

On his return trip to the little town of Webbwood, as he approached me with my thumb out, he said a quick prayer. The Holy Spirit had induced him to pick me up in a split second. He hit the brakes and pulled over. It actually took an act of God to get a ride with Richard that time.

I couldn't tell exactly how much divine intervention had occurred throughout the trip, but when you're exhausted from standing, or walking, you don't care why people stop. The only thing that matters is that they've exhibited an element of trust and have stopped for you. Webbwood was only about two miles down the road. I was walking, it was hot (believe it or not!), and I was happy to take a lift, short or long.

Richard had been a born-again Christian for about three years and was not very proud of his life up to the point of his conversion. With the partying and fighting part of his life now over, he was happy with his lot in life and had no worries regarding the safety of his soul on Judgement Day.

Upon reaching Webbwood, I didn't even bother waiting for a lift and started off walking down the road. I walked a couple of miles until I came to a nice pull-off spot, where I finally had a rest. The weather was looking good. So good that the sunny skies and warm temperatures made me feel sluggish. At about 60°F, it was like being in an equatorial torrid zone. I wasn't in a hurry at all and felt like taking a noontime siesta.

A few minutes into my rest, Charles Lacombe stopped. He worked as a roofer and really enjoyed his job. I mentioned my work as a painter on condominiums and ski lift tram towers. After too many dangerous close calls I now hated heights, and getting me on a ladder was as tough as giving a cat a bath. Charles was super friendly and good-natured. Our ride together was short and I was sorry to have missed visiting with him longer.

Charles left me in Massey, Ontario. The weather was perfect as I waited for a ride, right there in the middle of town. I was tired of walking and decided to soak up some solar rays and watch the people of this small town do their Saturday morning thing. There was a guard rail remnant where I waited and I was able to use it as a stool. I sat and read and watched and hitched and couldn't have cared if I'd had to wait all day for a ride.

This blissful physical and mental state of being ended when Tom Fitzpatrick loaded me up and took me the forty-five miles to Blind River. At the time, Tom was driving a station wagon, but normally drove a seventy-four-foot-long super truck. He put on 2300 miles a week along the 185 miles between Sudbury and Sault Ste. Marie. He could have driven that road with his eyes closed and one hand tied behind his back.

Upon our arrival in Blind River, Tom invited me home to meet his family and enjoy a couple of beers. Over a beer, Tom told me of the time he picked up a man who had just been the victim of a robbery. The poor guy had only 80 cents left in his pocket. It just so happened Tom was going to the town where the man lived. Like a delivering angel he took the unfortunate man 1600 miles. Tom seemed to be in the right place at the right time to give people a hand.

When I finished a second beer I decided to excuse myself. I figured I'd better hit the road before I had a third beer. I'm a cheap drunk, and after a mere three beers, I start singing songs I don't even know the words to. Tom returned me to the highway and I immediately started walking west.

It was late afternoon at the western edge of Blind River, Ontario, when Randy Johnson drove by to get a good look at me. He made a U turn a few blocks down and came back to load me up. It was a crazy situation. He was moving to Vancouver, British Columbia, and was using a tiny, Honda Prelude as his version of a moving van. Skis, backpacks, musical tapes, a kayak, climbing hardware, clothing, and everything else a twenty-three-year-old might need, was crammed into that little car. We jammed my big pack behind the front passenger seat and I held my small duffel bag on my lap. Randy was also 6'3" tall and we both slouched in our seats to keep from bouncing our heads on the ceiling headliner.

Randy picked me up on the advice of a friend who recommended picking up hitchhikers with backpacks. His friend had reasoned that someone with a backpack was a far safer bet than someone travelling light. It was another one of those recognition keys that people respond to. Whatever the reason, we were together and in for a grueling ride. Except for gas stops, we wouldn't slow down until we reached Thunder Bay, Ontario, over 500 miles away. I was incredibly lucky to be knocking off this huge hunk of road with a single ride. As I settled into my seat, I could almost taste the air of northern Minnesota again.

We had many similar interests to talk about, particularly outdoor pursuits. Randy had fallen in love with the western Canadian mountains and they were what was drawing him away from his home in Ottawa. There was a rafting guide position waiting for him in British Columbia, but he hoped to do some late spring skiing before settling down to work.

As we drove the long, lonely road along the north shore of Lake Superior, the hours ground on. The road was in pretty good condition despite its remoteness as it twisted and turned its way through the spruce forests. Occasionally, it would trace the shoreline. To see the vast, fresh-water ocean of Lake Superior, we had to look over massive ice floes which had piled up on the beach. After 7:00 pm, the towns that flashed by existed only in the abstract to us as we sped through the darkness.

I was certain I would be spending my last night on the road when Randy dropped me off in Thunder Bay. It was only about 250 miles from Thunder Bay to Willow River, but there were a lot of empty miles, and a border crossing still standing between me and an entirely successful trip.

In the city of Thunder Bay, I found a grassy spot along the highway right-of-way for my bed. As I lay under the stars, in my head I pictured the remaining miles. I was so close. I marvelled at my good fortune of the past four months. My mind raced like it did that first night I spent in the snow in Toledo, Iowa. Needless to say, I didn't sleep too well that night. I was impatient for the sun to come up. I wanted to continue down this familiar stretch of North American highway, and end my journey.

When daylight finally arrived I was packed up and walking south. The morning brought with it a light drizzle. It was a Sunday morning, traffic was thin, and I had no luck getting out of town. I just kept walking south on the Canadian version of Highway 61 until I reached an intersection that looked like it had the potential for success. The border was only about twenty-five miles away and I expected to walk the full distance. Rides up to, or through border crossings, are unusually hard to come by. Most people, even the nicest, aren't willing to face border Nazis with a stranger in their car. Even though the rider may be clean, the customs officials may delay the driver as well, just for fun.

NELL AND PAUL
DANLISKY
Thunder Bay, Ontario

After a long walk and an equally long wait, Paul and Nell Danlisky pulled right over. They were an elderly couple on a short Sunday morning drive to visit their daughter. I was grateful to be moving again under the power of something other than my feet. It didn't last long though. Paul and Nell turned off on a dirt covered back road in the middle of a rural area. The traffic was so sparse I didn't even bother waiting. I figured I'd have to walk to Minnesota, so I'd better get a move on.

I'd put on about four tiring miles on a long, empty section of highway, when Keren Chipeska stopped. Keren was a sweet, elderly woman with an excitable German Shepard cross named Hanna. She told of a time, about a year before, when she had passed by a "boy" who was hitchhiking. She'd felt guilty about that episode and it had apparently stuck with her. She was going to make up for it by taking me all the way to the border. I was elated by her generosity. My mood had been disintegrating with every hundred yards of walking. My crabbiness disappeared as I spoke with this woman.

We rode together for about a half hour before parting at the border crossing. Interestingly enough, it was my second ride to a border crossing with an elderly woman. The other was with Ella West in Eureka, Montana, and, like Keren, she had also taken me a few miles out of her way.

The first thing the customs guy did was interrogate me about Keren. Who was she? What did she do? Why was she dropping me off? What was she doing down here? I came up with satisfactory responses in each case. When he asked me to produce some identification he was surprised to see me whip out my passport. For some reason that impressed his socks off. He still did the usual make on the computer, to be sure I wasn't some criminal on the loose. He wasn't that impressed. I was still a low-life on foot and was shown the consideration that position deserved: little, if any. The agent took a cursory glance at my pack and figured I wasn't any more of a threat to the United States now, than I was before I had entered Canada.

As I repacked my pack, the guy who had processed me lit up a cigarette. I became furious. Surrounding us were notices regarding the non-smoking law that affected public places, such as that office. I wouldn't have cared much about it, except for the officer's blatant disregard for a law designed to protect the health of the citizenry. Here was a public servant, who specialized in knowing and enforcing laws, who absent-mindedly and inconsiderately broke a law he should have upheld. Surely he would have remembered that particular regulation and happily slapped a citation on me if I had been the one lighting up. I questioned his conduct, spoiling for a fight, and received cold stares in retaliation. Pardon my animosity, but the friendliness of America resides nowhere near a customs station.

Except for the dreaded border crossing, there is something uplifting about crossing a political boundary, an imaginary line on the earth's surface wherein lies your home. That feeling gets progressively stronger with each line that brings us closer. If we are coming from another country, the strangeness of being an alien leaves us as we enter our own country. Cultural differences, language barriers, unfamiliar climates, calculations of distances or monetary exchanges, unusual foods, and the appearance of another nationality or race of people, become but a memory as we step across that imaginary line onto home soil.

As we continue, crossing our own state line, names of cities and towns, highways, and regional accents become more recognizable, and prices better reflect the standards we're used to. With the passing of county lines and then city limits, we begin to feel like nobody knows their way around better than we do. This rapidly decreasing geographic space is becoming smaller and smaller on a map area, but larger and larger in our realm of understanding. We wave to the neighbors as we pull into the driveway and reach our domain. Rest and comfort can be had in this niche. It is here we live and plan our next excursion into unfamiliar territory. It is the going away that makes us ultimately appreciate home. Just ask Dorothy. She knows there's no place like home.

I was back in Minnesota and the United States and was feeling the beginning stages of arriving home. The invisible barriers were falling. Unfortunately, I still wasn't in control of my pace and had no idea how long I might have to stand around someplace before I would be on my way. It was six miles from the customs station to the little town of Grand Portage. I had already walked a lot to get out of Thunder Bay and wasn't excited at the prospect of wearing out even more shoe rubber.

I had only waited a short time before Bob Heinz stopped. He was a Canadian citizen who lived in a small town in northern Ontario. He was of German descent but was born and raised a French Canadian.

Bob said he'd done every job imaginable, and his last job was literally his last. Working as a logger, he had severely injured his back. That entitled him to a $2800 per month injury compensation/pension package, offset by a great deal of physical discomfort. He preferred the doctors in

Duluth to those in Toronto, for some reason. That preference forced him to drive many hundreds of miles from his home in Hearst, Ontario, to Duluth for medical attention.

Bob would be transporting me the entire length of the Minnesota north shore of Lake Superior into Duluth on U.S. 61. It is a neat drive. The road is constructed so close to the lake that cartographers mapping it can simply trace the shoreline with the symbol for a U.S. highway. The lake is visible from nearly every one of its 155 miles. Years of camping, canoeing, skiing, hiking, and excursions to watch the autumn color changes had brought me to the north shore time and time again. I knew it well. The rivers Brule, Cascade, Temperance, Manitou, Baptism, Gooseberry, and French; the towns Grand Marais, Lutsen, Taconite Harbor, Silver Bay, Castle Danger, and Two Harbors, welcomed me home.

I mentioned to Bob my good fortune at getting a single ride, along the Trans-Canada Highway, the entire distance from Blind River to Thunder Bay. He said I was indeed fortunate. Had I been dropped off in one of the little towns along the way, I could have had a very long wait to get out. He then related a story about the small town of Wawa, Ontario, one of the towns Randy and I had passed through the night before. There was a man who had been dropped off in Wawa a while back. He had tried hitchhiking a ride out of there for so long that he finally gave up waiting, found a place to live, got married, and was still there. One would assume that, now married, the man was no longer trying to leave town. My waits were blessedly short compared to that man's legendary hitch.

Bob dropped me off in downtown Duluth and it was a short walk to the entrance ramp of I-35. I-35 was a straight shot to Willow River, a mere fifty miles away. It was also a straight shot all the way to Laredo, Texas, 1300 miles away, where I had ridden with a carload of Spanish speaking men.

Duluth was reminiscent of my recent visit to St. John's, Newfoundland: the harbor with its ship traffic, the city clinging onto hills rising out of the water, and the freshening colors of spring.

Unusual for a Sunday afternoon, the top of the entrance ramp was a busy, crowded affair that would make it tough for a driver to stop and wait while I loaded. I had no other choice though, because walking down the ramp onto the urban freeway was an even less safe option. At least on top, the traffic was slow and everybody could see me.

Jim Crockett didn't think picking me up presented any sort of a problem. I had only waited about a half hour before he stopped. As I loaded up, he didn't insist that I hurry. I climbed into his big Chevy Blazer and stretched out to enjoy the last bit of pavement.

Jim was with the Coast Guard Reserve and had duty in Duluth for the weekend. That task completed, he was heading home to Minneapolis. Jim told me about a hitchhiking trip he had taken with a friend, to Colorado. He said they were young, dumb, unprepared, and they both froze. He also said he wouldn't have traded the adventure for anything in the world. They lived to tell about it and he was glad to have earned the memories. Carrying the memories I had earned over the past four months, I wouldn't have traded them for anything either.

The towns where our family went grocery shopping, checked out books at the library, and had supper out on special occasions were disappearing in the rear view mirror. Looking considerably different than it did on December 26th, I was thrilled as Jim pulled off the freeway at the Willow River exit. The snow was gone, the trees were turning green, car tires hummed along on dry pavement, and the air temperature hovered at a balmy 65°F.

Jim kindly offered to take me all the way to my folk's place. I accepted part of his offer and rode five miles to the dirt road that led to the farm. I didn't want to take Jim any farther out of his way and was happy to walk the two final, familiar miles home. As Jim drove county road 43 I anticipated every curve. I knew the houses, fields, and woodlands by heart. On the right was the barn with shingles arranged in a weird, colorful pattern. The farmers all had their cows out enjoying the spring pasture. As we passed under the power lines, held up by poles that once must have been the world's tallest trees, the names on the mailboxes identified familiar friends.

A few minutes later and it was time to be left off at another intersection. In high spirits I thanked Jim and bid my 291st ride, on the 119th day of my journey, farewell. It was Sunday afternoon, April 22. Coincidentally, it also happened to be Earth Day. A perfect day to celebrate the generosity of the earth and the humanity that occupied it.

Jim sped off, back toward Willow River. I looked around for a minute before starting my final, two mile walk. Just across the highway was our closest neighbor's farm. The barn roof was still sagging. They needed to get that shored up. Manure had been spread that day and its pungent odor was strong on a slight breeze that swept across the hayfields. The corner where I now stood, looking around, was not all that unique. It resembled every corner, any of millions in rural North America. It just so happened that I could walk up to the nearest farmstead, ask for shelter, and be welcomed by someone who had known me for fifteen years. Not unlike the welcome the farmers in Alberta and Saskatchewan gave me when I desperately needed shelter.

Neighborliness doesn't have much to do with who you live next to. It's an attitude, not a geographic concept. There is so much interaction between people in different residential areas, cities, states, and countries, that it's almost impossible to determine where neighborhoods begin and end. If there are no boundaries to define neighborhoods then the idea of treating someone as though they lived next door expands into an ever broadening range.

Each driver who picked me up contributed to the establishment of a continental neighborhood. People from every portion of America, driving all manner of vehicles, from all walks of life, with smiles on their faces, opened their doors to me, a complete stranger and treated me like a neighbor. Ignoring all geographic boundaries they treated me with respect and trust. They took a giant leap of faith and broke the bonds of fear.

County road 43 was decorated like any other highway. It had a yellow striped center-line with a solid yellow line on one side to warn drivers not to pass, solid white lines at the pavement edges, signs to inform drivers of regulations and locations, and mailboxes parked at the ends of driveways. If I wanted to, I could stand there, my feet outside of the solid white line, face the traffic, stick out my thumb as cars rolled by, and get a ride. I could meet someone new and eventually go someplace I'd never even imagined existed. It was that simple. It could happen on the strength of my own trust in human nature and that of those who would welcome me along for the ride.

The road beckoned to me to come out and play a little while longer. I thanked it for the opportunity it had given me to see into the soul of North America, but declined its offer this time. I chose to go no farther that day and turned my back on a road that could have been mistaken for any other two-lane highway on the continent. Stepping off the pavement and onto the red clay township road, I felt I had accomplished something good. It hadn't been a marathon trip, in an attempt to set some sort of record. It didn't have sponsors who would make money off of the efforts of others. It was a relatively simple thing to do with simple results. In a world that has proven itself to be decidedly unkind at times, the trip was ultimately a search for kind people.

I had found some of them.

The frost had left the ground at this late date so the road was in pretty good shape. There was still the occasional washboard, mud puddle, and rough spot where a culvert hadn't been buried deep enough when it had been originally installed. The weeds along the ditch were making a big push to occupy more terrain that spring, and encroached farther onto the roadway. The township didn't have the money to grade it as often as they should have and didn't even have a working brush cutter. The brush cutter had been sitting in some guy's yard for three years with promises of getting it fixed. It was nothing out of the ordinary for a road in the north-woods, or anyplace else for that matter.

When I had completed the first mile I had arrived at the far field of the farm. The pasture was greening up nicely. The cows were out and I could hear the faint clanging of Whitey's and Top's bells. Frogs were croaking in the ditches along the road and low spots in the woods. Low spots were always wet spots around there, just like outside of Washington, D.C. or Mountain Home, Idaho.

The sun was hot and I was sweating through my tee shirt. It reminded me of my hot walk outside of Tampa. That in turn reminded me of how different it was from my cold walk through Medicine Hat.

The memories of the places I'd been were now an intimate part of me. When something happened in those places I would now have a personal interest in what was going on. Each town was part of my neighborhood and my neighbors were important to me. Some places I would remember fondly while others less so. Either way they were etched forever onto my life's map.

When I was a quarter mile from the house I saw my brother and father out in a rough section of land picking rocks. They were busy clearing seven acres for new pasture. I jumped the ditch and set out across the field that separated us. The soil was still a little wet and it sucked at my shoes as I walked along. My dad was the first to notice me and pointed in my direction for the benefit of my brother. Then they both waved. I was looking forward to a big lunch that my mom would have whipped up a few minutes after I walked through the door.

The faces of my family weren't that much different from the faces of those whom I'd had occasion to ride with. My mother looked strangely similar to Ella West out in Eureka, Montana. My brother could have been mistaken for the big, sweet corn farmer in Batavia, New York, Allen Galbraith. My father could have been any of a dozen skinny, retired, balding men with glasses and crooked smiles.

I had heard the stories, and experienced the uniqueness of nearly three-hundred individuals. I could never be so foolish to say that they were are all alike. I witnessed no clones over the course of 17,000 miles. What I did witness was a brother and sisterhood. What bound them was an interest in sharing some goodwill. Membership in this group was entirely voluntary and required no dues, only an extraordinary leap of faith. It was a far higher toll to extract from a fearful citizenry than mere dollars. I had looked into the eyes of every member of this group and had seen a human being, flawed though we all are, who had taken that leap of faith. They, like my family, were to be cherished as a family of mankind.

As I approached the low trailer piled high with rocks and sticks, my pack no longer felt heavy. Compared to the distance I had travelled over the course of four months, the last two miles had felt like nothing more than a walk to the curb to pick up the morning paper.

I greeted my family with smiles, hugs, and tears. I knew then that there was a light at the end of our culture's long tunnel of fear. A spirit of cooperation and trust existed across the land. The very fact that I was greeting my family after such a trip was proof of its existence, far beyond a reasonable doubt.

Welcome to the neighborhood.

About the Author

When not involved in foolish and dangerous travel pursuits the author sorts mail in Glacier National Park and punches the occasional cow in east-central Minnesota. He also cooks breakfast sometimes and is rumored to break golf clubs if he hits too many bad shots in a row.